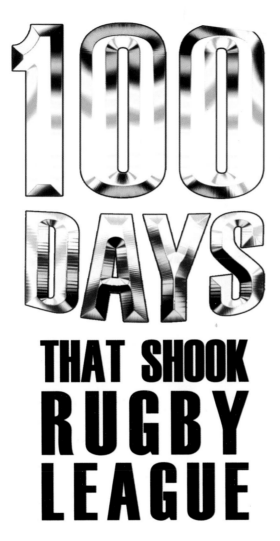

THAT SHOOK
RUGBY
LEAGUE

Richard de la Rivière

FOREWORD BY ALEX MURPHY OBE

First published in Great Britain in 2017 by
League Publications Ltd, Wellington House, Briggate, Brighouse,
West Yorkshire, HD6 1DN

A CIP catalogue record for this book is available from the British Library
ISBN 978-1-901347-34-0

Printed by H Charlesworth & Co Ltd, Wakefield

For Katy and Finlay

CONTENTS

FOREWORD

Alex Murphy OBE

It's a pleasure to write a foreword for Richard's new book, '100 Days that Shook Rugby League', especially as I feature heavily in a few of them! It goes without saying that two of my career highlights are the second match of the 1958 Ashes series with Australia and the 1971 Wembley final between Leigh and Leeds.

Everyone knows the story of Alan Prescott breaking his arm and deciding to continue in that wonderful Test match in Brisbane nearly 60 years ago. It was such an extraordinarily brave thing to do. He knew if he went off, then we would lose the series. But he stayed on, helping us level the series and made himself an all-time great in the process. I was just 18 at the time and having had a poor game in the first game, it proved to be the day which launched my international career. To be selected to tour at that age was just amazing. I was the youngest player to have been selected in Lions history. I had my 19th birthday out there and to tour with clubmates Glyn Moses, Alan, Dick Huddart and Vince Karalius was very special. I'd never been out of England before, never mind all the way to Australia. I didn't even know I was going to be selected. Jeff Stevenson cried off from Leeds, and I thought Frank Pitchford would be ahead of me. I thought I'd be lucky to get into the side.

We went to a race meeting one day and when I was introduced to the Australian scrum-half Keith Holman, someone said "this is the best scrum-half in the world." I jumped in and joked "it's nice of you to say that about me." It didn't go down well and Keith outplayed me in the first test. Alan gave me a rocket, putting me in my place. But the second Test was different. I made sure they had to chase me and we went on to win the Ashes. We all know about Alan's injury, but there were others too. We played with just nine men! But too many of us thought we were unbeatable, and we came through. Then the Australians were saying I was the best scrum-half in the world and it was music to my ears.

Before I went to Leigh, they didn't look like a club who could win the major trophies. I'd left St Helens under a cloud because they insisted I went to an Australian club. I had an agreement to go to North Sydney, but I didn't really want to go. I was in limbo and had to find a job, until Tommy Sale, one of the Leigh directors, asked me to join his club as coach. I said "You're joking! You're bottom of the league and I've never coached in my life." So I went as a coach and learned so much. The 1958 tour had taught me how good you need to be to succeed. I only signed a couple of players and built a side around players I could trust, because I couldn't play for a year. I told the chairman I'd run the team right if he sorted out the business side of things and we'd be fine. That 12 months with me not playing was vital to us and we wouldn't have had the success at Wembley if it wasn't for that.

Again, most people know what happened in the 1971 final with the sending-off incident. Syd Hynes and I are still best friends. We always have been. According to the bookies we had no chance, but the bookies don't play Rugby League. We'd played them twice that season and had beaten them. I knew what Holmes, Dyl, Smith and Atkinson were going to do. But they didn't know what I was going to do. I'd coached Leigh in a certain way. We could score tries and stop tries. We put Leeds back in their half, time and time again. They scored just one obstruction try. It was the greatest achievement anyone has produced at Wembley. The people of Leigh were so proud. It's the same as what Leicester City did in 2016.

This book also includes the story of my infamous dressing-room team talk from 1983 which was shown on ITV when I was coach of Wigan. I wasn't happy about it at the time, and neither was my mother! So what was behind it? Well, I do not like losing! That's as a player or a coach or even in a game of conkers. I didn't want to go to Wigan to be honest, but Maurice Lindsay persuaded me. I signed players who didn't really want to do what they were getting paid for. We signed David Stephenson, a great player, but he was always late for training and he took some stick off me after that game. The public were getting sick of the performances, and rightly so. I like people who train properly, but I had a problem with David, a rugby union lad. In the match in question, I couldn't believe we had performed like that. Once I get something off my chest, I don't hold grudges. But it was captured on television! The cameras had been left on without me knowing. It went out and I watched it with my mum and dad, two strong Catholics, so I had some explaining to do! It was an eye-opener to many people because that must have been a time when no TV company had ever access to dressing rooms. The players reacted very well to be honest, and we moved on very quickly from the episode. And David was always on time for training after that!

INTRODUCTION

'100 Days that Shook Rugby League' doesn't need much explanation. It's exactly as you might expect. This isn't a definitive list of the most dramatic Rugby League stories – that would be impossible. It is merely a collection of 100 out of the thousands of extraordinary events that have taken place since the first clubs were formed in the nineteenth century.

Just over half the stories focus on the breathtaking, classic matches that have shaped this wonderful sport for well over a century – internationals, cup finals, State of Origins and many others. Also included are the great tours, historic milestones, transfers, new dawns, structural changes with an abundance controversy scattered throughout. There are some tragic tales too, although there wasn't room for all of them. I hope this causes no offence. No one death is more important than another, but in seeking to get the balance right over the course of the book between the types of stories chosen, some difficult decisions had to be made.

This is my second book on a sport I have written about since 2005, having fallen in love with the game at Workington's Derwent Park many years earlier. I can be found on Twitter - @richdelariviere.

FIRST BRITISH LIONS
CAPTAIN DIES ON TOUR

For many years before the great schism of 1895, it was the northern players and teams who dominated rugby. Yorkshire won six of the first seven County Championships from its 1889 inception, with Lancashire winning the other. Over 40 per cent of England players between 1890 and 1895 came from clubs that would later become members of the Northern Union, the forerunner to Rugby League.

So it was no surprise that when the first British Lions tour took place in 1888, when there was only one code of rugby, 14 of the 22 players selected to tour were from such clubs as Batley, Swinton, Runcorn, Salford, Rochdale, Bramley or Halifax. Two Dewsbury players, William 'Buller' Stadden and Dicky Lockwood, were also chosen, but declined to tour. The captain was the 28-year-old Swinton forward Robert Seddon, who had previously played for Broughton Rangers. Tragically, Seddon lost his life shortly after the mid-point of the tour, drowning in a boating accident in Maitland, part of the Hunter Valley in New South Wales. This saddest of days remains the blackest in British Lions history, in either of the rugby codes.

The tour was set up as a private enterprise by a trio of England international cricketers - Alfred Shaw, Arthur Shrewsbury and James Lillywhite - who had previously taken tours to Australia. Their ventures had given them a high profile which, in turn, had boosted Shaw and Shrewsbury's sporting-goods business and they were keen to use their experience to profit from another sport. Given rugby's amateur status, however, and the fact that the players would also be taking part in Australian Rules matches, the Rugby Football Union refused to sanction the tour, and no Test matches were played. They also dictated that the players must receive no payment at all. They went as far as banning Halifax's Jack Clowes from playing in any of the matches, upon hearing he had received a clothing allowance of £15, although every player had received the same payment. Bizarrely, he was still allowed to travel with the party.

"The sods lie lightly and the grass grow green where poor Bob Seddon sleeps his last long sleep so far from home and kindred."

The 'Kaikoura' set sail from Tilbury in early March 1888 and, after stopping in London, Plymouth, Tenerife, Cape Town and Hobart, they arrived in Dunedin in New Zealand a month and a half later. Seddon had almost fallen overboard. "I don't think I was born to be drowned," he wrote in a letter to a friend, blissfully unaware of his eventual fate.

The 54-game schedule, which bizarrely included 19 Australian Rules matches, stretched from April to October. Despite the Clowes fiasco and any on-field success, the 1888 Lions Tour will always be remembered for terrible events of 15th August when Seddon drowned in the Hunter River. The story is poignantly told in Sean Fagan's 2013 book, 'The First Lions of Rugby'.

The players were afforded some leisure time before heading to Newcastle in the afternoon. A few of them went to the river, with the skipper happy to watch and not participate in any sailing. Andrew Stoddart and Jack Anderton decided to remain in Maitland for the afternoon and get a late-evening train to Newcastle. Seddon told the management he would do the same, as he wanted to write some letters home. "We left him outside his hotel at Maitland with no hat upon his head and a cigarette in his mouth, in the very best of health and spirits," said Shrewsbury.

Seddon accompanied Stoddart and Anderton back to the River Hunter. He hired a small boat, with his teammates sharing another. They stopped near Horseshoe Bend with Anderton and Stoddart "lying in an old punt, smoking and taking it easy." There are varying accounts of what happened next. The press reported that Seddon rowed ahead on his own, before his boat overturned. He drowned, suffering asphyxiation. His body was recovered nearly half an hour later by his distraught teammates. Twenty miles away, in Newcastle, an emotional Tom Haslam, the team's fullback, ran into the hotel shouting "Bob Seddon is drowned!" The players could scarcely believe what they were hearing.

The 'Newcastle Morning Herald' reported that "two men saw him swimming and encouraged him by shouting, but could render no assistance as no boat was available. [He] swam about 15 yards on his back, and then sank twice – the last time for good." Another newspaper wrote: "His death has caused a painful sensation in athletic circles in Sydney … The sods lie lightly and the grass grow green where poor Bob Seddon sleeps his last long sleep so far from home and kindred."

Seddon was buried at Campbell Hill Cemetery in Maitland the day after his death with around 3000 mourners in attendance. Enough money was raised for a tablet to be erected inside St Paul's Church and a monument to mark his final resting place. The latter reads: "In memory of Robert L. Seddon, Captain of the English football team, drowned in the River Hunter at West Maitland, August 15 1888, aged 28 years."

Before the next fixture on the 18th in Brisbane, the players lined up for a pre-match photo, with the seat traditionally occupied by the captain poignantly remaining empty, with a ball where his feet would have been. Stoddart took over as captain, but refused to talk about Seddon's death. The tour was completed, with the last match drawn with Wanganui on 3rd October.

The first British Lions line up following the death of their captain Robert Seddon, whose seat is poignantly left empty

In February 1889, many of the tourists, including Stoddart, were re-united, playing against Swinton in the Robert Seddon Memorial Match at the club's Chorley Road Ground. Tom Kent scored the only try of the match as 'The Anglo-Australian Team' won 3-0.

The lives of two other prominent tourists ended in tragic circumstances many years later. Shrewsbury resumed his cricket career, playing in the next two Ashes series, in 1890 and 1893, but ended his life in 1903, at the age of 46, paranoid that he was falling ill. Stoddart, with financial problems and on the verge of an attack of pneumonia, which can trigger depressive symptoms, died at the age of 52 in 1915. Both men shot themselves.

Rugby League has dutifully honoured Seddon's memory, as the 'Sydney Morning Herald' reported in 1975: "The monument was covered in leaves and disrepair until a British Rugby League team visited the site in 1954. Although it was a League tour, the British manager felt strongly about the condition of the grave and asked a local Maitland Rugby League official, Frank Taylor, if he could arrange for the grave to be repaired and kept in good condition. Mr Taylor undertook the job himself and for the past 21 years has meticulously cared for the monument."

RUGGBY LEAGUE IS BORN

It didn't just come down to broken-time payments, although compensation for players missing work on a Saturday afternoon was the main reason why a group of the best rugby clubs in the land broke away from the Rugby Football Union in 1895 to form the Northern Union.

In the late 19th century, those who played rugby often had to miss work, resulting in calls for compensation from working-class players in the north, but this was classed as professionalism by the London-based RFU, which had been fighting for years to maintain their flawed ideologies of amateurism.

The Yorkshire and Lancashire clubs had an unhealthy relationship with the autocratic RFU, which had long resented them for being so good. In their eyes, rugby was for enjoyment and the northerners were taking it too seriously. The RFU, which was formed in 1871, had even objected to the inauguration of the Yorkshire Cup in 1877 because they regarded competition to be against their gentlemanly ideals. There was a genuine fear that the working-class player was driving his wealthier counterpart from the game. In 1874 the Half Day Holiday Act reduced the working week from six days to five and a half. Now that Saturday afternoon was free, sport could be played and watched by the masses. The face of rugby was to change forever, but the RFU and their established clubs even disliked crowds watching matches.

Frightened that the sport was in danger of losing its roots, the RFU further embraced amateurism in 1886 by introducing tighter legislations - a move designed to hurt northern players and clubs, many of whom would soon end up in trouble for flouting the new rules. But there were numerous examples of RFU hypocrisy when it came to amateurism, not least the experiences of 1888 British Lions tour of Australia. "The committee will look with a jealous eye upon any infringement of [amateurism]," read an RFU statement, but James Lillywhite, one of the trio of entrepreneur organisers, told New Zealand's 'Evening Post' that "we ... believe that each man has been guaranteed £200."

Halifax's Jack Clowes had even been outed as a professional by the RFU prior to departure because he had received a clothing allowance, despite every other player receiving the same payment. The RFU decided not to professionalise any of the other tourists on condition they signed, upon their return, "an affidavit that they received nothing beyond hotel and travelling expenses." All of the players did, bar the high-profile Andrew Stoddart, who

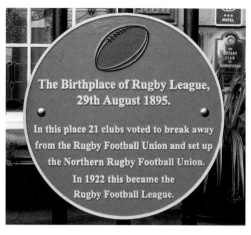

Dicky Lockwood was central to some of
the ill feeling between the RFU and the northern clubs

had taken over the captaincy following Bob Seddon's death. The RFU decided not to pursue Stoddart, fearful of the consequences of having to take on such an influential personality. The governing body feared being overthrown or seeing a rival organisation being formed.

England captain Dicky Lockwood, a diminutive three-quarter who hailed from Dewsbury, wasn't so lucky and had his amateur status regularly challenged by the RFU and their chief attack dog, the Reverend Frank Marshall, although always unsuccessfully. Lockwood was treated appallingly, and was even banned from playing for Heckmondwike because work commitments meant he had to miss England's Calcutta Cup match in Scotland in 1894, despite the RFU allowing Cyril Wells, a housemaster at Eton, to play for Harlequins in identical circumstances. Such gross hypocrisy did little to calm the troubled waters.

In September 1893 a vote to allow broken-time payments took place at the RFU's annual general meeting in London, but the motion was defeated by 282 votes to 136. The issue didn't disappear. Marshall even had his own club Huddersfield suspended because they had made payments to George Boak and John Forsyth, a couple of three-quarters from Cummersdale Hornets in Cumberland. Leigh, Salford and Wigan were among other clubs found guilty of professionalism. In November 1894 the leading 21 Yorkshire and Lancashire clubs met for the first time to discuss the RFU's over-zealous behavior and forced the RFU to drop a controversial clause in a six-point manifesto on amateurism. It was a minor victory, at least.

"We breathe pure air in being freed from the stifling atmosphere of deceit in which we previously existed."

By 1895, the elite Yorkshire clubs were unhappy because they were under pressure to accept promotion and relegation. Hull and Wakefield had finished bottom of the competition but were under no obligation to make way for the top two sides in the next division down, Morley and Castleford. Later in the summer, the RFU passed new rules stating that any club accused of professionalism would be banned until their innocence was proven, and so the leading clubs decided to jump before being pushed. After a meeting at the Mitre Hotel in Leeds on Tuesday 27th August, 12 Yorkshire clubs decided to break away from the RFU with a view to forming a Northern Union. They were to be joined by nine Lancashire clubs, which had simultaneously convened at the Spread Eagle Hotel in Manchester.

The 21 clubs would meet up two days later at 6.30pm at Huddersfield's George Hotel and after a meeting chaired by Harry Waller, it was agreed that "the clubs here represented decide to form a Northern Rugby Football Union, and pledge themselves to push forward, without delay, its establishment on the principle of payment for bona-fide broken time only."

One of those clubs, Dewsbury, decided not to join immediately, but did sign up to the Northern Union three years later. Stockport and Runcorn were absent from The George, but jumped on board in time to be part of the new organisation. The first matches were played on 7th September, although many players did not play, having not yet decided to commit to the new venture.

Rules concerning payments would still be strict in the Northern Union and aspects of amateurism were maintained. A list of jobs was drawn up that would see players compensated when they missed work. The maximum a player could receive was six shillings at a time.

The day after the historic meeting, the 'Wigan Observer' reported that "all along the feeling has been expressed that freedom from the thraldom of the Southern gentry was the best thing that could happen." A letter in the 'Yorkshire Post' in September said: "I say with Mark Twain's bold, bad boy, that we glory in the sentence of outlawry pronounced on us, as freeing us from the tyrannical bondage of the English [Rugby] Union, and we breathe pure air in being freed from the stifling atmosphere of deceit in which we previously existed."

Within two years, Northern Union membership grew from 22 clubs to 150. Rugby union in the north

THE ORIGINAL NORTHERN UNION CLUBS

Batley
Bradford
Brighouse Rangers
Broughton Rangers
Halifax
Huddersfield
Hull FC
Hunslet
Leeds
Leigh
Liversedge
Manningham
Oldham
Rochdale
Runcorn
St Helens
Stockport
Tyldesley
Wakefield Trinity
Warrington
Widnes
Wigan

was decimated, although they only had themselves to blame. Clubs which remained were forbidden from playing Northern Union clubs. In January 1898 Goole were even prevented from playing a charity match against a touring Little Red Riding Hood pantomime troupe, because the troupe had previously played Batley.

Free from RFU shackles, rule changes were gradually implemented as the Northern Union looked to become the more entertaining sport. The line-out was abolished in 1897 and the game became 13-a-side in 1906, the same year that the play the ball was introduced. The new code was fast gaining its own identity, and in 1922 the Northern Union changed its name to the Rugby Football League.

Saturday, 24th April 1897

THE FIRST CHALLENGE CUP FINAL

Summer rugby may have been to the detriment of the Challenge Cup, but for 100 years, this much-cherished competition was the be-all and end-all for Rugby League clubs and their supporters. And so the first final between Batley and St Helens is naturally one of the most important dates in the sport's history.

In the Northern Union's second season, 52 clubs entered the first-ever Challenge Cup competition, which began on 20th March, at the conclusion of the league season. There were 30 clubs from the Lancashire and Yorkshire Senior competitions, and 22 'junior' sides. Neither of the finalists had enjoyed a successful league campaign, with Batley coming sixth in the Yorkshire Senior Competition, winning just half of their 30 games and finishing 13 points behind leaders Brighouse. In the Lancashire competition, St Helens had finished even lower, in ninth, winning only ten matches out of 26 and coming in 19 points behind the top-placed Broughton Rangers.

The Cup matches were played on successive Saturdays, with the final taking place on 24th April in front of 13,492 spectators at Headingley Stadium. It was a hugely significant occasion for the infant sport.

The Gallant Youths of Batley, who had beaten Warrington 6-0 at Huddersfield in their semi-final, went on to become the first winners of the sport's most famous competition after a 10-3 win. Gate receipts totalled £624 and the general consensus was that the occasion had been a great success.

The Yorkshiremen had been one of a dozen teams to enjoy a bye in the first round. They won 11-0 at Bramley in the next before enjoying a magnificent win in the third round, unexpectedly beating the Yorkshire Senior Competition champions, Brighouse Rangers, 6-3 at home. A 10-0 win saw them overcome an injury-hit Widnes, who were down to 12 men in the first half, having lost three men – the sport was still 15-a-side at this stage. They beat Warrington 6-0 in the semi-final at Huddersfield, with their opponents protesting that the match should have been called off due to the sodden conditions. They also accused the referee of ending the match six minutes early.

Saints beat Lees, a non-major league club, 58-0, Castleford 17-3 and Wigan in the third round 11-0. All three were at home and the crowd of 5,000 for the Wigan game had been over four times higher than in their last league clash. They enjoyed another home draw when they beat Tyldsley 12-0 to reach

Batley, the first winners of the Challenge Cup

the semi-final. Heavy rain saw their last-four clash with Swinton initially postponed, but when it was played the following Monday at Broughton in front of 20,000 fans, they prevailed 7-0.

St Helens won the Cup Final toss and elected to play with the wind. The Batley stand-off Joe Oakland, who had earlier split the Saints defence with a fine run from inside his own half, scored the first points when he dropped a goal from a scrum-base. Such a score was then worth four points. Saints hit back, threatening the Batley line but Richard O'Hara's pass was intercepted by Dai Fitzgerald, who took play back into the Saints half. Jim Barnes, the St Helens centre, had to be alert enough to kick dead when a Batley try seemed likely, but they couldn't hold out for long and the honour of scoring the first Challenge Cup Final try went to Batley's John Goodall, assisted by Welsh winger Wattie Davies, although reports suggested the try scorer may have been offside. Davies missed the goal, but these two first-half scores against the wind went a long way to deciding the match. The half-time score was 7-0.

Saints rallied in the second half and when centre David Traynor beat four men from the halfway line to score the first try that the Gallant Youths had conceded in their Cup campaign, it was the culmination of a wonderful length-of-the-pitch move. But the goal was missed. St Helens had to cope without their injured halfback Freddie Little, who had scored against Swinton in the semi-final, for a spell. With no substitutes, they were down to 14 men, and although he later returned, Batley regained control by pinning Saints in

"This day will be remembered for as long as the Cup is played for."

their own half.

Fitzgerald's kick for Shaw looked like yielding Batley's second try but Saints scrambled the ball clear. They didn't hold out for long though, and when John Munns added another try from a loose scramble, there was no doubt where the £60 trophy, made by the Bradford jeweller Fattorini & Sons, was going. The 189-ounce cup was presented to the Batley captain, John Goodall, by Mrs Henry Hirst Waller, the wife of the Northern Union president.

After a celebratory meal at the Exchange Restaurant in Leeds, the Batley players caught the train from Leeds, and were welcomed home by 160 celebratory fog signals. They spent the evening toasting victory at Batley Town Hall in the company of the mayor, with the Batley Old Band playing 'See the Conquering Heroes Come'. The civic-reception speech claimed that "this day will be remembered for as long as the Cup is played for."

People flocked in from all parts of the surrounding district, for both the telegraph, the telephone, and the carrier pigeon had been the means of widely spreading the news of Batley's victory at Headingley. Trade for an hour or two was at a standstill, and shopkeepers and their assistants were constrained to join in the general reception. From the windows of hotels, shops, warehouses, and every-day residences people caught up the enthusiasm from below, and for more than an hour the passage of the victorious team through the streets was one "triumphal march." Flags and banners, and the

---

BATLEY 10 ST HELENS 3

BATLEY
1 Arthur Garner
2 Wharton 'Wattie' Davies
3 Dai Fitzgerald
4 Jack Goodall (C)
5 Ike Shaw
6 Joe Oakland
7 Harry Goodall
8 Mark Shackleton
9 Jim Gath
10 George Maine
11 Bob Spurr
12 Fred Fisher
13 Charlie Stubley
14 J Littlewood
15 John Munns

Tries: J Goodall, Munns
Drop goal: Oakland

ST HELENS
1 Tom Foulkes (C)
2 Bob Doherty
3 David Traynor
4 Jim Barnes
5 Billy Jacques
6 Richard O'Hara
7 Freddie Little
8 Tom Winstanley
9 Billy Briers
10 William Winstanley
11 Tom Reynolds
12 Joe Thompson
13 Peter Dale
14 Sam Rimmer
15 Bill Whiteley

Try: Traynor

Half-time: 7-0
Referee: J H Smith
Crowd: 13,492

MANNINGHAM SWITCH TO SOCCER

P layers now move freely between the two codes of rugby and into other sports, but of all of the cross-code activity which has involved Rugby League down the years, the one which stands out as perhaps the most surprising came in 1903, just before the Northern Union's eighth birthday. It wasn't just one player switching sports. It was an entire club.

Manningham FC, the inaugural champions of the Northern Union, decided to end their association with the oval-ball game and switch to soccer. They became Bradford City, and went on to win the FA Cup eight years later. It proved to be a great decision for the club, but the move was a significant blow for the infant code of rugby. Manningham may have been struggling on and off the field, and were failing to compete with the richer and more successful Bradford FC, but the Northern Union wasn't strong enough to be losing clubs, especially not the iconic first champions of the sport.

Having been a successful club since their formation in the 1870s, Manningham finished top of a 22-team league in the 1895-96 season. The clubs were then split into Yorkshire and Lancashire competitions for the next five seasons with Manningham, who played at Valley Parade, coming second, fifth, seventh, ninth and twelfth. In 1902-03, two national divisions were created – the first and second divisions – with Manningham finishing tenth out of 18 teams in Division Two, winning 14 and drawing five out of 34 matches. That was to be their last involvement in the sport.

Soccer was growing quickly and sought to rectify the fact it had no professional representation in the city of Bradford. Manningham had initially expressed interest in 1901 after missing out on a place in the Northern Union's new first division in 1902. Secretary Harry Jowett said at a later date: "Manningham had no chance if they were not in the same rugby league as Bradford. They were ready to leave the rugby game to the Bradford club and put their energies into the association game if they received enough support."

One of the instigators of the switch was James Whyte, a Scotsman who

"It is a sad thing to have to do but I propose that Manningham Football Club should abandon the rugby code for the present."

was the sub-editor of the 'Bradford Observer'. He met with John Brunt from the Football Association at Valley Parade at the end of January in 1903 to debate the merits of bringing the sport to the city. By March, the Manningham committee was prepared to allow a professional soccer club to play at its Valley Parade ground. Initially the plan was for soccer to be played on Saturdays, with rugby on Sundays.

In the end, the round-ball proposal gained such momentum that the plan to maintain rugby in any form was quietly shelved. The 11-a-side game was desperate to gain traction in West Riding of Yorkshire, so the new club was likely to be welcomed with open arms. Sheffield United sent a team to Bradford to play at Valley Parade on 25th April, and 12 players were signed despite, at this stage, no guarantee of a Football League place. The wheels were in motion. A month later, the application was made formal when a delegation travelled to London to meet soccer chiefs. With no problems arising, the club was admitted to the Football League by 35 votes to 30, without having played a single match.

There remained just one issue. The members of Manningham still had the power to veto the move. The fate of the club would be decided at St John's Church School on Friday 29th May 1903, at the club's 23rd annual meeting. "It is a sad thing to have to do but I propose that Manningham Football Club should abandon the rugby code for the present," said Jowett.

Alfred Ayrton, the club president, argued that soccer was "a game that would pay", and perhaps that line swayed those who were still undecided because the club had been in such a parlous state. Only a successful archery tournament had kept them afloat earlier in the season. The opposing argument - to remain as a rugby club – "was met with great cheers" but, in the end, the motion to switch sports was carried by 75 votes to 34. Manningham, now known as Bradford City AFC, were to replace Doncaster Rovers in soccer's Division Two.

The new club struggled financially, reporting a loss in its first four years, but they won promotion to the top flight at the end of the 1907-08 season. Three years later they beat Newcastle United 1-0 in a replay at Old Trafford to win the coveted FA Cup – not bad for a second division rugby team!

Four years later, history repeated itself in the city when Bradford FC decided to take the same route, becoming Bradford Park Avenue Association Football Club in a move which was described as "a great betrayal" to the Northern Union game. They were immediately replaced by Bradford Northern, who went on to become one of Rugby League's great iconic clubs.

Tuesday, 25th December 1906

'BULLER' STADDEN MURDERS HIS WIFE

As one of the first genuine stars of Welsh rugby, William Stadden excelled long before the Northern Union breakaway of 1895 for both Cardiff and Dewsbury. He was also responsible for an incident which shocked the West Riding town to its core at Christmas in 1906 when the former international footballer staggered into the local police station and announced: "I want to give myself up. I have killed my wife!" After murdering her, he slashed his own throat and eventually died on the 28th.

'Buller', as he was nicknamed, scored the only points of the game in a Home Nations match against England in 1890 when just one code of rugby existed. His try on that day from a line out was as opportunistic as it was controversial. He had also scored Wales's only try in the same fixture in 1886. He made his international debut in 1884, scoring a drop goal against Ireland in the Home Nations Championship, the pre-cursor to the Five Nations, helping Wales to their first win on home soil. In all, he played in eight internationals, with seven coming in the Home Nations. He was on the winning side five times, scoring twice. He turned down the chance to go on the first British Lions tour in 1888 because he wasn't happy with the terms offered by the private entrepreneurs organising the tour, despite the official line that rugby was a strictly amateur sport.

The talented halfback had been a member of one of the great Cardiff sides, but shocked everybody by moving to Dewsbury in September 1886, making him the first of many Welshmen over the next century to make such a move. But Stadden wasn't turning professional, as Rugby League hadn't yet been born. He revealed that he left Wales due to the lack of employment opportunities. It later came about, rather controversially, that he was working for Mark Newsome, the president of the Dewsbury club, at his mill factory. Even though the Northern Union breakaway was still nine years away, the concept of amateurism was a thorny issue. Dewsbury came in for much criticism as Newsome's actions were frowned upon, although there was no rule in place at the time that stopped players from working for a member of a club's committee.

"I want to give myself up. I have killed my wife!"

Stadden continued to play for Wales while at Dewsbury and after retiring from the game he ran a grocery business. But his family's world came crashing down on Christmas night in 1906, when he strangled his wife in their bed, with his five children in the house, before attempting suicide. Together they had attended the Dewsbury v Wakefield fixture on Christmas Day.

After his police-station confession, Stadden was taken to Dewsbury and District Infirmary where he was left under the supervision of a constable. It was initially believed that he would survive. A blood-stained carving knife was found in his home, and Mrs Stadden was discovered on the floor in her night attire with strangulation marks on her neck. The five children were located in another room, four in one bed, while Abraham Evans, a professional footballer who lodged with the Staddens, was in another room.

Historian Stuart Stanton, from Dewsbury, helped shed more light on Stadden's incredible story. "Buller was one of a number of siblings and he became a first-choice player for Cardiff in 1883," he said. "He went on to play for Wales and then moved to Dewsbury to play for that team. On their ground in January 1890 playing for Wales, he scored the only and winning try. The story concludes – and I have unearthed all the original reports – with him running a large grocery business in the Yorkshire town. On Christmas night 1906 he strangled his wife in their bed and, with five children and a lodger asleep on the premises, he attempted to slash his own throat before surrendering to the police. He died three days later and I have recently found his unmarked grave.

"I was a bit taken aback by the full scale of the story. On a pure rugby front, I think he is the greatest underwritten Welsh hero. If you look at the first decade, 1881-1891, Stadden is the most important figure and his crowning moment was scoring that try to beat England. He also was the first Welsh player to be bought by an English club and he evolved into a star player in Yorkshire, which was the best in England by a country mile. He did what Jonathan Davies did in the 1980s – he went up north and proved he was better than any of the players up there."

As for the horrific events of Christmas 1906, Stanton added: "I have absolutely no idea what happened. That coroner's report is very open – there were no hints of marital discord or that he had been drinking. And what is disturbing about it is he had obviously premeditated it because he moved the youngest child from his own bedroom up to the bedroom with the other children."

Another historian, Gwyn Prescott from Cardiff, had no doubts about Stadden's rugby talents and noted that he played for "the finest Cardiff side in history" and that "he was an outstanding player. He was also the first genuinely working-class player to represent Wales and for that alone he deserves to be remembered."

But no matter how impressive Stadden's on-field talents were, he will always be recalled with infamous notoriety for the appalling events of Christmas Day in 1906.

NEWS EMERGES OF A PROFESSIONAL NEW ZEALAND TEAM

Having stood alone since 1895, Great Britain was finally joined in the professional code by two more countries in 1907. News broke on 13th May, courtesy of the 'New Zealand Herald', that a group of high-profile players in New Zealand intended to tour England and Wales, playing against Northern Union sides. They were soon to be nicknamed the All Golds – a professional version of the All Blacks.

The report read: "A circular has been issued to the football clubs in the union by the Northern Union committee respecting the proposed visit of a New Zealand team to the Northern Union clubs next season. The committee has had this matter under consideration, and they are very favourably disposed to the visit."

The newspaper's scoop stunned many of its readers. The All Blacks were a sporting phenomenon, winning game after game. It was inconceivable that such a revolt could occur, but for the same reasons as in England 12 years earlier, union's strict amateur ethos was seen as flawed by too many. The game was thriving, with the All Blacks tour of Britain in 1905 netting the New Zealand Rugby Union a handsome £10,000 profit, and players were beginning to resent putting their

THE NEW ZEALAND "PHANTOM."

DUNCAN McGREGOR
W. MACKRELL
G. W. SMITH
W. JOHNSTON

A DIATRIBE AGAINST PROFESSIONAL RUGBY

London writers have no sympathy with professional Rugby, and probably it is a case of the wish being father to the thought when "The Times" critic declares: "The Northern Union is fighting a losing battle. . . . All the finer points of true Rugby have been sacrificed by the professional union in order to secure a rushing rough-and-ready spectacle, which proceeds continuously. The tour of the New Zealand professionals is increasing the interest in this chaotic and meaningless pastime for the time being. But it is doomed to extinction in the end, and the growing frequency of foul play (which the referees are tacitly forbidden to check) is a symptom of approaching dissolution. After all, a professionalised pastime always dies of its professionalism, sooner or later."

DUE AT DOVER ON MONDAY.

Mr. Joseph Platt, secretary of the Northern Union, has received a cablegram from Mr. Baskerville, manager of the New Zealand team, dated Naples, Friday, confirming the list of the New Zealand team already published, and adding the names of Messenger and Fraser.

Messenger is the Australian centre three-quarter, and is considered the finest exponent of Rugby football in Australia. He is described by experts as the Valentine of Australia.

Fraser is a forward, of Petone, and has inter-provincial honours. This makes six Petone players.

The team arrives at Dover on Monday afternoon.

The All Golds line up before the third Test against the Northern Union at Cheltenham Dally Messenger is on the far left

bodies on the line for no reward. One official asked: "Was it reasonable to ask those young men to absent themselves from their homes for months, perhaps lose their positions, and then expect them, after enriching the NZRU to the extent of thousands of pounds, to rest satisfied with an allowance of three shillings a day?"

The fact there were so few details of the 1907 tour in the report also sent tongues wagging. Who would be involved? How competitive would the team be? How certain was the tour to go ahead? And how would the NZRU react? The last question was the easiest to answer. The players would be banned, of course. And over the coming weeks, the NZRU and friends trashed the tour in the press, attempting to scaremonger players from signing up to it. Later in May, they thought they had been successful in stopping the tour by forcing players to sign declarations of amateurism, but their efforts were in vain.

The man behind the venture was a player from Wellington called

"Was it reasonable to ask those young men to absent themselves from their homes for months, perhaps lose their positions, and then expect them, after enriching the NZRU to the extent of thousands of pounds, to rest satisfied with an allowance of three shillings a day?"

Albert Baskerville, a modest, quietly-spoken man, whom rugby union underestimated. Baskerville had done a wonderful job in organising the tour and keeping it from the union authorities for so long. He also had the support of George Smith, a genuine star of not just rugby but other sports. An increasing number of other players including Lance Todd were also interested in the proposals. Many had toured England with the All Blacks in 1905 and had come across the Northern Union game, which became 13-aside a year later with the play-the-ball introduced. Baskerville was confident they would learn the game quickly and he wrote to the Northern Union and some of the leading clubs, hoping to be invited to lead a tour. The positive reply came in March 1907 and Baskerville had three months to make the necessary arrangements. There were around 200 rugby players in New Zealand. Over 150 wanted to join his party.

Before long, the Rugby League wheels were also in motion across the Tasman. On 8th August, Rugby League in Australia had its 'George Hotel' moment, when around 50 rugby union officials met at Bateman's Crystal Hotel in George Street in Sydney and took the decision to form the New South Wales Rugby League. However, the meeting was less of a defining moment than the birth of the game in England because they didn't have anything like the number of clubs and players on board. They needed a big name to secure the future of the new sport and that man turned out to be Herbert Henry 'Dally' Messenger, a wonderfully talented player. In a significant coup for Vic Trumper and J.J. Giltinan, who were leading the efforts to establish the new sport, Messenger decided to come on board.

The 24-year-old three-quarter would be unveiled on 17th August in the first match played under Rugby League jurisdiction in the Southern Hemisphere, as he lined up for New South Wales against Baskerville's New Zealand side, who had agreed to play three matches in Sydney before sailing for England. The New South Wales Rugby Union knew how big a blow to them Messenger's decision was and responded by deleting his career statistics from their official records. They weren't reinstated until 2007. Alan Whiticker and Glen Hudson's 'The Encyclopedia of Rugby League Players' in 1999 stated that "it is doubtful the new game would have caught on had he not changed codes."

It was estimated that Messenger's presence in the New South Wales team put an extra 20,000 on the crowd at the Royal Agricultural Society ground. Played under union rules, New Zealand won 12-8, but Messenger excelled, scoring five of the points. A British reporter concluded: "It was only Messenger, first, middle and last." Four days later, New Zealand won again, 19-5, before completing a whitewash with a 5-3 win on the 24th. Messenger captained New South Wales in the final match.

The story didn't end there.

The New Zealand party, led by Baskerville, agreed with Messenger that he would join them on tour – a wonderful compliment given how highly regarded the New Zealand team was. The party left on 25th August, travelling via Melbourne to Colombo where it played against Ceylon on 12th September, although still under union rules. The All Golds won 33-6.

The first game in England came against Bramley - the tourists' first match under Northern Union rules – and the All Golds ran out 25-6 winners. They also prevailed in the Test series with the Northern Union, by two matches to one, having lost the first. The prolific Messenger had scored over a century of points. More importantly, the tour was a fiscal triumph. But it ended in tragedy on its Australian leg in May 1908 when Baskerville contracted pneumonia after a match with Queensland and died in hospital three days later. An exhibition match to raise funds for Baskerville's mother took place on 13th June at Athletic Park in Wellington. It was the first game of the new code to be played in New Zealand.

While Messenger had been touring with the All Golds, the new NSWRL body concentrated on setting up their new competition, which would kick off on Easter Monday in 1908. The nine clubs involved in the first season were Glebe, Newtown, South Sydney, Balmain, Messenger's Eastern Suburbs, Western Suburbs, North Sydney, Newcastle and Cumberland. Souths were later crowned the inaugural champions. At the end of the season, Messenger returned to England, this time with the inaugural Kangaroos. He was now a global star, courting attention from soccer clubs Glasgow Celtic, Newcastle United and Tottenham Hotspur.

This time Messenger failed to inspire international success as the first Ashes series was won by the Northern Union - but he had more than played his part in launching Rugby League down under, as had Bert Baskerville and his pioneering All Golds.

Saturday, 9th May 1908

HUNSLET SEAL 'ALL FOUR CUPS' AFTER CHAMPIONSHIP FINAL REPLAY

It goes without saying that Rugby League has boasted numerous outstanding teams down the years, but Hunslet's 1908 vintage are widely regarded as the sport's first truly great side.

The men from south Leeds produced the most stunning achievement in the code's 13-year history, when they won 'All Four Cups' in the 1907-08 season. Only a handful of clubs have subsequently produced similar feats.

The team was captained by Albert Goldthorpe who, in 2015, was inducted into the British Rugby League Hall of Fame, an honour which sees him regarded as one of the best 25 players to have played in this country. Billy Batten, Hunslet's winger who played alongside Goldthorpe, is another whose name belongs in that finest of groups.

Goldthorpe's brother Walter played in the centres, and scored the only two tries of the Championship Final replay against Oldham, which saw Hunslet win their fourth Cup of the season. Their elder three brothers, William, James and John, had also played for the Hunslet, underlining the fact that they were a local, community-based club, with 24 of the 25 players used in that glorious

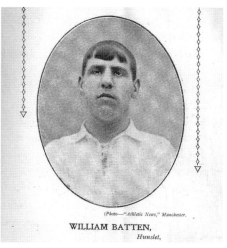

(Photo—"Athletic News," Manchester.

WILLIAM BATTEN,
Hunslet,

season coming from within a 25-mile radius of the ground.

In front of the Goldthorpe boys were the 'Terrible Six', an apt nickname for the Hunslet pack. Prop Harry Wilson was described as "the greatest forward in the Northern Union." The 'Yorkshire Post' regarded the forwards as "an irresistible force, the fiery ardour of the whole combination was simply unnerving."

The Hunslet team cost less than £500 to assemble and won its first trophy on 21st December, beating Halifax in the Yorkshire Cup Final. The next piece of silverware was the Yorkshire Senior Competition. The 27-team Northern Union table shows that Hunslet came second to Oldham. A separate table was calculated from games involving only Yorkshire teams – and likewise for Lancashire - in order to establish the leading side from each county. Hunslet topped the 13-team Yorkshire League, nine points ahead of Halifax.

John W Higson was the only player to win 'All Four Cups' twice, with Hunslet in 1908 and Huddersfield in 1915

The Challenge Cup came next. Hunslet beat Leeds 14-5, Oldham 15-8, Barrow 8-0 and Broughton Rangers 16-2 to set up a final with Hull FC, which was played at Fartown in Huddersfield. It had been a tough run - in the first two matches, Hunslet had needed to overturn half-time deficits, but the final was more straightforward. Tries from Fred Farrar and Fred Smith, along with three Albert Goldthorpe goals, and a drop goal from Billy Eagers, worth two points, gave them a 14-0 win in front of a crowd of 18,000.

An unprecedented Grand Slam was now on.

The Championship Final was played a week later at The Willows in Salford in glorious sunshine in front of 14,000 fans. The game finished 7-all, with Albert Goldthorpe scoring all of his side's points with a penalty, a try and a conversion. Tom White kicked two penalties for Oldham and Jim Wright scored a try. White was left with a difficult conversion to give the league leaders the lead, but he missed.

The governing body convened that night at Manchester's Grand Hotel and decided to stage a replay on the following Saturday at Wakefield Trinity's Belle Vue stadium. The crowd was marginally higher second time around, with 14,054 in attendance. Both figures were regarded as slightly disappointing with the 'excessive' admission charge of one shilling blamed.

Albert Goldthorpe, captain of Hunslet's all-conquering 1907-08 team

"The triumphant march of the footballers of Hunslet will go down in history as the most notable affair of football, ever known in the north of England."

Hunslet led 7-0 at half-time, with all the points coming in the final ten minutes of the half. White had missed a number of shots at goal for Oldham, but when Goldthorpe was given chances in the 30th and 35th minutes, he was successful. Two minutes before half-time, his brother crossed for the game's first try, hacking ahead after a George Tyson error. Albert failed to convert Walter's try, but Hunslet had a handy lead.

Oldham made their life uncomfortable in the opening stages of the second half with White finally landing a kick at goal to reduce the deficit to a converted try. It soon looked like parity would be restored when stand-off David Beynon touched down, but he was ruled to have stepped out of play. Oldham continued to press but there were no further points until the 65th minute when Hunslet fullback Herbert Place kicked a drop goal to edge his side 9-2 ahead.

The Championship and the magnificent achievement of All Four Cups were finally sealed when Walter Goldthorpe scored his second try. Batten broke clear before Billy Eagers and Fred Smith combined to create the chance. The try scorer's brother missed the goal, but it mattered not. The glory was Hunslet's.

Two days later, the 'Yorkshire Evening Post' summed up the club's triumph quite succinctly: "The triumphant march of the footballers of Hunslet will go down in history as the most notable affair of football, ever known in the north of England."

We've swept the seas before boys
And so we shall again
So we shall
So we shall
So we shall again
We've swept the seas before boys
And so we shall again

- Hunslet's anthem

HUNSLET 12 OLDHAM 2

HUNSLET
1 Herbert Place
2 Fred Farrar
3 Billy Eagers
4 Walter Goldthorpe
5 Billy Batten
6 Albert Goldthorpe (C)
7 Fred Smith
8 Harry Wilson
9 Bill Jukes
10 Jack Randall
11 John Higson
12 Tom Walsh
13 John Smales

Tries: W Goldthorpe 2
Penalties: A Goldthorpe 2
Drop goal: Place

OLDHAM
1 Dicky Thomas
2 Arthur Oldershaw
3 Billy Dixon
4 Tom Llewellyn
5 George Tyson
6 David Beynon
7 Tom White
8 Joe Ferguson (C)
9 Arthur Smith
10 Albert Avery
11 Joe Wilkinson
12 Jim Wright
13 Billy Longworth

Penalty: White

Half-time: 7-0
Referee: E Tonge
Crowd: 14,054

SOUTH SYDNEY CROWNED CHAMPIONS IN THE MOST DRAMATIC CIRCUMSTANCES

South Sydney are the most successful club in Australian Rugby League, with 21 Premierships to their name. Their most recent came in 2014 when an injured Sam Burgess inspired them to glory against the Bulldogs. The circumstances of their second title were quite different, however. They won the competition because their opponents, Balmain, failed to turn up for the final.

1909 was a testing year for the new sport in Australia with its very future all too often in doubt. The first Kangaroos had returned home in May, having incurred significant financial losses to the extent that the Northern Union had to pay for their fares home. The Ashes had been lost and English clubs had snapped up 15 of the players, which would impact badly upon domestic crowds in Australia. In contrast, the simultaneous Wallabies

The 1909 Balmain side

rugby union tour had been a considerable success. The momentum achieved a year earlier, when the signing of Dally Messenger helped launch the new code, had evaporated.

Two showpiece matches between the Kangaroo side and a 'Rest of New South Wales' team, meanwhile, attracted just 3,000 spectators. Three of Australian Rugby League's founding fathers, J. J. Giltinan, Henry Hoyle and Victor Trumper, were sacked from their positions.

The 1909 season comprised just ten matches for each club with South Sydney, the 1908 premiers, again finishing top - one place above Balmain. What happened next was quite extraordinary. Balmain, captained by Joe Regent, the great uncle of future Australia coach Tim Sheens, won their semi-

"The club has come down wallop from its high position in public esteem since its childish actions of last week."

final 15-8 against Eastern Suburbs to qualify for the 'club final'. Without realising it at the time, it was to be the final match in Regent's career. At least he went out with a try.

The problems began when the match was not immediately diarised because the league wanted to press ahead with a series of promotional matches between the Kangaroos and rugby union's Wallabies, whose players would be banned from their sport for taking part. They would then switch codes and give League the boost it needed.

Three exhibition games were initially planned, with the Kangaroos winning the first match on the back of Messenger's brilliance, and the Wallabies the next two. The concept had been underwritten by an English businessman called James Joynton-Smith, who funded the payments to the Wallabies, totalling £1,850, with individual fees ranging from £200 paid to the brilliant halfback Chris McKivat and £25 to Ray Gavin. To put that into context, the average Australian annual salary at the time was £100.

The entrepreneur wanted to be repaid, so when three matches still left him £130 short, a fourth game, which had been raised as a possibility in the contracts, was promptly arranged. The Kangaroos received nothing for the matches, despite 1909 being the first year of professionalism in Australia - something which led to considerable ill feeling.

When the domestic final was eventually pencilled in for the Agricultural Ground on 18th September, it was to be a curtain-raiser to the fourth Kangaroos-Wallabies game. Angry Balmain officials stated that having to play second fiddle was unconstitutional. They wanted the match moved to the following week, or they wouldn't turn up. Nobody backed down and so, on the big day, around 4,000 people in filthy weather saw Souths kick off and score a symbolic try with no opposition. They were awarded the match and, consequently, the Premiership. To entertain the crowd, Souths instead played a 'Combined' team, made up of players from various clubs all in different jerseys, and beat them 18-10.

A later interview with the Balmain player Chook Fraser suggested that Souths had initially agreed to join their opponents in boycotting the match, only to renege. A long-standing feud between the clubs developed, which lasted until the 1970s, although Souths denied they had agreed to any such thing.

What the Balmainiacs, as they were known due to their trouble-making reputation, seemed particularly upset about was the league's desire to sign union players. On the day before the final, they complained to Ted Larkin, the secretary of the NSWRL, that "they had been badly treated, and they should not be asked to play an early match." Balmain were also adamant that funds raised from the final should not be used to reimburse Joynton-Smith, and they sided with the many who resented individual entrepreneurs from getting involved with the sport. "It is reducing football to private enterprise and making it a wild scramble for cash," was one opinion aired in 'The Bulletin'.

Balmain's players had even stood outside the ground to dissuade supporters from attending the final, but garnered little sympathy, with 'The

Sydney Sportsman' suggesting that "the club has come down wallop from its high position in public esteem since its childish actions of last week. Outside of their own following, there is not a single voice upholding the action of the club, and nothing but disgust is expressed for their despicable behaviour."

It was also suggested that Balmain might not have fancied their chances of winning the title, knowing they would have had to beat Souths twice. Had they beaten them, the league leaders would have been granted a rematch in what would have officially been the Grand Final, such was the competition format in those embryonic days.

A difficult 12 months for the game in Australia might have ended in farce, but with an influx of star players, the seeds of recovery were sewn and Rugby League had the upper hand over union again. It has remained the bigger code in Australia ever since, although that was further cemented by the visit of the 1910 British Lions. Enough money was raised from the fourth exhibition game, which the Rugby League side won 8-6 to tie the series, to reimburse Joynton-Smith. The governing body even finished the most challenging of years with £39 in the bank.

The only losers in the episode were the Balmainiacs, who remain the only team to lose a Premiership in such bizarre circumstances.

SOUTHS
1 Howard Hallett
2 Tommy Anderson
3 Arthur Conlin
4 Jim Davis
5 Frank Storie
6 Arthur Butler
7 Son Fry
8 Dick Green
9 Harry Butler
10 W Conlin
11 Jack Coxon
12 Billy Cann
13 Pat Carroll

Try: unknown

BALMAIN
1
2
3
4
5
6
7
8
9
10
11
12
13

Half-time: n/a
Referee: W P Finnegan
Crowd: 4,000 (approx)

THE FIRST ASHES TEST DOWN UNDER

The Northern Union had conquered the Kangaroos in England in the inaugural Ashes series of 1908-09. Now it was the time for Australia to be beaten on their own soil.

The first Anglo-Australian Test match to be played in the Southern Hemisphere took place in June 1910 at the Royal Agricultural Showground in Sydney, with the Lions beating Australia 27-20 to take the lead in the two-game series. Their performance was described as "a perfect exhibition of Northern Union rules." What made it so special wasn't just that it was the first Ashes match to be played in Australia, but that the tourists had to overhaul a sizeable deficit with a numerical disadvantage to record such a glorious victory.

With established players like Wigan's James Leytham, the captain Jimmy Lomas who played for Salford and Hunslet's Billy Batten - the highest-paid player in the game, the tourists would have been justifiably confident of maintaining their unbeaten record against an Australian side, which had just beaten New Zealand by two matches to one. The star name in the opposition's line-up was Dally Messenger, who took part in a goal-kicking contest before the match with Lomas, which the West Cumbrian won by three to two from six attempts each.

The hero of the day was Billy Jukes, the second-row forward from Hunslet, who scored a second-half hat-trick. He did more than most to compensate for his team being at least a man down for a prolonged period after the Wigan fullback Jim Sharrock had been stretchered off with concussion and a broken nose following an accidental blow to the head. Forward Bert Avery had to replace him at the back, which was far from ideal. In the second half the tourists also lost Billy Ward - albeit temporarily – and so were down to just 11 men.

Australia, wearing blue and maroon, the colours of New South Wales and Queensland, scored first following a British mistake when Billy Farnsworth set up a try for Darb Hickey, who touched down after beating Batten. Messenger converted.

The Northern Union soon hit back. After Lomas had taken play out of his 25-yard area, the tourists charged forward with a dribbling rush - a tactic used frequently in rugby's early days when a player dribbled ahead soccer style, with several players immediately behind him. The ploy brought the

Lions their first try on foreign soil, with the prolific winger Leytham touching down. Lomas failed with the conversion – one of several missed attempts.

Following a spell of heavy pressure exerted by the home side, Messenger kicked a penalty for a 7-3 lead. The captain, who played his club football for Easts, then extended the lead with a try while Sharrock lay injured. Con Sullivan, the Australian forward who had also represented New Zealand, had been first to handle, before William Farnsworth, Robert Craig and future captain Chris McKivat became involved in the

move. The halfback's pass found his captain on the wing, and Messenger came in-field to touch down near the posts. He converted his own try to take the score to 12-3.

The red-and-white hooped Northern Union produced a stunning comeback, despite playing into the wind. Wigan stand-off Johnny Thomas took Tommy Newbould's pass from a scrum in the opposition 25 and scored near the corner, with Lomas adding the goal.

Just before half-time, another attacking scrum yielded a try for the tourists with every back handling before Leytham scored his second in the corner. Lomas again failed to convert, but the Northern Union were just a point behind at 12-11 and would have the wind advantage in the second period, but Sharrock had been taken from the field five minutes before the break.

After an early second-half skirmish on the Australian try line, Jukes scored his first try in the corner after beating an attempted tackle by the fullback

"A perfect exhibition of Northern Union rules."

Charlie Russell. Although Leytham missed the tricky conversion attempt, the Northern Union now had a 14-12 lead which they would not relinquish. "The Englishmen played up like bulldogs," reported 'The Referee', a Sydney newspaper. Lomas missed with a couple of penalty attempts before Batten produced a try-saving tackle on Albert Broomham. There was no denying that the visitors were on top - they were "in great fettle" according to another local newspaper, although they were soon to lose Ward.

Their prospects were dramatically improved when Sharrock and Ward returned to the field. There was no stopping them now they had their full team on the paddock again. Lomas launched another raid before finding Ward, who fed the marauding Jukes to score his second. Leytham goaled for a 19-12 lead. Lomas was soon haring downfield again, which led to Jukes' hat-trick and a conversion for Thomas.

Batten, who had to play in an amateur game for Hemsworth before the tour to prove his fitness to the selectors, was the next to score, with man-of-the-match Lomas yet again providing the assist. The Australians did pull back a couple of tries. First, Jack Barnett scored after a great run by the halfback McKivat, and then Charlie Woodhead went in under the posts, but there was no escaping the fact that they had been comprehensively outplayed.

The game was played before the sport's then-record crowd of 42,000 spectators. A fortnight later, with Leytham scoring four tries, the Northern Union wrapped up the series with a 22-17 win in the second Test at Brisbane.

The Ashes was on the way to becoming a Rugby League icon and the British were proving far more adept than Australia at this new code of rugby.

AUSTRALIA 20
NORTHERN UNION 27

AUSTRALIA
1 Charlie Russell
2 Charlie Woodhead
3 Jack Hickey
4 Dally Messenger (C)
5 Albert Broomham
6 William Farnsworth
7 Chris McKivat
8 William Noble
9 John Barnett
10 Con Sullivan
11 William Spence
12 Robert Craig
13 Edward Courtney

Tries: Hickey, Messenger, Barnett, Woodhead
Goals: Messenger 4

NORTHERN UNION
1 Jim Sharrock
2 James Leyham
3 Jim Lomas (C)
4 Bert Jenkins
5 Billy Batten
6 Johnny Thomas
7 Tommy Newbould
8 Albert Avery
9 Dick Ramsdale
10 Ephraim Curzon
11 Bill Jukes
12 Fred Webster
13 Billy Ward

Tries:
Leytham 2, Thomas, Jukes 3, Batten
Goals: Lomas, Leytham, Thomas

Half-time: 12-11
Referee: Tom McMahon
Crowd: 42,000

THE RORKE'S DRIFT TEST MATCH

On New Year's Day in 1912, Australia won their first Ashes series, sealing a two-nil series victory with a resounding 33-8 at Villa Park in Birmingham. The Northern Union had more than two years to stew over the humiliation before being able to regain international superiority and they did just that, courtesy of one of the most incredible games in the history of the sport. The deciding Ashes Test of 1914 was a match won by the British Lions despite them being down to nine men at one point. As well as that, the match had been brought forward against the tour party's wishes, with several players unavailable.

Jack Robinson, Stan Moorhouse and Fred Longstaff had scored two tries apiece, as the tourists won the first Test of the series 23-5 on 27 June in Sydney, although the match had originally been scheduled to be played in Brisbane on 20th June. The Lions had agreed to move the match to save the Australian players a 700-mile journey. Australia hit back with a 12-7 win just two days later to square the series.

An argument broke out between the New South Wales Rugby League governing body and the touring managers, Joe Houghton and John Clifford, as a result of a request to bring the deciding Test forward by six weeks in order to capitalise on the rocketing public interest.

A total of 95,000 people had attended the two matches and instead of the decider being played in Melbourne after the Lions' matches in New Zealand, the NSWRL demanded the match played on 4th July, just five days after the second Test. Houghton and Clifford refused because they could barely scrape together a team, not unreasonably pointing out that they had already changed the schedule once in agreeing to move the first Test.

The NSWRL went over their heads and cabled the Northern Union, threatening to withhold gate receipts unless they agreed to move the third Test. Inexplicably, agreement came back from England and the tourists had no choice but to comply with the Australians' demands.

Clifford was incandescent, telling his players: "You are playing in a game

"You are playing for right versus wrong. You will win because you have to win."

of football this afternoon but, more than that, you are playing for England and more, even, you are playing for right versus wrong. You will win because you have to win." Harold Wagstaff, the captain, remembered the meeting well. "The men in my team were moved," he said. "I was impressed and thrilled as never before by a speech. You could see our fellows clenching their fists as Mr Clifford spoke and I know that when we left the room none of us spoke."

Not only did the Lions have injured men unable to take to the field, they suffered further casualties during the match meaning that their 14-6 win remains perhaps the greatest team achievement in the history of Rugby League. The game - aptly named after Rorke's Drift where 150 British troops had manfully defended a ford over the Buffalo River in the 1879 Zulu War against a brutal assault by well over 3,000 African Warriors - was described by the Rugby League historian Robert Gate as a Test which "stands pre-eminent as the perfect example of a team winning against all the odds."

Winger Frank Williams, loose forward Douglas Clark, centre Billy Hall and stand-off Stuart Prosser were the four men who needed to leave the field, having sustained injuries during

ABOVE: Douglas Clark

BELOW: Frank Burge gets a pass away

the match. Clark's predicament, in particular, went down in folklore. Having already broken a thumb, he dislocated his collar bone after a collision with Arthur 'Pony' Halloway, but managed, briefly, to return to the field before tearfully accepting that he could not carry on. By then his side had something to cling on to as, despite the various turmoil, they had managed to pose a more considerable attacking threat than their opponents. Avon Davies had scored a magnificent try after kicking ahead for himself. Alf Wood had also landed three goals.

With only four men in scrums, the Northern Union managed to win their fair share. Then they produced a gem of a try. Wagstaff broke from deep before finding John Johnson on the wing. Primarily a back-rower, Johnson didn't

AUSTRALIA 6
NORTHERN UNION 14

AUSTRALIA
1 Howard Hallett
2 Dan Frawley
3 Sidney Deane (C)
4 Robert Tidyman
5 Wally Messenger
6 Charles Fraser
7 Arthur Halloway
8 Con Sullivan
9 William Cann
10 Frank Burge
11 Edward Courtney
12 Sid Pearce
13 Robert Craig

Tries: Messenger, Deane

NORTHERN UNION
1 Alf Wood
2 Frank Williams
3 Billy Hall
4 Harold Wagstaff (C)
5 Avon Davies
6 Stuart Prosser
7 Fred Smith
8 Dave Holland
9 Percy Coldrick
10 Dick Ramsdale
11 Albert Johnson
12 Jack Chilcott
13 Douglas Clark

Tries: Davies, Johnson
Goals: Wood 4

Half-time: 0-9
Referee: Tom McMahon
Crowd: 34,420

have the pace to finish so instead, toed it forward and dribbled the ball for half the length of the field to score a miraculous, game-winning and series-clinching try with the Aussie fullback, Howard Hallett, beaten all ends up. Wood's goal saw the tourists with a scarcely believable 14-3 lead. Wally Messenger, younger brother of Dally, had scored Ausrtralia's first try.

Even more incredibly, most of the crowd appeared to be cheering for the British out of sheer admiration for their Herculean efforts. Hall heroically returned to the field with ten minutes left to shore up the tourists' defences, although they did concede one late score to the Australian captain Sid Deane.

Even though the second half had gone on for 54 minutes, the Northern Union held firm for the last few moments to regain the Ashes, attracting a standing ovation from the Australian crowd in the process. It was the most remarkable of achievements.

JIMMY LEYTHAM DIES AT SEA

One of Rugby League's first great players - the man who scored the first-ever Test try - was tragically killed in a boating accident near Lancaster in August 1916, at the age of 36. Along with Bert Jenkins, Lance Todd and Joe Miller, James Leytham was part of the great Wigan three-quarter line which helped the club win three trophies in the 1908-09 season. The tragedy shocked Lancaster, where Leytham had started his professional career before he was transferred to Wigan.

His greatest achievement was scoring four tries in an Ashes Test in Brisbane in July 1910, and he remains the only British player to accomplish such a feat against Australia in an international. In the two-match series that year, he scored six times as the Northern Union overturned half-time deficits in both games to prevail 27-20 and 22-17.

Nicknamed 'Gentleman Jim of the Football Field', Leytham was a megastar of the still comparatively new Northern Union code of football. Born in Lancaster in 1880, he signed for his hometown club who joined the Northern Union in 1897. According to 'Rugby League Myth', a book written by Mike Latham in 1993, which charted the histories of extinct north-west clubs: "Lancaster had one jewel shining brightly in a struggling team and this was Jimmy Leytham, who was destined to become one of the finest players of his or any other era. Leytham was destined for great things, not with Lancaster but with Wigan."

Wigan signed him for £80 in late 1903, with the player receiving £10. It represented fantastic business as Leytham went on to amass 1,308 points in just 280 games, after scoring 258 (three-point) tries and 267 goals. His first

Wigan try came in a 14-0 home win over Batley in December 1903 and a fortnight later, on Christmas Day, his hat-trick helped the side to a 12-6 win over St Helens. The new boy was a fans' favourite already.

The tries kept on coming. He came up with a hat-trick as Wigan beat the New Zealand All Golds in November 1907. Leytham passed through the 1,000-point barrier in December 1909. He was the club's leading try scorer in each of his first five seasons at Central Park, and was second only to Miller in 1908-09.

The winger played in Rugby League's first international match for England against Other Nationalities in 1905 at Central Park, finishing on the losing side, 9-3. The game did not have Test-match status, but when the real thing did arrive in January 1908, Leytham marked the occasion by scoring the first try. Scrum-half Jim Jolley had already put the Northern Union 2-0 up against the New Zealand All Golds with a drop goal when the prolific wingman scored in the corner courtesy of Johnny Thomas, Tom Llewellyn and Jenkins. In total he played five matches for the Northern Union, all against New Zealand or Australia, scoring in all five, registering an impressive ten tries. He scored a further eight tries in five matches for England.

He retired in 1912, but was to live for just another four years.

The 'Lancaster Guardian's' front page didn't even carry the story of the deaths of seven fishermen on 20th August 1916 because there were numerous casualties from the Great War on which to report. They still ran a significant story which began: "While the Sabbath bells were ringing on Sunday evening, several Lancaster families were plunged into mourning, not through brave men facing the deadly foe on the field of battle, but through being overwhelmed by the waters of the silvery-streaked bay."

Leytham had led a party of eight men, whose ages ranged from 18 to 44, on a Sunday-afternoon fishing trip at the mouth of the River Lune estuary. All was fine until, on their return, the boat capsized near Cockersand Abbey, leaving the men clinging to the top of the upturned vessel. Only two of the party - Leytham and Richard Wright - could swim. Seeing himself as the leader of the group, Leytham selflessly insisted that he would look after the others, and so Wright swam a mile for help instead.

Wright later gave evidence to the inquest. "As I was swimming to the shore, I could hear the men calling out "Help!" many times, and I could see them on the top of the upturned boat. The sea was choppy, and two or three times I was on the point of giving up hope and drowning with the rest of them, but I had promised to try and get ashore." Mr Wright staggered into a nearby farm and collapsed, having successfully raised the alarm. A lifeboat was sent from Fleetwood at 4pm, but none of the remaining men could be found. The body of Leytham was one of the last to be washed up, six days

"Lancaster had one jewel shining brightly in a struggling team and this was Jimmy Leytham."

after the accident - a tragic ending for a great rugby player. Two of the dead were brothers-in-law of Leytham's. Survived by his wife and two children, the British Lion was buried in Lancaster Cemetery and was later commemorated by a plaque at Wigan's Central Park ground.

The 'Lancaster Guardian' said of Leytham: "[He] was a foreman in the Stores department at Lune Works, residing with his wife and two children and 24, Lodge Street. He was best known in the Rugby football world. For many seasons he delighted Rugby followers at Lancaster with his brilliant play, but it was with the Wigan Northern Union club that he won his many honours. As a three-quarter back he was considered one of the smartest exponents of the game, and has many times been selected for his country and for international games both home and abroad. Mr Leytham's service at Wigan had frequently received recognition, and his loss is deplored in that borough, as he was always looked upon as the most gentlemanly player on the field."

In 2003 Leytham's great nephews, Brian and Steve Leytham, contacted the newly-formed Lancaster RLFC, which had entered the totalrl.com Summer Conference competition, to tell them of the Leytham story. The club duly named its player-of-the-year award after the tragic hero. "As a club we felt it was important to honour the greatest player to ever wear a Lancaster jersey, and the greatest rugby player this city has ever produced," said the club's chairman, John Thomason.

Monday, 8th November 1926

ALL BLACKS COACH SUSPENDED DURING SHAMBOLIC TOUR

It is hard to imagine that any rugby tour could disintegrate into the chaos and misery experienced by the 1926-27 New Zealanders in England - the first tour from the land of the long white cloud since that of the pioneering All Golds in 1907-08.

Seven players went on strike and only made themselves available for selection again when the coach, Ernest Mair, was suspended. He returned to the post after a month and so the players downed tools again. Not surprisingly, the All Blacks, as they were still known, were whitewashed in the Test series against England and incurred crippling losses at the gate.

In 1925 New Zealand had taken the brave step of appointing as coach Mair, an Australian official, who had enjoyed great success in his native Queensland. However, the success of his team, the Toowoomba Clydesdales, was most probably down to the legendary player Duncan Thompson, the captain-coach. Mair convinced the New Zealanders he could replicate Thompson's success, but in reality he was a coaching novice. Mair set about picking the touring squad – not an easy task when the 'Possibles' beat the 'Probables' in a trial match – but he erred in not choosing a genuine hooker. Alphonso 'Phonse' Carroll stepped into the role on tour, but he was to be one of the seven strikers.

The incredible story of what unfolded in England was told by the New Zealand historian John Coffey in his 2012 book, 'Strike! The tour that died of shame'.

Along with Carroll, the striking players were the vice-captain Neil Mouat, Bill Devine, Lou Petersen, Arthur Singe, Jack Wright and the English-born Frank Henry. All were ex-rugby union players, with four of them having switched codes under a cloud of controversy. Doubt has remained over the real cause of the friction between the coach and the striking players. The post-tour inquiry, which was never made public, saw the players banned for life from Rugby League. The 19 loyal players made a pact not to discuss what happened on tour, and stuck to it. When another inquest was launched in

"All the major parties, with the exception of the English Rugby League, were at fault."

43

1962, the life bans were lifted. There were suggestions that Mair was too authoritarian. It was also mooted that religious issues may have caused a problem. Mair once suggested that he had been assaulted and had items stolen, but he never repeated those allegations.

The problems began on board the ship, the 'Aorangi', with arguments surfacing over a variety of issues including laundry expenses, the compulsory wearing of ties at meal times, fines for players missing on-board training and the refusal of some players to perform a haka in an almost empty Canadian train station.

Trouble escalated after the opening match of the tour on 11th September which saw New Zealand beat Dewsbury 13-9. Fullback Craddock Dufty was involved in a stand-up fight with Singe. The forward was ordered home, with Dufty receiving no punishment. Petersen criticised the management's handling of the decision and received his marching orders as well. The other five declared their intentions to walk out on the tour. Mair changed his mind, allowing Petersen to remain, but that Mouat should join Singe in returning home. In the end, nobody went home but the Australian's credibility was in tatters. The English Rugby League Council began to hear murmurs of unrest in the All Blacks camp and contacted Thomas Cook and Son to instruct that no early ship reservations from the New Zealanders should be honoured.

Mair and the striking players weren't responsible for all of the tour's failings. Mining strikes throughout the north of England meant that many could not afford to attend games. From a financial viewpoint, the tour was always going to be a struggle, especially when compared to the lucrative 1921-22 Kangaroo Tour.

The opening dozen matches saw the tourists win nine times, although they went down 28-20 to England at Wigan in a drab first Test. Matters came to a head before the next match at the Watersheddings against Oldham on 23rd October when the rebels refused to play. Winger George Gardiner had to line up at prop with Dufty moving into the second row. Oldham won 15-10. The impasse lasted for another four games, which saw just one win against

Hec Brisbane kicking against Oldham

Mildred Mair (wife of Ernest) leading out captain Bert Avery, vice-captain Neil Mouat, George Gardiner, Lou Petersen and Craddock Dufty for the opening game at Dewsbury

Salford, until, on 13th November, it emerged that Mair had been suspended for a month by the English Rugby League Council, with the blessing of their New Zealand counterparts. The septet were available again for the second Test in Hull, but England won 21-11. In the next seven matches, the tourists won just twice - against Wigan Highfield, when all six forwards were rebels, and Keighley. An international against Wales was lost 34-8.

Mair resumed his position a month later, and so the seven players went on strike again. The last nine matches of a punishing tour went ahead with just a skeleton pack. To their credit, New Zealand won four of these matches, but lost the third Test at Leeds 32-17 on 15th January – the last match of a nightmare tour.

Six of the strikers were sent home early – Henry remained in England to play for York. Upon the tourists' return, they were banned from Rugby League for good. Debate raged whether the decision was fair with the banned players protesting their innocence. The captain, Bert Avery, sided with Mair, as did the other tour manager, George Ponder. Both blamed the striking players for the disastrous tour. Records of meetings were not kept and with the players refusing to discuss the matter ever again, too many questions have gone unanswered, despite Coffey's research. Little in Rugby League's international history has been as dramatic as the events of this tour. The author concludes that "all the major parties, with the exception of the English Rugby League, were at fault."

Mair was arrested in 1929 and charged with attempting to persuade two men to set fire to a hotel he owned which was struggling financially. Despite considerable evidence against him, the case collapsed. He was struck by a car in 1957 and killed.

Sadly four of the players did not live long enough to see their life bans lifted on 24th September 1962. Singe died from an illness in 1936, as did Wright. Devine passed away in 1956 and Petersen in 1961. Mouat did see his exoneration before he was killed in a work accident in 1967. Carroll died in 1974.

Saturday, 4th May 1929

THE FIRST WEMBLEY CUP FINAL

The first Challenge Cup Final at Wembley, played 34 years after the birth of the sport, is obviously one of the most famous Rugby League occasions. The Cup was won by Wigan for the second time after three tries helped them beat an outclassed Dewsbury by 13 points to two.

The Northern Union Challenge Cup was first competed for in 1897 when Batley beat St Helens in the final at Headingley and by the 1920s, interest in the competition was growing rapidly. In 1924 the crowd for the Wigan-Oldham final was 41,831 and John Leake, an exiled Yorkshireman and chairman of the Rugby League's Welsh Commission, suggested that "the final tie for the Challenge Cup be played each year in London." Despite opposition from many in the north, the motion was seconded by Hunslet and eventually the vote succeeded by 13 to 10. It was the biggest gamble in the sport's 34-year existence.

It took five years for the move to go through, with there being an abundance of opposition. There was also doubt over which venue in the capital would be chosen, with Crystal Palace in with a shout, but the cheaper terms offered by Arthur Elvin, the managing director of Wembley Stadium, became the deciding factor. The ground could cater for 94,000 people and it was hoped by the Rugby Football League that enough Londoners would be interested in the first final to swell the crowd by 30,000. After a big marketing push in the north and the south of the country, the figure was a commendable 41,500, just 331 under the British attendance record, and there was no question that Wembley would be used again the following year. Over 20,000 northerners attended and for many it had been a monumental journey as the journalist Ernest Cawthorne noted: "Thousands of northern people who in their highest flights of fancy have only dreamt of a visit have made the metropolis their Mecca today." One man even walked to Wembley from Wigan in a pair of clogs.

A preview of the 1929 final appeared in 'The Manchester Guardian' and read as follows: "If they are sensible in the south they will take some interest in it as a spectacle, even if they do not play it as a game for it is a fast and furious business and the standard of skill in the best teams is very high." They also warned, however, that "the Rugby League game will not catch on in the south, and that is for two reasons: the amateur game [rugby union] is firmly rooted

Wigan's Jim Sullivan collects the
Challenge Cup

and the northern revolution through 'broken time' to full professionalism has found no echo in the south." Even King George V sent a message, via Lord Stamfordham, which read: "I am commanded to convey to the Rugby Football League an expression of the King's best thanks for the loyal message of greeting to its patron on the occasion of the first cup final in London, and to wish all present at the match an enjoyable afternoon."

Wigan were widely tipped to win the final with 'The Manchester Guardian' also noting that "the cosmopolitan Lancashire side may not be allowed to show the brilliance frequently displayed, but all spectacular effect should not be lost." 'Cosmopolitan' referred to the fact that the Wigan side was made up of two New Zealanders, five Welshmen and a Scot. Dewsbury's only non-Yorkshireman was their Welsh fullback, Jack Davies.

Arthur Caiger led the singing of the annual Cup Final hymn 'Abide With Me' and a band of the Welsh Guards entertained the crowd. Lord Daresbury had been invited to present the Cup and a number of other dignitaries including Knights, Lords and Brigadier-Generals were present, as were two former England rugby union captains, Wavell Wakefield and Ronald Cove-Smith. The game was broadcast on BBC radio with Reverend Frank Chambers, a former referee, providing the commentary. A year earlier, Chambers had suggested that the Cup Final move to London, pointing out how excitement had gripped his home town of Huddersfield when the local club reached soccer's FA Cup Final.

Wigan kicked off the match at 3pm and Wembley's first piece of Rugby League action saw Dewsbury's prop William Rhodes field the ball and pass to

DEWSBURY R.L.F.C.   WEMBLEY CUP TEAM, 1929.
[Hartley]   Departure from Dewsbury Station.   [Dewsbury]

one of his centres Clifford Smith who kicked to touch. The first points came from Wigan fullback, Jim Sullivan, who kicked a penalty from 30 yards. Wembley's first try came on 14 minutes with the honour of scoring it going to Syd Abram, the Wigan stand-off. His halfback partner, Arthur Binks, fielded a Dewsbury kick and passed to Abram who set off on a 40-yard run before scoring in the corner. Sullivan couldn't convert, but the favourites were 5-0 up. The only other points in the first half came from a magnificent drop goal from Davies from just inside his own half. Dewsbury had played well, but Wigan led 5-2.

The Yorkshire side continued to pressure Wigan at the start of the second half and launched a 50-yard raid with captain Joe Lyman, Herbert Hirst and Henry Coates prominent. Lyman seemed to be in the clear but, with a tackle that altered the momentum of the game, John Sherrington took him down and Dewsbury's threat thereafter was markedly lessened. There were no points in the third quarter of the game but Scotsman Roy Kinnear, who had signed for Wigan from rugby union in a big-money move in 1927, soon set up a try for his winger, Lou Brown. Ten minutes later Kinnear, who tragically died during a wartime game of rugby union, scored the match-clinching try from Binks' kick. Sullivan's conversion took the final score to 13-2.

The final returned to Wembley in 1930 when league leaders St Helens were surprisingly beaten by 15th-place Widnes. Interest grew until the capacity was satisfied in 1949 by a bumper attendance of 95,050. Until the Super League era came along, the Challenge Cup Final remained the sport's

"Thousands of northern people who in their highest flights of fancy have only dreamt of a visit have made the metropolis their Mecca today."

most iconic occasion.

Dewsbury's Jim Rudd, thought to be the last of the 1929 Cup Finalists to die, had his Ashes scattered at Wembley after his death in 1998. "We do receive occasional requests of this nature, but we were especially touched by Mr Rudd's desire for his ashes to be scattered by the hallowed turf," said a stadium spokesman. "Rugby League is an integral part of the Wembley magic, and we are only too pleased to adhere to his wishes. He holds a unique place in the history of Rugby League at Wembley."

WIGAN 13 DEWSBURY 2

WIGAN
1 Jim Sullivan (C)
2 Johnny Ring
3 Tom Parker
4 Roy Kinnear
5 Lou Brown
6 Syd Abram
7 Arthur Binks
8 Wilf Hodder
9 John Bennett
10 Tommy Beetham
11 Frank Stephens
12 Len Mason
13 John Sherrington

Tries: Abram, Brown, Kinnear
Goals: Sullivan 2

DEWSBURY
1 Jack Davies
2 Tommy Bailey
3 Clifford Smith
4 Herbert Hirst
5 Henry Coates
6 John Woolmore
7 Jim Rudd
8 James Hobson
9 Percy Brown
10 William Rhodes
11 Harry Bland
12 Joe Malkin
13 Joe Lyman (C)

Drop goal: Davies

Half-time: 5-2
Referee: Bob Robinson
Crowd: 41,500

Saturday, 4th January 1930

CHIMPY'S DISALLOWED TRY

Scoreless Rugby League matches are a thing of the past. The last time it happened in a professional match was in December 1993 when Whitehaven played host to Workington Town, but there was a time when such results didn't raise too many eyebrows.

A nil-nil draw has only occurred once in Test football and it couldn't have come in a more important match, nor could it have been any more controversial. The occasion in question was the third and deciding Ashes Test of the 1929-30 Kangaroo Tour. The series was locked at a game each after Australia had won 31-8 in Hull, with Great Britain winning 9-3 win in Leeds.

A crowd of 34,709 crammed into Swinton's Station Road ground on a freezing afternoon in early January 1930 to witness the final match of a magnificent series. They saw Australia dominate proceedings, although the tourists had failed to create much. With a couple of minutes left, however, one of the most famous incidents in international Rugby League history took place when Joe 'Chimpy' Busch, the Eastern Suburbs halfback, picked up at a scrum base inside the 25-yard line and made a darting run on the blindside, going past Stan Smith, the English winger, en route to the corner.

Despite a mass of bodies, the general consensus seemed to be that Busch had scored the try to win the Ashes, but referee Bob Robinson was alerted by touch judge Albert Webster

Joe 'Chimpy' Busch

that Busch had touched the corner flag. With the light fading, confusion reigned. The try was disallowed, despite subsequent suggestions that the referee admitted that it was a fair try but that he had been persuaded otherwise.

Rugby League Australian Tour.

LAST TEST MATCH, at Swinton,
JANUARY 4th, 1930.

H. SUNDERLAND (Jt. Manager).   J. L. DARGAN (Jt. Manager).

To the Australasians.

The Australasian Tour of 1929-30 opened on the ground of the Rochdale Club on September 7th, and to-day with the playing of the third and last Test Match, the climax has been reached. In the four months the tourists have been in the Mother country, many things have happened, but either in success or otherwise they have played the game as it should be played and have proved themselves a credit to the great Commonwealth to which they belong.

Healthy competitive rivalry is essential between Britain and the Dominions and of national value that few people realise. These tours help to focus attention on Australia and to knit bonds of friendship that will be unbreakable.

We congratulate the Australasians upon the splendid all round ability they have shown, although they have had more than their fair share of injuries to players, and we are pleased that Rugby League supporters have so far recognised their merits as to ensure the tour being a financial success.

Win or lose, to-day—whether they regain the "Ashes" or not—we wish them on their return God speed! Bon Voyage!

Busch was furious, later stating that he got the ball down between 18 inches and two feet inside the line. He always maintained that his opponent Fred Butters, the Swinton loose forward, had knocked the flag down in making the tackle. Busch later said of the incident: "I beat Smith and could only see the white line ahead of me. I knew it was a certainty, and dived across the line and placed the ball down for a try. Butters did not even touch me. I had the try scored when he dived at me, missed, and he hit the corner flag. Then, when we thought we had the game and the Ashes won, the linesman waved his flag. It was ruled no try and after all we did not win."

England believed they had retained the Ashes with a draw, having gone into the series as holders. This was the line that 'The Observer' took the following day, but a fourth Test, at the suggestion of the Australians, was hastily arranged and played 11 days later at the Athletic Grounds in Rochdale. Harry Waller, who had chaired the historic meeting at the George Hotel in 1895, was appalled at the staging of such a match and sent a telegram to the RFL, complaining that 'Mammon' had triumphed over sportsmanship.

The English agreed to play but there has always been uncertainty as to whether they really considered the Ashes to be on the line. England captain

"When we thought we had the game and the Ashes won, the linesman waved his flag."

Jonty Parkin who had announced his decision to retire after the series, elected not to take part.

Jim Sullivan took the captaincy and England prevailed by three points to nil with Smith again involved in late drama, this time snaring a try with just six minutes left to play. One way or another England had retained the Ashes, which they went on to dominate in the 1930s, but Chimpy Busch and the Australians always maintained they should have won at Swinton.

He did have the last laugh – of sorts. At the end of that third game, Busch ran to the corner flag, yanked it out of the ground and took it home as a souvenir of perhaps the most famous moment in Test football history. "All England could not have taken it from me unless they brought out their navy," he said. On the boat home, Busch met a Glaswegian girl called Josephina, whom he later married. After leaving Easts in 1930, he moved to England to play for Leeds. He represented the club in a Yorkshire Cup final replay against Wakefield Trinity in 1934. He returned home in the role of captain-coach at Balmain before his career was ended by injury in 1936. No matter what the talented halfback achieved in an outstanding career, Chimpy Busch's name will forever remain in Ashes folklore for what happened on that bizarre afternoon at Station Road in 1930.

Nearly nineteen years later, the 1948-49 Kangaroos stood silently around that same corner of the Station Road pitch to pay homage to Busch before their match against Great Britain. "We looked at the corner patch of with hallowed feelings of an incident that caused a terrific sensation in Rugby League at the time," wrote Clive Churchill in his autobiography. "Even to this day of 1962, the Joe Busch try raises controversy. Having gazed at the revered spot we dipped our lids and walked back to the dressing room."

ENGLAND 0 AUSTRALIA 0

ENGLAND
1 Jim Sullivan
2 Alf Ellaby
3 Artie Atkinson
4 Hector Halsall
5 Stanley Smith
6 Jack Oster
7 Jonty Parkin (C)
8 Arthur Thomas
9 Nat Bentham
10 William Burgess
11 Alec Fildes
12 Martin Hodgson
13 Fred Butters

AUSTRALIA
1 Frank McMillan
2 William Spencer
3 Tom Gorman (C)
4 Cecil Fifield
5 Bill Shankland
6 Eric Weissel
7 Joe Busch
8 Herb Steinohrt
9 Arthur Justice
10 Bill Brogan
11 George Treweek
12 Vic Armbruster
13 Jack Kingston

Half-time: 0-0
Referee: Bob Robinson
Crowd: 34,709

Saturday, 18th June 1932

AUSTRALIA'S RORKE'S DRIFT

Australia kept the Ashes series alive in the second Test of 1932 with one of their most celebrated victories, in a match dubbed 'The Battle of Brisbane' due its sheer brutality and the lengthy rollcall of injuries.

The Australians went into the match on the back of a tight 8-6 defeat in the first game at Sydney, played in front of a world-record crowd of 70,204. Alf Ellaby and Artie Atkinson had scored the only tries of the match for the victorious Lions. Twelve days later, the sides met again at the Brisbane Cricket Ground with 26,574 in attendance, in a game that was to go down in Ashes folklore, described as being "as hot as fire and as hard as steel".

Australia suffered five injuries during the match, and were at one point reduced to ten men, although they did at least get off to the perfect start when halfback Hector Gee scored from a Fred Laws pass. The big English prop Joe Thompson had been carried off after the first scrum and Australia took advantage, posting another try when Gee set up Joe Wilson. The young stand-off Eric Weissel converted the first before kicking a penalty, and the score remained 10-0 until half-time.

Earlier in the half, England wing Ellaby had what would have been a glorious try controversially disallowed with even the match report in 'The Referee', an Australian publication, claiming that it should have stood. At the other end, the Australian captain, Herb Steinohrt dropped a Weissel pass with the line begging. Desperate to stay in the game, the tourists cranked up the physicality. Australia's 19-year-old centre Ernie Norman had to leave the field three times on his maiden Test appearance after struggling to get to grips with the bigger English centres Atkinson and Stanley Brogden - but each time he returned. Gee needed a torn lip to be stitched up and a stray English boot meant that Frank O'Connor picked up a sizeable gash above his eye. Thompson had returned for the Lions, and even though Martin Hodgson and Les White also needed treatment, they began to claw their way back.

"It became the most desperate and rugged game imaginable. Players were strewn like dead men on the field, or were carried off to the touch lines to recover. They were chiefly Australians."

When Stan Smith scored shortly after the break from Brogden's pass, the complexion of the match was changed again. Jim Sullivan couldn't convert, but at 10-3, and momentum with the tourists, things were now a lot more interesting.

With the Rorke's Drift Test of 1914 still rankling, Australia produced a similar effort in a sensational last 15 minutes. Weissel badly injured his ankle. It was initially thought that he had broken a bone, but tests later showed that not to be the case. Gee was stretchered off. Weissel came back on. Norman was still struggling and Dan Dempsey broke his arm, but heroically decided to play on despite medics trying to persuade him otherwise. When they finally got their way, Dempsey cried on the sideline. England could smell blood. Brogden thought he was over the line, but O'Connor knocked the ball from his grasp in the act of his opponent scoring and the referee ordered a 25-yard drop out. An enormous slice of luck made up for that when a cross-kick fooled all of the Australian players in the path of the ball and Ernest Pollard was able to touch down. But Sullivan missed another goal. Just four points down, England would win the Ashes with a converted try.

Things got even harder for Australia when they were down to just three in the scrums with Steinohrt, Les Heidke, now at hooker, and Madsen

AUSTRALIA 15 ENGLAND 6

AUSTRALIA
1 Frank McMillan
2 Cliff Pearce
3 Ernest Norman
4 Fred Laws
5 Colin Wilson
6 Eric Weissel
7 Hector Gee
8 Herb Steinohrt (C)
9 Dan Dempsey
10 Peter Madsen
11 Les Heidke
12 Sidney Pearce
13 Frank O'Connor

Tries: Gee 2, Wilson
Goals: Weissel 2, Pearce

ENGLAND
1 Jim Sullivan (C)
2 Alf Ellaby
3 Artie Atkinson
4 Stan Brogden
5 Stanley Smith
6 Ernest Pollard
7 Les Adams
8 Nat Silcock
9 Les White
10 Joe Thompson
11 Martin Hodgson
12 Bill Horton
13 Jack Feetham

Tries: Smith, Pollard

Half-time: 10-0
Referee: Joe Simpson
Crowd: 26,574

taking on the English pack. Norman, having gone off, re-emerged and Gee hobbled back into battle. Amazingly, Weissel was still out there, and when Joe Pearce hammered Les Adams, the English scrum-half, the ball came free and into the hands of the crocked five-eighth who managed to hobble 75 yards downfield, side-stepping Sullivan, with half-a-dozen opponents in pursuit. This bravest of runs was ended just five yards short of the try line and in the next phase of play, Gee, also barely able to walk, picked up the ball and crashed over for the clinching try. With Weissel incapacitated, Pearce landed the goal, and at 15-6, Australia were home and dry at last.

'The Australian Worker' wasn't impressed with some of the foul play: "It is all very well to speak of Tests being a game for "he-men". If that sort of thing is to be accepted as a part of big football it is bound sooner or later to bring the game into disrepute." 'The Referee' praised Australia's courage. "It became the most desperate and rugged game imaginable," they said. "Players were strewn like dead men on the field, or were carried off to the touch lines to recover. They were chiefly Australians." Australian journalist Claude Corbett had a stark warning for the game that such violence should be curtailed "otherwise there will be a fatality on the field which will not be accidental."

Australia had finally avenged Rorke's Drift and in 1959 the new football ground at Wagga Wagga was named The Eric Weissel Oval,

The 1932 Lions

honouring a man who had produced one of the most remarkable performances international Rugby League had ever seen.

Friday, 7th July 1933

RUGBY LEAGUE IN MERGER TALKS WITH AUSTRALIAN RULES FOOTBALL

In early July 1933 the Sydney publication, 'The Referee', published a sensational scoop, revealing that Rugby League and Australian Rules Football had entered into serious dialogue about the two sports merging.

The thinking behind the proposed venture was to develop "one common code of football for Australia. This new football code would stand unrivalled in the winter, just as cricket does in the summer." Similar ideas had been floated in 1908, when Rugby League was still in its infancy in Australia, and in 1914 when the outbreak of the Great War saw the proposal forgotten about. Nobody had expected it to resurface.

The idea was perhaps founded on anti-British feelings which existed at the time in Australia. In the last two Rugby League Ashes series, there had been Chimpy Busch's contentiously disallowed try and the violent scenes at the Battle of Brisbane. In cricket, meanwhile, Douglas Jardine's 1932-33 'Bodyline' tour saw hostile English bowling push back the accepted boundaries of sportsmanship. Animosity between the two nations lingered with Australia's next tour of England now in serious doubt. Unlike Rugby League, such a newly merged football code would have no British origins or connections. It would be a totally Australian sport, and that appealed to many.

The men behind the proposals were Horrie Miller, the secretary of the New South Wales Rugby League, and Con Hickey, a high-ranking Australian Rules official. Miller had been in Melbourne to wave off the fifth Kangaroo Tour of Europe and had travelled back to Sydney with Hickey who was preparing for the Australian National Football Carnival. Miller suggested the merger to Hickey, and the idea blossomed. It was announced in 'The Referee' that formal talks would be held during the carnival in August.

"Just imagine it - the game featuring that outstanding high-marking and cultivated drop-kicking of the Australian Rules, and those brilliant passing movements, sizzling wing runs, and the side-stepping and dodging of rugby."

The new sport, it was hoped, would become as common as cricket and better supported than any existing winter sport in Australia. Hickey spoke of the game "incorporating the best features of the Rugby League code and the Australian" which would allow "the game to operate throughout Australia and eventually the world."

One outspoken supporter of the proposal was James Joynton-Smith, the man who had done so much to ensure that Rugby League stayed alive during its tumultuous second year of 1909, when his wealth managed to attract most of the Australian national rugby union side. "Just imagine it," he said. "The game featuring that outstanding high-marking and cultivated drop-kicking of the Australian Rules, and those brilliant passing movements, sizzling wing runs, and the side-stepping and dodging of rugby."

The story progressed on 27th July when the same publication revealed how Miller's suggestion of the hybrid game would work. Rugby League fans would still see rugby posts, tackles, play the balls, offsides, running with the ball, knock-ons, forward passes, three-point tries and two-point goals. However, changes included an oval pitch, each side having 15 men, the scrum being replaced by the referee bouncing the ball and no tackling above the waist.

With little support from the public, significant opposition to the plan soon surfaced. On 4th August the 'Sydney Morning Herald' wrote that "each game is too well-rooted in its own sphere to be shaken and any attempt thereat would almost surely bring nothing but disappointment and disaster." Furthermore, in an interview published on 8th August, the great administrator Harry 'Jersey' Flegg told 'The Referee' that he wouldn't be attending the talks because they were of no interest to him. He was happy to be involved in a sport which had deep British connections. "It involves matters much greater than drafting the new rules ... the original and existing games have their own powerful appeal to their players and public, and [have] the sentiments which history inspires." The Queensland Rugby League shared Flegg's sentiments.

A fortnight after Flegg's comments, the proposals were dealt a severe blow when a match played at Sydney Agricultural Grounds, under hybrid rules, on 11th August failed to satisfy anybody. Instead of Miller's proposed rules, Australian Rules Football was played in the middle two quarters of the pitch with Rugby League rules deployed in the other quarters. The two teams of junior Queenslanders appeared confused, and the idea of a hybrid game soon fell away.

At a meeting in Sydney the following week, the League's George Ball (better known as S.G. Ball) suggested that the proposals should not be circulated to the clubs. Miller disagreed and so Flegg accused him of disloyalty to Rugby League. Nobody else spoke in favour of the hybrid, and the vote to take it to the clubs was defeated by 15 to 10. Such a proposal between the two sports has never been raised again.

KANGAROO TOURIST DIES ON JOURNEY TO ENGLAND

One of Rugby League's saddest stories occurred in August 1933 when the Kangaroo tourist Ray Morris died in a Maltese hospital en route to England. It was a desperate tragedy that was felt in both hemispheres.

Born in 1908 in Ashfield, New South Wales, Morris made his first-grade debut for Western Suburbs in 1927 and his try helped them win the 1930 Grand Final against St George. He also played in the 1932 decider when the Magpies lost to South Sydney. He played wing in the first final, centre in the latter and was also adept in the stand-off position. He made his New South Wales debut in 1931 and was called up again in the following two seasons.

At club level, Morris, described as a "forceful player, dashing in attack and strong in defence", transferred to the Sydney University club and, despite only playing five matches in 1933, he was selected to tour with the Kangaroos at the end of the season. The University club played in the New South Wales Rugby League Premiership from 1920 to 1937 and were perennial wooden spoonists, finishing bottom on 12 occasions, although they were third in the table when the party departed. Morris was the only player from the club chosen to represent Australia, even if he wasn't destined to pull on the green and gold.

The fifth Kangaroos tour party departed from Darling Harbour in Sydney on 4th July with a happy Morris "looking forward to a wonderful experience," according to 'The Rugby League News'. It is believed that Morris's difficulties started when he took a blow to the ear whilst sparring on the Jervis Bay ship somewhere between Perth and Colombo. Later he swam in the ship's pool where his burst ear-drum became infected. He lay in the ship's hospital for ten days.

On 9th August Sydney newspapers carried a cable from Harry Sunderland, the tour manager, reporting that "the managers of the Kangaroos met a difficult situation in the Mediterranean, where the surgeons of the Jervis Bay, Dr Gordon and Dr Clough, held a consultation and decided to send a radio message to Valetta for a specialist." Sunderland also assured Morris's relatives that "every care is being taken and risk avoided", although he did admit that Morris was in a "low condition".

Morris, a member of the New South Wales police force and a talented wrestler and swimmer, was met by specialists and taken to the Blue Sisters Hospital in Valetta along with a travelling Rugby League supporter called Sam Haron who wished to keep him company. Tragically, Morris died following an operation which had led to meningeal complications. On the morning of 11th August, the Australian papers carried news of the operation and described Morris's condition as "critical".

It was not long before the terrible news broke throughout Australia that the popular 25-year-old had lost his life. "Advice has been received that Ray Benjamin Morris, the member of the Australian Rugby League team, en route to England, who was put ashore at Malta with ear trouble, died last night following an operation," reported 'The Queensland Times'. The 'Rugby League News' carried the following poem: "Ray, you've heard the final whistle, full time's sounded, life's game is o'er." 'The Manchester Guardian' reported that "Australia's Rugby League team will be without their most brilliant centre three-quarter, R Morris, who died at Malta." Some compared his death to that of Swinton's Bob Seddon, the British Lions captain who drowned in the Hunter River halfway through their 1888 tour of Australia.

There was a memorial service on the ship which was still on its way to England. Australia decided against replacing Morris in their squad. With the Australian domestic season still in progress, minute silences were held before games and flags were flown at half-mast at Australian Rules Football matches. The Western Suburbs club was stunned, with the president, E McFayden, paying this tribute: "Dear Ray Morris has passed away. One that cannot be forgotten; his manliness and sportsmanship could not be surpassed."

Haron, who was with Morris throughout his final hours, later said: "I was with Ray until the end. Ray knew he was dying. He gripped my hand, mentioned his mother and then died peacefully. Everybody had hopes that Ray was recovering. The doctor suggested that it was safe for me to relax my bedside vigil. I went motoring and on my return Ray asked me about the trip and seemed cheerful; but early the next morning I awakened feeling instinctively that all was not well. When I visited Ray I found him apparently

"Ray knew he was dying. He gripped my hand, mentioned his mother and then died peacefully."

worse and called the doctor, also the military doctor, who told me the case was then pretty hopeless and that he had only one chance out of 600. Ray died within a few hours. I attended the simple funeral ceremony on August 18th. The body has been placed in a vault to await transference to Australia."

Morris was buried at Waverley Cemetery where a huge crowd assembled to pay their respects, including Harry Jersey Flegg and J.J. Giltinan from the New South Wales Rugby League and the former Kangaroo captain Dally Messenger. Ross McKinnon, Tom Monaghan, Gordon Favelle and G Sullivan, teammates of Morris at The University Club, carried his coffin.

Over in England, Morris's teammates were unable to bring the Ashes home, despite the presence of magnificent players like Wally Prigg, Dave Brown, Vic Hey and Ray Stehr. They lost the three Tests to England by scores of 0-4, 5-7 and 16-19. They won 27 of their 37 matches, with the tour making a healthy profit. The Morris family received Ray's £200 tour fee.

Many of the 1933-34 Kangaroos visited Morris's grave when they returned from Europe. His headstone reads: "Ray Morris. Who died at Malta while on tour with Aust. Rugby League Team. (KANGAROOS) 10th August 1933. Aged 25 Years. Loved and Remembered By All."

In his 'ABC of Rugby League', published in 2006, Australian journalist Malcolm Andrews described Morris as "Rugby League's most tragic player." In 2008 the Malta Rugby League governing body changed the name of their player of the year award to the Ray Morris Medal, a small but poignant tribute to a largely forgotten hero of the sport's early years.

Sunday, 31st December 1933

THE FIRST RUGBY LEAGUE MATCH IN FRANCE

Dimanche 31 Décembre 1933
Stade Pershing
L'ECHO DES SPORTS
présente sous les auspices de la
Rugby League
La première partie jouée en France de Rugby à treize

Match International

Angleterre
contre
Australie
■
Ce PROGRAMME
comprend une analyse des règles du nouveau
jeu, la composition des équipes,
et les numéros des joueurs.
PRIX : UN FRANC

With French rugby union tearing itself apart amid a backdrop of widespread thuggery and shamateurism, the time was right for Rugby League to be launched across the English Channel. The first-ever match took place on the last day of 1933 as an England XIII were hammered 63-13 by Australia in Paris in an exhibition designed to showcase the game to a new audience. Despite the one-sided score, the event was an enormous success and led to the birth of the sport that the French call Rugby à Treize.

Such plans had been in place in 1921 with the manager of that year's Kangaroos, S.G. Ball, and the Rugby Football League confident of launching Rugby League in France, but rugby union threats to boycott the Stade Pershing should any 13-a-side match be staged there, among other problems, saw the venture quietly dropped. At least seeds had been sewn at the governing bodies of Great Britain and Australia. "The Rugby Football League had been considering for some time the possibility of introducing the game into France and had set up a working party in April 1933 to look at the viability of the project, wrote Mike Rylance in 'The Forbidden Game'. "Six months later, October 3rd 1933, a five-man delegation arrived in Paris to make specific arrangements. Their plans coincided with the arrival of the Australian touring team, whose manager,

"Galia was 'astounded by the fitness, mobility and intelligent passing of the Australian pack.'"

Harry Sunderland, a journalist with a reputation for a pioneering spirit, joined the Paris delegation."

John Wilson was the chief executive of the RFL at the time, a post he had held since 1920. "Ordinarily I am a cautious man," he said. "I want to see the plan clearly before I make a move. In this matter of extending the Rugby League game to France, however, I believe that the time is opportune for us to make a move forward."

The New Year's Eve match was scheduled for the Stade Pershing, with the original venue ruled out due to pressure from rugby union. Wilson's days as a cyclist - he had represented his country in the 1912 Olympics - gave him the opportunity to liaise with the French sporting media. Victor Breyer, an official of the International Cycling Federation and the editor of 'Echo des Sports', was immediately interested in Wilson's plans and managed to book the stadium, despite opposition from the 15-man code. Breyer, in turn, put Wilson in touch with Maurice Blein, a journalist at a publication called 'Sporting'. He advised the five-man working party, which also included Hunslet's Joe Lewthwaite, Bramley's Walter Popplewell and Barrow's Wilfred Gabbatt, that "it had to be skilful and attractive to play and watch, otherwise it wouldn't be able to persuade players to want to play it." Blein was asked which French union players would be most able to lead a Rugby League tour of England. "Without the slightest hesitation, I gave them the name of Jean Galia," he said, according to 'The Forbidden Game'.

Hopes were high of a huge crowd, with Wilson worried that the stadium would not cope with Parisian demand to see the game. Unfortunately a blizzard kept the figure to around 10,000 with £650 taken in gate receipts. The prolific Easts point scorer, Dave Brown, provided the stand-out contribution

---

AUSTRALIA 63 ENGLAND XIII 13

AUSTRALIA
1 Frank McMillan (C)
2 Vic Hey
3 Cliff Pearce
4 Dave Brown
5 Jack Why
6 Frank Doonar
7 Leslie Mead
8 Mick Madsen
9 Arthur Folwell
10 Ray Stehr
11 Jimmy Gibbs
12 Sidney Pearce
13 Wally Prigg

Tries: Brown 4, Gibbs 3, Mead 2, S Pearce 2, Prigg 2, Stehr, Hey
Goals: Brown 9

ENGLAND XIII
1 Jim Sullivan (C)
2 Jack Morley
3 Artie Atkinson
4 Joe Oliver
5 Tommy Thompson
6 Stan Brogden
7 Bryn Evans
8 Norman Fender
9 Les White
10 Nat Silcock
11 Ken Jubb
12 Bill Horton
13 Ted Sadler

Tries: Morley, Evans 2
Goals: Sullivan 2

Half-time: 20-10
Referee: A E Harding
Crowd: 10,000 (est)

with four tries and nine goals, giving him 30 points in the match. The margin of their victory was even more incredible given that nine of the Kangaroos had played the day before against Wales at Wembley, with Brown scoring 21 points in that game. While Brown led the way with his points haul in Paris, the honour of scoring the first Rugby League try on French soil went to the Australian Wally Prigg.

England had whitewashed Australia in the 1933 Ashes series, but only five of their Ashes players figured in this exhibition match. Many had been in action the day before either for their clubs or for the Welsh at Wembley, and took a later ferry than their opponents. They didn't adapt to the freezing conditions. It was reported in 'The Kangaroos' by Ian Heads that they were "reluctant to put their bodies on the line on the cruel, cold surface, and Australia tore them apart, playing football of dazzling quality." At the end of the match, the joyous crowd threw the red cushions from their seats into the air, and "showered the Australians with kisses". Brown and Vic Hey were led from the field on the shoulders of fans.

Unsurprisingly, the President of the International Rugby [union] Federation talked the occasion down: "It is less diversified and owing to the lack of combination it is quickly exhausted as a spectacle capable of arousing emotion," he said, but he was in a minority. The exhibition was a triumph and, crucially, Galia was "astounded by the fitness, mobility and intelligent passing of the Australian pack." He was soon on board and along with Wilson, according to 'The Times', "signed an agreement under which M Galia will form and captain a French team which will play four matches in England during March."

Even though it was an exhibition match, the game had the desired effect of sparking interest in the country. Galia's pioneers played their first international match on 17th March 1934, losing 16-32 to a 'Rugby League XIII' at Warrington. Shortly after the players' return, the Ligue Française de Rugby à XIII was formed on 6th April in Paris with ten clubs, and it went from strength to strength for the remainder of the decade.

Before long, the game in France would grow quicker than anyone had dared imagine, much to the chagrin of rugby union officials.

Wednesday, 21st August 1940

NAZI-SUPPORTING GOVERNMENT BANS RUGBY LEAGUE

T he following story ranks quite justifiably as one of the most outrageous injustices in sporting history. With Rugby League fast overtaking union in France in the 1930s and early 1940s, rugby union shamefully collaborated with the Nazi-supporting Vichy government to have League banned and its assets seized. The tale was told extensively for the first time in Mike Rylance's 1999 book, 'The Forbidden Game'.

When Rugby League was introduced to France in 1933 and 1934, its growth exceeded all expectations. Shortly after Jean Galia's pioneers returned from their six-match tour of England, ten teams kicked off the inaugural professional competition. Four years later, there were as many as 3,000 open-age players and 1,500 juniors. Union players were switching codes en masse, including the France captain Jep Declaux who moved to Bordeaux for 80,000 francs. He was an exception in monetary terms, though. The majority of players barely earned any more than expenses or what they would have earned in the shamateur union code.

Rugby union was in a parlous state in France throughout the 1930s. In the first year of the decade, an international player called Jean Taillantou was handed a suspended prison sentence for a late tackle, which killed an 18-year-old opponent, Michel Pradié. Three players had died in similar circumstances the previous autumn. Thoroughly disillusioned with the shambolic running of the sport and the relentless on-field violence, 12 leading clubs broke away to form their own competition. The national team was then booted out of the Five Nations in 1931, guilty of routine thuggery and the regular flouting of union's amateur ideologies. Rugby League came along at just the right time in France, and made significant inroads immediately.

As in England, union's governing body was situated in the capital city, but the best players and teams were located at the other end of the country. "By the 1920s and 1930s, French rugby had become a game administered at national level by toffs in Paris but played by peasants in the South-west," explained John Lichfield in a feature in 'The Independent' in 2007. "The toffs soon lost control." The southerners played rugby union with flair, vision and panache, and so took to the more aesthetically pleasing Rugby League instantly. The new game spread like wildfire across the south west, as rugby (union) had done in the late 1800s. Even after a promising first five

Colonel Joseph Pascot, an instigator of the ban on Rugby League in France

years, leading union clubs like Carcassonne, Narbonne and Brive were still switching to League by 1939. Typically, union responded by making life as awkward as it could for League, getting the new game banned from various stadia, whilst the Ligue Française de Rugby à XIII was blocked from joining the Comité Nationale des Sports, making the administration of the game that much harder. Nevertheless, rugby union still had more to worry about than Rugby League with clubs and players deserting them in droves. They had boasted nearly 900 clubs in the 1920s. Fifteen years later, there were 471. As one Treiziste put it: "By 1939 we'd killed them off! Rugby union was dead."

Only one thing was able to halt the commendable progress of Rugby League in France: the Second World War. "The rival sport stormed through the South-west like the word of Martin Luther through the corrupt 16th-century Catholic Church," wrote Lichfield. "It was to take a war and one of the shabbiest tricks in sporting history to save French rugby union." In May 1940, the Germans invaded and subsequently occupied northern and much of central France. The south was controlled by a right-wing government based in the town of Vichy. Senior rugby union administrators were cynical enough to convince the Vichy government that professional sports, like the new code of rugby, had contributed to the corruption of the French youth, whose

"The fate of Rugby League is clear. Its life is over and it will be quite simply deleted from French sport."

collective laxity and ill-discipline had allowed the Nazis to conquer their country. It was an outrageous line, but unfortunately the government, with ex-union international Colonel Joseph Pascot as its Director of Sports, took little persuading in falling for it.

On the weekend of 21st-22nd August 1940, the Vichy sports minister, Jean Ybarnégaray, was quoted in newspapers as saying: "The fate of Rugby League is clear. Its life is over and it will be quite simply deleted from French sport." In December, the head of the government, the 84-year-old Marshal Philippe Pétain, ordered Rugby League to 'merge' with union, but that League could continue at amateur level. Vichy even reneged on that, and, quite shamefully, League's assets including stadia, money, players and kit were seized and handed over to rugby union.

XIII Catalan official Marcel Laborde, who was summoned to Vichy to be told that Rugby League was to be banned

Evidence that rugby union was paying its players was ignored and other professional sports - football, wrestling, cycling and boxing - escaped Rugby League's fate despite a newspaper headline on 13th July which read: "No more professional sport in France." Only one sport was to suffer. "Professionalism must disappear totally," Ybarnégaray continued. "Professionalism, whether open or covert, has done much harm. I have seen it in the sport I know very well – pelota. It is professionalism which, in most of France, has turned the public away from rugby matches and which has corrupted certain teams. Rugby was no longer being played for the sake of playing, but to win, sometimes for reasons which had nothing to do with sport. No more Rugby League!"

The 1940-41 Rugby League season kicked off on 13th October, but after just one round of games, the Ligue Française de Rugby à XIII threw in the towel. "We will be playing rugby union from now on," said the Ligue's Marcel Laborde, who came under fire for not fighting back. Players, fans and clubs were devastated. On 19th December 1941, the collaborationist dictator Petain formalised the suppression of Rugby à Treize.

Re-born after the war as 'Jeu à Treize', not even allowed to use the word 'rugby' nor re-claim the assets which were stolen from it, Rugby League in France never fully recovered, despite the wonderful achievements of Puig-Aubert's post-war team. There have been no apologies from the rival code, nor any compensation paid, despite the French government finally recognising in 2002 that the Rugby à Treize had been terribly wronged.

BITING SENSATION MARS FIRST TEST MATCH IN EIGHT YEARS

Domestic Rugby League continued during the Second World War in the UK and in Australia, but the international scene went into an eight-year hiatus. The last Test match had taken place in January 1938 when the touring Kangaroos beat France 16-11 in Marseille.

Britain was as good as bankrupt at the end of the war, but crowds still flocked to watch sport and Rugby League benefitted from healthy attendances. Australia had also been affected by hostilities, feeling isolated from Britain, with whom it had previously enjoyed close ties. Australia were therefore keen to host a touring party, but cricket and rugby union authorities decided they were not in a position to consider the issue. The Rugby League Council, however, thought differently, putting the matter to a vote, and on 24th October the motion was carried by 19 votes to four. The touring party set sail on 3rd April on the aircraft carrier, HMS Indomitable, which led to one of the great sporting nicknames. The Lions would emerge unbeaten from a three-match Ashes series down under, a record which still stands, and so the squad became known as 'The Indomitables'.

Willie Horne, Jim Lewthwaite and Bryn Knowelden, the three Barrow players, had actually helped build the vessel in the town's shipyards, although, of course, at the time they didn't know its destiny. The arduous journey took a month with the players training and taking part in numerous activities to stave off the boredom. Seven-a-side deck hockey proved most popular and the team with the Wigan players called themselves Wigan Warriors, half a century before their club assumed that moniker. During a game of hand football, the ball went overboard. Eric Batten dived into the water, estimated to be 60 feet below the deck. When he returned with the ball, he was chastised by the captain because the waters were shark infested. Upon docking in Western Australia, there followed a painstaking train ride across the country lasting four days, during which the tourists couldn't even change their clothes.

"When the Australians found they couldn't outplay us in the tests they tried rough tactics. These methods were a great mistake, for you cannot produce good play by these means."

'The Indomitables' depart for Australia, April 1946

The Australian public couldn't get enough of the tourists. Star players like the 35-year-old captain Gus Risman, a veteran of the 1932 and 1936 Lions tours, Ike Owens, Ernest Ward and Batten - son of Billy, a 1910 Lion - were mobbed when they stepped outside their hotel. Grounds were so full that spectators climbed onto grandstand roofs to watch games, and many injured themselves falling off.

Despite the Australian press writing Risman's men off, the Lions were good enough to beat New South Wales twice at the Sydney Cricket Ground by scores of 14-10 and 21-7 before crowds of 51,634 and 47,431. They approached the Ashes series with confidence. The official crowd for the first post-was Test was officially 64,527, but many more found their way in. Numerous fans fainted and a skirmish of litter throwing broke out between Sydney Cricket Club members and Rugby League fans, which was later referred to as the Battle of Sydney Hill.

The Lions got off to a great start when the Barrow stand-off Horne touched down in the second minute, but Risman, who would join Workington Town after the tour, missed the relatively simple conversion. He had also missed a penalty shot in the first minute. It would prove to be a difficult day with the boot for the skipper. Australia hit back with a penalty from their captain, Joe Jorgenson, but an unconverted try from the colossal Welsh prop Frank Whitcombe, one of 11 players from the Valleys, put the Lions ahead at 6-2.

The big moment of the game, and indeed the whole tour, came in the 27th minute, and it remains one of the most controversial incidents in Anglo-Australian Tests. Jack Kitching, the Bradford Northern centre, was sent from

Great Britain take to the field for the first Test match of the 1946 Ashes series

the field by referee Tom McMahon for punching Jorgenson. As he left the field, he showed off a bruise to his chest, claiming that he had been bitten by the Australian skipper. The story became front-page news for days, and even when the two nations settled their differences, the media and the public refused to drop the issue. Jorgenson threatened to sue Kitching for the accusation, but eventually dropped the matter. The incident was a sensation, becoming almost as notorious as cricket's 'Bodyline' tour, 14 years earlier.

England - as the team was still called despite the presence of numerous Welshmen, with the Great Britain name still a year away from being used in Rugby League - held on until half time and then sought to protect their lead and earn a famous victory. With one exception, Risman continued to miss penalty goals, although with Horne partnering the magnificent Tommy McCue behind the scrum, England, wearing squad numbers, were still a threat. But it was Australia who scored the second-half tries with Ron Bailey and Lionel Cooper crossing. Fortunately for the tourists, Jorgenson was also profligate with the boot. England tried to pinch the game late on but Owens was tackled into touch near the line and Risman missed with a long-range penalty. But as holders of the Ashes, a draw suited the Lions. Australia needed to win each of the remaining Tests.

The fall-out from the biting controversy dominated the news for days. Cinemas advertised that they had the footage and people flocked to watch it, while the media successfully whipped up an anti-Lions feeling. That, in turn, led to an amusing story of an elderly woman on the same train as the tourists who was helped with her luggage by 'a portly gentleman'. She thanked him, and told him she was relieved to be in her carriage without coming into contact with Lions, of whom she was frightened. The portly gentleman was, inevitably, Whitcombe, the 17-stone Bradford Northern prop.

The brilliant Risman had some harsh words for his opponents. "Compared with the standards revealed in my two previous tours, play in Australia has deteriorated 50 per cent. When the Australians found they couldn't outplay us in the tests they tried rough tactics. These methods were a great mistake, for you cannot produce good play by these means."

England sealed the Ashes by beating Australia 14-5 in Brisbane, with debutant wing Arthur Bassett scoring a hat-trick. He scored a further two tries in the third Test in Sydney, helping the Lions to a 20-7 win – a match which Risman was offered £500 to throw. "Bribery to make the British team lose a rugby match?" Risman wrote in his 1958 autobiography. "A thing unheard of, and I know every British player that day would sooner have died than lose."

England had now won nine consecutive Ashes series and would go on to make it ten in a row, before Australia finally triumphed again in 1950, 30 years after their last series win.

AUSTRALIA 8 ENGLAND 8

AUSTRALIA
1 Dave Parkinson
2 Edgar Newham
3 Joe Jorgenson (C)
4 Ron Bailey
5 Lionel Cooper
6 Pat Devery
7 John Grice
8 Frank Farrell
9 George Watt
10 Roy Westaway
11 Arthur Clues
12 Reg Kay
13 Noel Mulligan

Tries: Bailey, Cooper
Goal: Jorgenson

ENGLAND
5 Gus Risman (C)
3 Eric Batten
6 Ernest Ward
9 Jack Kitching
11 Albert Johnson
12 Willie Horne
14 Tommy McCue
18 Ken Gee
19 Joe Egan
16 Frank Whitcombe
22 Doug Phillips
23 Les White
26 Ike Owens

Tries: Horne, Whitcombe
Goal: Risman

Half-time: 2-6
Referee: Tom McMahon
Crowd: 64,527

RUMOURS OF SECTARIANISM SURFACE AS AUSTRALIAN CAPTAIN IS DROPPED

Sectarianism has rarely reared its ugly head in Rugby League, yet it remains regarded as perhaps the only logical explanation for the incredible omission of the Australia captain, Len Smith, from the 1948-49 Kangaroos Tour.

The decision ranks as one of the most baffling in Australian sporting history. The 30-year-old centre was the captain of Newtown, New South Wales and Australia and had just inspired his country to a comfortable win in Brisbane against the Kiwis. The series was drawn, with Smith attracting most of the plaudits. Playing centre, he was the New South Wales player of the year and seemingly a certainty for tour selection. It was initially believed that the omission was a simple error, and no credible explanation was ever forthcoming. The episode became an embarrassment to Rugby League in Australia, with Smith retiring at the end of the season, and the Kangaroos enduring a miserable time in England. Smith's absence overshadowed the entire tour. In 'The Kangaroos' by Ian Heads, the chapter which deals with the 1948-49 tour is aptly titled 'The Enduring Mystery of Len Smith'. Heads observed: "The omission of Len Smith from the 1948 Kangaroo touring team ranks as both the greatest injustice and the greatest mystery in the history of Australian Rugby League."

With Smith as captain-coach, Australia had lost the first of their two Tests to New Zealand in 1948, by 21-19 in Sydney. Before the next game, the governing body applied pressure on Smith to produce a positive result. With Clive Churchill making his Test debut, Australia did indeed win, and convincingly, by 13-4, as they scored three tries to none. Smith was credited by many for the win, with his tactic of targeting the Kiwi centres proving decisive. More importantly, the win gave Australia new hope ahead of the Ashes series with Great Britain. With Smith at the helm, victory was possible.

The official NSW Rugby League yearbook named Smith as its best player of 1948 and was glowing in its praise of his second-Test performance. Yet of the 15 players on duty for Australia, 14 were chosen to tour England. Smith was the exception. Something didn't quite add up. Smith was in Queensland on the day the squad was announced, having just captained New South Wales to victory in an inter-state match. With the assembled players only listening for their own name, nobody other than Smith realised what had happened.

When they did learn of his omission, they were stunned. The public outcry was unprecedented. Newtown even declared that they planned to raise £700 to send Smith on the tour as its 29th player, but Harry 'Jersey' Flegg, chairman of the Australian Rugby League Board of Control – the man who ran the game - told the club that such a move could not be sanctioned, but he did describe Smith's omission as a tragedy. Former Kangaroo Ross McKinnon called it "one of the greatest injustices ever perpetrated against any man in any sport." The St George official Sid Pert said: "Smith's rejection is vicious. It is an insult to Rugby League." Eddie Burns, the Canterbury prop who was also overlooked, called the decision "the cruellest thing I have known in football." The great Clive Churchill labelled it "the greatest blunder ever made by Australian Test selectors." He continued: "We were like a leaderless legion. His omission is a blot on Test selection administration."

A broken Smith walked away from Rugby League, becoming an administrator in the sport of trotting and a sports writer. Shamefully, he was rarely invited to Rugby League functions.

Gradually, as time passed, the idea that sectarianism had played its part began to surface. Smith was a Catholic, while many of the selectors, and others in influential positions in the game, were Masons. It was later reported that Masonic meetings had taken place on the boat on the journey to England, something which had also happened on the 1937-38 tour. "Some of the players told me they'd been pushed through the Masonic Lodge," said Smith, in an interview with Heads. "I'm a Catholic – I'm not a particularly religious man, but I'm not ashamed of it either. In my view religion was one aspect of what happened." Other players have agreed with the theory.

There were suggestions that two of the selectors wanted the coaching job for themselves, but neither got it. In another surprising twist, the captain-coach role was awarded to a player recently dropped by both Wests and New South Wales – the uncapped Colin Maxwell, who wasn't even sure he would be selected to tour. Chaos reigned. That they started the tour going down 22-3 against Huddersfield was little surprise. Australia went on to lose all three Ashes Tests to Great Britain.

Fifty years later, Smith was interviewed by Sean Fagan, one of Australia's most prominent Rugby League historians. He recalled: "I asked Len whether he thought the decision to exclude him from the tour to England was based on religion. He reluctantly said 'Yes'. Len said he thought he was omitted because he was Catholic. At the time, he did not even consider that it would be an issue, after all he was the incumbent captain-coach and they had beaten the Kiwis as demanded by 'Jersey' Flegg. Although he never said, it was apparent

"The omission of Len Smith from the 1948 Kangaroo touring team ranks as both the greatest injustice and the greatest mystery in the history of Australian Rugby League."

The 1948 Kangaroos

that the pain of missing that tour never really subsided. By the account of every other player and League expert I have met or read about, Smith should have led the tour as captain. It is difficult to understand the implications or enormity of the incident 60 years later, although whenever the matter is raised with any of the remaining 1948 Kangaroos you can see in their responses that it still causes great anguish to all."

Fagan said recently of the interview: "Whenever I raised with Len his 1948 tour non-selection, his eyes immediately welled-up. You could see it hurt him very deeply inside, even if his spoken words were more circumspect and restrained about it."

PUIG'S BRILLIANT FRENCH TEAM BEAT AUSTRALIA

Rugby union and the Vichy government may have done their best to kill off Rugby League in 1940 and 1941, but seeds of recovery were sewn after the war. Although the sport never fully recovered from those crimes, the French established a foothold strong enough for them to tour Australia in 1951. Incredibly, they returned victorious. The tourists didn't just edge past the Green and Golds, who were skippered by the great Clive Churchill. They beat them in games one and three with consummate ease and with a style of play rarely seen before. The Australians couldn't live with a team throwing 40-yard passes, or popping the ball up between the legs.

On their maiden tour of Australia, France were the first Rugby League side to travel by air. Their champion player was the legendary Aubert Puig, better known as Puig-Aubert, the classy chain-smoking fullback, who remains widely regarded as the greatest Treiziste of them all. The French travelled in great heart, having won the 1950-51 European Championship, but were poor in their opening matches and suffered a 20-10 loss to Riverina five days before the first Test.

The Australians were worried about the impact the French form might have on gate receipts, with one pundit calling one of their early tour performances "the worst display that any international Rugby League team has ever given in Australia." But he was shown to be no judge when Aubert's superlative kicking game helped France win the first Test 26-15 in front of a mammoth crowd of 60,160 in Sydney. The Aussies hit back with a 23-11 win in Brisbane and the much-anticipated decider was played in front of a huge 67,009 crowd on Saturday 21st July. One of the spectators was 'The Master' himself, Henry Herbert 'Dally' Messenger, Australian Rugby League's first hero and a self-confessed fan of the French fullback.

One Australian reporter concluded that France's win was down to "fast, nippy forwards and greater speed in the backs. [They] out-generalled and outplayed Australia." Mike Rylance in 'The Forbidden Game', said: "The French didn't just beat the Aussies, they did so in a style that left the

"The French didn't just beat the Aussies, they did so in a style that left the opposition looking clueless."

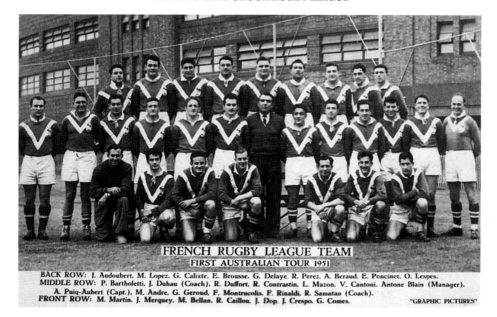

FRENCH RUGBY LEAGUE TEAM
FIRST AUSTRALIAN TOUR 1951

BACK ROW: J. Audoubert, M. Lopez, G. Calixte, E. Brousse, G. Delaye, R. Perez, A. Beraud, E. Poncinet, O. Lespes.
MIDDLE ROW: P. Bartholetti, J. Duhau (Coach), R. Duffort, R. Contrastin, L. Mazon, V. Cantoni, Antone Blain (Manager).
A. Puiq-Aubert (Capt.), M. Andre, G. Geroud, F. Montrucolis, F. Rinaldi, R. Samatan (Coach).
FRONT ROW: M. Martin, J. Merquey, M. Bellan, R. Caillou, J. Dop, J. Crespo, G. Comes.   "GRAPHIC PICTURES"

opposition looking clueless." Even without their influential half Jean Dop, the Chanticleers won the match 35-14, with Lyon scrum-half Jo Crespo scoring three tries, Bordeaux winger Raymond Contrastin crossing for two and Lyons second-row Ellie Brousse and XIII Catalan centre Gaston Comes scoring one apiece.

Aubert, who played his club football for Carcassonne, and who had by now passed Jim Sullivan's record tour points haul of 132, kicked seven goals. He was later crowned France's sportsman of the year, even receiving a telegram from Sullivan before the match, saying: "Congratulations. Keep it going!" Not surprisingly he was courted by Sydney clubs, many of whom offered him a lucrative contract.

The battle between Aubert and Churchill had been built up heavily by the press with one Australian reporter, at a tour match before the first Test, commenting that "Churchill stamped himself, on Saturday, as the greatest fullback playing League, when he overshadowed the much-publicised French champion, Puig-Aubert." They were less forthcoming with their views on the subject following the Tests after the genius Frenchman had more than proved his worth. Puig reportedly said: "I have found Churchill out. I know how to beat him. Churchill is now just another fullback." There was clearly quite a rivalry between the two, given Churchill's scathing comments about his French counterpart in his autobiography. "Puig-Aubert was not, contrary to popular belief, a great fullback," he wrote. "I could name dozens of fullbacks who would leave him for dead in football ability. Puig-Aubert was only a kicker."

The Australian players were even derided by their own supporters. "When France, early in the second half, went to a 25-4 lead the crowd, resigned to the inevitable, laughed ironically as man after man of France pounced on the ball and ran yards through the Australian forwards, scarcely touched by a hand," read another report. The only Australians to emerge with any credit were Duncan Hall, Wally O'Connell, Keith Holman and Denis Flannery. Brian Davies and Hall scored their tries with Noel Pidding kicking four goals.

It was 'a Black Saturday' according to the 'Sydney Morning Herald'. "It was Puig-Aubert and his merry men all, or practically all, the way! Few can doubt that the hundreds of thousands of Australians who saw these French footballers play will think more appreciatively of the land from where they came." The newspaper's reporter also harboured hopes that France's "fast open game with brilliant backing-up and split-second passing" would rub off on the Australians. The tourists had certainly been buoyed by Australia's five-yard rule at the play-the-ball which allowed them to exercise their expansive brand of football. With no strict rules in place at the time, defences were sometimes taken back only a yard in other parts of the world, which tended to result in more forward-dominated games.

According to Rylance, the streets of Marseille were lined with around 150,000 people who welcomed back their heroes. Even the Parisian L'Équipe newspaper, which has ignored Rugby League in recent times, carried the headline 'Antipodes Shattered', and later crowned their hero fullback as sportsman of the year. The Australian 'Sun Herald' was happy to admit that Puig was 'the finest fullback in the world,' even above Churchill, although the Australian later wrote that he was no fan of his French counterpart.

Coming so soon after Vichy's infamous strangling of French Rugby League, the achievements of Puig-Aubert's men were truly remarkable.

AUSTRALIA 14 FRANCE 35

AUSTRALIA
1 Clive Churchill (C)
2 Noel Pidding
3 Noel Hazzard
4 Norman Hawke
5 Denis Flannery
6 Wally O'Connell
7 Keith Holman
8 Denis Donoghue
9 Kevin Schubert
10 Duncan Hall
11 Brian Davies
12 Bernie Drew
13 Harold Crocker

Tries: Davies, Hall
Goals: Pidding 4

FRANCE
1 Aubert Puig (C)
2 Raymond Contrastin
3 Gaston Comes
4 Jacques Merquey
5 Vincent Cantoni
6 Rene Duffort
7 Joseph Crespo
8 Paul Bartoletti
9 Gabriel Genoud
10 Louis Mazon
11 Elie Brousse
12 Édouard Ponsinet
13 Gabriel Calixte

Tries: Crespo 3, Contrastin 2, Brousse, Comes
Goals: Puig 7

Half-time: 4-20
Referee: Tom McMahon
Crowd: 67,009

The 1951 France squad on the plane to Australia

Puig-Aubert, 'The finest fullback in the world'

Saturday, 10th November 1951

RUGBY LEAGUE'S TV DEBUT

Great Britain wrapped up their Test series against New Zealand in 1951 at Station Road in Swinton by landing a penalty goal with just three minutes to play. That in itself made it an occasion to remember, but their 20-19 victory is better known for being the first-ever live nationally televised game of Rugby League.

A fortnight earlier in 'Rugby League Review' magazine, Eddie Waring had spoken of a trip to America in 1950, where bars had shown sporting events. In his opinion, Rugby League needed the benefits such exposure brought. "At last we have the opportunity to go big in a big way, through the channels of the television set," he wrote. A fortnight later the vision became reality as the nation was given a chance to watch Great Britain and the Kiwis do battle. The Saturday afternoon coverage, which started at 2.50 and ended at 5 o'clock, was one of just seven programmes on that day's standalone BBC channel. Three of those were news shows. The commentary was performed by Alan Dixon and Harry Sunderland, with Waring providing half-time analysis. He also conducted post-match interviews with the two captains, Dickie Williams and Maurie Robertson.

Great Britain had won the first Test at Odsal 21-15, a game in which Hunslet second-rower Cec Thompson became the second black player to play for Great Britain, four years after Roy Francis' two-try debut against the same opposition. The match had been filmed by Movietone News and was shown a few days later in cinemas, with Waring commentating.

This time they were outscored by five tries to four, but Desmond White's profligacy with the boot cost the tourists dearly. Dick Cracknell, Vince McKeating, Ken Traill and George Wilson scored for Great Britain, with Jimmy Ledgard kicking three goals, although that still left the hosts 19-18 down with just minutes to play. The big moment came in the 77th minute when Great Britain were awarded a penalty following a scrum offence by the Kiwi halfback Des Barchard. Ledgard sent the ball between the posts and the series was won.

"At last we have the opportunity to go big in a big way, through the channels of the television set."

GREAT BRITAIN 20
NEW ZEALAND 19

GREAT BRITAIN
1 Jim Ledgard
2 Dick Cracknell
3 Doug Greenall
4 Ernest Ward
5 George Wilson
6 Dickie Williams (C)
7 Alf Burnell
8 Ken Gee
9 Vince McKeating
10 Alan Prescott
11 Cec Thompson
12 Billy Blan
13 Ken Traill

Tries: Cracknell, Wilson, McKeating, Traill
Goals: Ledgard 4

NEW ZEALAND
1 Desmond White
2 Bruce Robertson
3 Tommy Baxter
4 Maurie Robertson (C)
5 Jack Forrest
6 Cyril Eastlake
7 Des Barchard
8 Cliff Johnson
9 George Davidson
10 William McLennan
11 Charlie McBride
12 Frank Mulcare
13 Alistair Atkinson

Tries: B Robertson 2, Forrest, Eastlake, McBride
Goals: White 2

Half-time: 7-11
Referee: Albert Dobson
Crowd: 28,246

It may have been anticipated that this thrilling international would herald the beginning of a healthy relationship between Rugby League and television, but unfortunately that was not the case. The BBC were keen for more, but live coverage was likely to cause not just a reduction in attendances for the televised match, but also for the rest of that day's fixtures. Moving games to Sunday was not possible at the time.

Leeds were given the chance to host the first televised club match when they played Warrington on 12th January 1952 but they turned it down, fearing a smaller crowd. Instead, the cameras went to Wigan to broadcast the second half of their match with Wakefield Trinity. When Workington played Featherstone Rovers in the 1952 Challenge Cup Final, the first to be televised nationally, the crowd was around 20,000 down on the four previous finals – although perhaps that was also down to the participants hailing from small towns. Either way, Rugby League fans would have to wait another six years for another televised Wembley final, with the Rugby Football League continually rebuffing bids from the BBC, concerned with television's impact upon gate money.

The 1952 Kangaroo tourists were also against matches being televised.

Eddie Waring

Harry 'Jersey' Flegg, chairman of the Australian Board of Control, said: "The propaganda angle of television does not interest Australia." Others who were against televised games pointed to the fact that when England's game against France was broadcast in 1953, that day's domestic crowds were halved. It was also suggested that the BBC were getting Rugby League on the cheap, and many were disgruntled with what they saw as knockabout commentaries from Waring, which were harmful to the game's image.

So, back to 1951 – what did Rugby League supporters make of being able to watch a game from the comfort of their armchair for the first time? Vincent Firth described the experience in positive terms for 'Rugby League Review'. "I would say that while a televised version would never keep me away from a match I was able to attend, television is a good substitute for the real thing and it must be a wonderful channel for really successful propaganda." But he pointed to some minor flaws: "What I missed was the warm, intimate contact with the normal Rugby League crowd; the colour; the frustration of not being able to put in the occasional personal cheer; and an inability to recognise the players as easily."

Despite the presence of the cameras, Station Road still housed 28,246 people at the match, although that was some way from its 45,000 capacity. "Television must not be made the scapegoat for the failure to fill the Station Road ground with a forty-five thousand crowd," wrote Stanley Chadwick, editor of the Review, and a constant thorn in the side of the RFL. "The responsibility rests entirely with the RL Council who failed to put the match over in a big way."

In 1958, Workington were again in the Challenge Cup Final when it was next beamed into the nation's living rooms. Rugby League and Eddie Waring were well on the way to becoming a staple part of the BBC's Saturday afternoons via their new programme, 'Grandstand'.

Friday, 13th March 1953

BILLY BOSTON SIGNS FOR WIGAN

One of Rugby League's bona-fide legends signed professional forms with Wigan on 13th March 1953 and a major reason he switched codes was the colour of his skin.

Desperate to play for Cardiff and to win an international cap in the 15-man code, Billy Boston was forced to accept that the chances of a black player playing for Wales were virtually non-existent. Never having happened before, such an occurrence wouldn't take place for decades more. Rugby union in Wales was inherently racist, as Professor Tony Collins pointed out in his 2009 book, '1895 & All That'. "Black rugby union players were disadvantaged by the link between the sport and Welsh national identity," he wrote. "As expressed through rugby union, Welsh nationalism was closely tied to British imperial identity: indeed, Welsh rugby was profoundly pro-British. Rather than being separatist or oppositional, it took pride in proving that the Welsh nation was the best representative of the British imperial ideal - which meant that a white skin was a prerequisite for success. Faced with open hostility in their daily lives and institutionalised racism in their sport, there can be little wonder that young black rugby union players eagerly accepted contracts from Rugby League clubs in the north of England."

Between the 1930s and 1960s, prominent Welsh talent like George Bennett, Alec Givvons, Roy Francis, Johnny Freeman, Colin Dixon and Clive Sullivan left the Valleys for the north of England, all having failed to become Wales's first black rugby union international. Not for the first time, the prejudices embedded in that sport were to benefit Rugby League. "I was disappointed that Cardiff never showed any interest in me and I think that was because of my colour," Boston told 'The Western Mail'. "They certainly wouldn't let me into their clubhouse after I turned professional. I don't think I would ever have been picked for Wales at union." The contrast with his new sport could not have been greater, as he recognised when penning the foreword to 'The Glory of their Times', a history of black players in Rugby League, edited by Collins and Phil Melling. "It's no good writing a book about Rugby League and talking about the colour bar," he said. "In this game there isn't one."

Numerous Rugby League clubs wanted to sign 'Billy B', the 18-year-old sensation from the multiracial Tiger Bay, where blacks were barred from working on the Cardiff docks in 1935. But it was Wigan who claimed the scalp. Before he signed, Boston was in the Army, based in Catterick, proving himself a prolific try scorer for the successful Signals rugby union team. With many of their games in Yorkshire, he was able to showcase his talents on the doorstep of Rugby League clubs.

Wigan entered the bidding in January 1953 and first saw him in action the following month when the Signals beat Old Roundhegians 24-8 in the sixth round of the Yorkshire Cup. On 11th March in the Army Cup Final, Boston's team came up against the Welsh Guards, the holders of the competition. Many tipped a close game, but a tearaway Boston romped in for six tries, further underlining his sublime ability. Representatives from Wigan and Oldham tried to speak to Boston, but were refused entry to the post-match celebrations, although it was suggested that an approach from Hunslet would be welcomed. Coached by the great Welshman Gus Risman, Challenge Cup holders Workington Town were also interested.

Wigan directors knew they had to act quickly and on Friday 13th March they set off to visit John and Nellie Boston in Tiger Bay, withdrawing £3,000 from the club's account on the way. They hoped they could persuade them to accompany them to Catterick where they could all sit down with their son. The chances of such a scattered approach coming to fruition must have been slim, but they were to get very lucky.

Upon arrival, they were delighted to hear that Boston was due home later that evening on leave as he was due to play for Neath the following afternoon. When he arrived, a bid of £1,000 was rebuffed. They then placed £1,500 on the kitchen table in five-pound notes. Boston left the room, leaving the decision to his mother, who tried to get rid of them by demanding double. To her surprise, the club agreed. The worlds of both Wigan and Billy Boston were about to change forever.

Boston said later: "I'm not ashamed to tell you that when the two Wigan directors left our house that night, I burst into tears wondering what lay ahead of me as a professional Rugby League player. I didn't sleep at all that night. Suddenly I realised that now I would never wear the red of Wales in a rugby union international and I can't say I was happy about it. I honestly thought that when my mother told Wigan I wanted £3,000 to turn professional … it would frighten them off. I suppose I could have got more than £3,000 even in those days. Soon after I signed for Wigan, another club offered me an open cheque."

Boston's parents demanded that the signing initially remain a secret

"Faced with open hostility in their daily lives and institutionalised racism in their sport, there can be little wonder that young black rugby union players eagerly accepted contracts from Rugby League clubs in the north of England."

while his army commitments continued, and even though the deal had to be registered with the Rugby Football League, their secretary Bill Fallowfield kept the details to himself. The news eventually broke in August, with Boston making a try-scoring debut for Wigan against Barrow in November, eight months after putting pen to paper.

He scored in each of his first five games and went on to make his Great Britain debut in the same season, posting a try against France in a 17-8 win at Bradford, although the match didn't have Test status. He was selected to tour at the end of the season, becoming the youngest-ever Lion, before setting a record for the number of tries scored by a tourist. That eye-watering sum of £3,000 was beginning to look a very astute piece of business. In all, he scored 478 tries for Wigan in 488 matches. Including internationals and a short stint at Blackpool, he ended his glorious career with 571 tries in 564 games, a tally which remains second only to Warrington's Australian winger Brian Bevan.

Boston was appointed Member of the British Empire in 1986. He was in the first group of players to be inducted into British Rugby League Hall of Fame in 1988 and is one of five greats on the Rugby League Wembley statue, unveiled in 2015.

The considerable success of men like Boston, Bennett, Francis and Sullivan failed to change Welsh rugby union attitudes. It wasn't until 1986 that a winger called Glen Webbe became their first black international when he was chosen for a match against Tonga.

Time and again, their self-inflicted losses were Rugby League's gain.

THE YANKEES ARE HERE!
THE CURTAIN IS UP! THE BIG SHOW IS ON!

Of the stories that are hardest to believe from Rugby League's wonderful history, the American All Stars' 26-match tour of Australia and New Zealand in 1953 surely sits near the top.

With hindsight, the whole amazing story appears completely surreal. But it actually happened. A motley crew of college gridiron players, wrestlers, athletes and low-level rugby union players, all but one of whom hadn't heard of Rugby League, were rounded up and handed a gruelling schedule which saw them come up against numerous Australian Test stars. The All Stars actually won seven and drew two of those games, and played in front of several five-figure crowds, with the biggest a quite unbelievable 65,453.

Six decades later, the tale was brought to life in Gavin Willacy's compelling book, 'No Helmets Required'.

The scheming Mike Dimitro was the tour leader. He had failed to make the grade as a professional footballer, but continued to work in sport in California, determined to make a name for himself. He had seen one game of Rugby League in Australia and, remembering it vividly, corresponded with the governing bodies in Australia and New Zealand, convincing them that he had a squad of competent Rugby League players. Desperate to see League crack America, the tour was given the green light. But the fantasist Dimitro didn't have a single player, nor enough money. Neither had Rugby League ever been played in America.

Dimitro did eventually assemble a squad of 20, but failed to inform the players what would be playing. "We had no idea what Rugby League was," said one of the forwards, Alfred D Kirkland. "Mike must have known we were going there to play Rugby League but just didn't tell us." In the nick

"More than 500 people – many of them young girls – mobbed the American Rugby League team at Mascot last night. They broke through barriers to surge around the Americans. Eighteen-year-old Maree Morgan, Miss American Valentine 1953, kissed the captain Vince Jones."

AMERICAN ALL STARS RUGBY LEAGUE TOURING TEAM

FIRST AUSTRALIAN-NEW ZEALAND TOUR, 1953

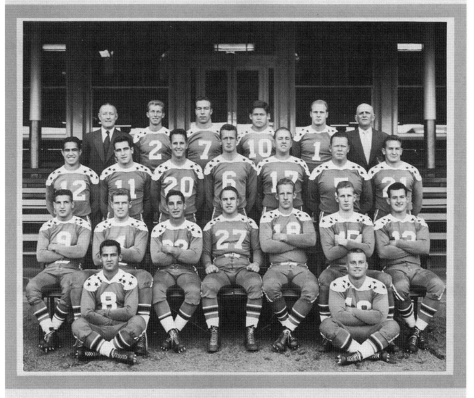

Back Row: BILL MOORE (Trainer), TED GROSSMAN, PAT HENRY, HAROLD HAN, AL E. KIRKLAND, LATCHEM ROBINSON (Coach).
Middle Row: SOL NAUMU, GARY KERKORIAN, GEORGE KAUFFMANN, BILL ALBANS, STEVE DRAKULVICH, RAY TERRY (Assistant Manager), FRAN MANDULAY.
Front Row: ED. DEMIRJIAN, JACK BONETTI, BOB BUCKLEY, MIKE DIMITRO (Manager-Coach), VINCE JONES (Captain), AL. D. KIRKLAND, XAVIER MENA.
In Front: AL. ABAJIAN, SYD. WALKER.

of time, with many in Australia doubting the tour would go ahead, Dimitro found a backer to stump up the cash. The All Stars were up and running at last, and, in a genuine coup, Norman 'Latchem' Robinson, the Kangaroos coach, would lead the team. What he must have thought at the first training session at Coogee is anyone's guess.

The All Stars landed at Mascot Airport in southern Sydney on 18th May and were greeted by hordes of autograph hunters and well-wishers. It was an incredible scene. "More than 500 people – many of them young girls – mobbed the American Rugby League team at Mascot last night," reported 'The Telegraph'. "They broke through barriers to surge around the Americans. Eighteen-year-old Maree Morgan, Miss American Valentine 1953, kissed the captain Vince Jones."

'The Mirror' splashed with "The Yankees are here! The curtain is up! The Big Show is on! Despite rumours to the contrary the Yankee Boys are here, see." Jack Bonetti, one of the players, was stunned: "When we got to Sydney there were about 25,000 at the airport to meet us. We didn't know what was going on." Journalists swarmed all over the bemused players, with

The All Stars arrive in Australia

Dimitro cranking up the hyperbole. Five articles appeared in 'The Daily Telegraph' the next day. The story was a sensation.

Looking back, it is incredible that the All Stars won a single match, but they managed to triumph in their tour opener – against Southern Divisions in Canberra by 34-25. Former Test half Joe 'Chimpy' Busch said: "Their handling is phenomenal. I've never seen such bewildering passing," after watching the All Stars beat the Royal Australian Engineers 41-10 in a 60-minute friendly. Al E Kirkland, who later played for Parramatta and Leeds, was sensational. But former Test skipper Len Smith wasn't so complimentary, pointing to their farcical scrummaging.

Perhaps the win in Canberra, allied with memories of Puig-Aubert's incredible Frenchmen just two years earlier, are the most likely explanations for the tour statistic which is the hardest to believe, and that is that a crowd of 65,453 turned up to watch their next game, against Sydney at the Sydney Cricket Ground. The All Stars were the hottest ticket in town. Eager fans slept outside the turnstiles and 5,000 failed to get into the ground. Sydney, with Clive Churchill at fullback and many other notable players, were far too good for the All Stars, winning 52-25. An even stronger New South Wales side beat the Americans 62-41 at the same venue in front of 32,554 people, on the day of Queen Elizabeth's coronation. Despite the losses, the Americans were scoring tries.

Fourteen further matches brought ten defeats, although Western Division pinched their game in the closing minutes. The All Stars beat Newcastle 19-10, drew with Far North Queensland 17-all and only went down 39-36 to Queensland at The Gabba before a crowd of 24,397, after leading for most of the game. They recovered to beat Ipswich 17-16 and draw 33-all with Wide Bay. Their last game in Australia saw them lose 27-18 to New South Wales at the SCG in front of another sizeable crowd – 19,686.

65,453 fans packed out the Sydney Cricket Ground to see the All Stars

By now, Dimitro was being pursued by numerous organisations in both states for money he owed. More seriously, Bonetti was struck down with polio. It was front-page news. He flew home before the end of the tour seriously ill, with his sporting career over, although he eventually recovered.

The tourists won four out of eight games played in New Zealand. Later in the year, with most of the original All Stars refusing to go anywhere again with Dimitro, a new-look All Stars toured France, winning one match out of five. The final game was a Test against a Puig-inspired France, who won 31-0 at the Parc des Princes before a crowd of 20,000.

THE RUGBY LEAGUE NEWS

June 2, Vol. 34 — No. 13.

AMERICA VERSUS NEW SOUTH WALES

SYDNEY CRICKET GROUND

TUESDAY, JUNE 2 1953

UNDER THE AUSPICES OF THE AUSTRALIAN RUGBY LEAGUE BOARD OF CONTROL

Unfortunately the tours didn't lead to Rugby League's big breakthrough in the United States, despite interest from the LA Rams and the San Francisco 49ers, and two matches between Australia and New Zealand on their way home from the 1954 World Cup. Failure to establish the game in America represents, perhaps, the biggest missed opportunity of them all. All the same, Dimitro's tour remains one of the great Rugby League tales.

Sunday, 26th July 1953

WORLD FAMOUS SPRINTER SIGNS FOR LEIGH

Imagine Widnes signing Usain Bolt. Or Wakefield Trinity unveiling Linford Christie or Carl Lewis in their pomp. Completely unthinkable now, but such a signing did happen in the 1950s when Leigh pulled off the most audacious coup with the help of the renowned Rugby League journalist Eddie Waring. Having finished seventh in the 1952-53 season, the club entered into a remarkable deal by signing the joint world-record holder of the 100 metres. His name was Emmanuel McDonald Bailey and few could believe what they were reading when Waring broke the news one Sunday morning in July 1953.

A year earlier, the Trindadian had won the bronze medal for Great Britain in the Helsinki Summer Olympic Games with a time of 10.4 seconds, having come sixth four years earlier in London. He was also just one position away from a medal in both the 100 metres relay and in the 200 metres, a race in which he led with 40 metres to go. More notably, he had equalled Jesse Owens' world record of 10.2 seconds in Belgrade in 1951, a time which stood until 1956. He was a world-famous athlete, and now he was going to play Rugby League for Leigh.

Earlier in the year, Bailey had become embroiled in a high-profile court case when he successfully overturned a suspension imposed on him by the Amateur Athletic Association. They had been angered by a photograph of him advertising starting blocks, because athletics was strictly amateur. Bailey became disillusioned with the sport and, having met him at an athletics meeting, Waring convinced him that he could make a successful transition into Rugby League.

Under the headline "Sports sensation of the year", the signing of Bailey was announced by the BBC commentator in the 'Sunday Pictorial' amid a blaze of publicity for the Leigh club. The report began: "E. McDonald Bailey, fastest runner in the world, has decided to turn professional in Rugby League Football. He signed agreements with the Leigh Rugby League Football Club in the Sunday Pictorial office a few days ago." Bailey commented that the

"I thought I was dead a couple of times when the man with the ball ran straight at me and ploughed his knees into my chest."

offer was so attractive that he "was bound to accept it," and that "I cannot lose out of it even if I am not successful." According to reports, he had been running as well as ever at the time of the move, but the move to a professional sport ended his athletics career at the age of 32. "From now on I can do things without fear or suspicion," said Bailey. "As you know, I have had my setbacks in the past, but I think I can look forward to a clear and successful future."

Things weren't so simple, however. Bailey suffered a groin injury in an early training session which would sideline him until December. He played his first game in a specially-arranged friendly with Wigan on the 16th, which saw Hilton Park's floodlights used for the first time. Before a crowd of 14,996, the sprinter scored a try in an 11-3 win, after quick passing to the right created an overlap. 'The Manchester Guardian' was less than positive about his display, though. "He seemed lacking in proper grim determination both on attack and defence," read their report. "Much experience is needed before any player becomes competent, and usually several seasons pass before a young player becomes outstandingly good. Bailey is not young. His chances of achieving in this game, [producing] performances comparable with those he achieved in athletics, do not seem bright on his display last night."

In the closing stages, Bailey aggravated his groin and the match turned out to be his only appearance for the Leythers. The club later revealed they had paid out £1,350 for Bailey, while their share of the gate receipts for his one game had been just short of £1,000. Bailey and the board of directors came to an agreement in February 1954 which saw him leave the sport. Leigh's chairman, James Hilton, said: "Such factors as the difficulty in attuning muscles to the demands made upon them, the intense cold and the persistence of a groin injury which had delayed his efforts to prepare himself for the game were points discussed. The directors and McDonald Bailey have ended their relationship in an atmosphere of cordiality and goodwill on both sides."

Bailey admitted of his adventure: "I was not a success. They threw me straight in with no time to learn even the fundamentals. I thought I was dead a couple of times when the man with the ball ran straight at me and ploughed his knees into my chest. And being trained as a straight-line sprinter, when I was given the ball my groin kept tearing every time I tried to sidestep. But I enjoyed the experience all right. By jove, those young guys in the north had a terrific sporting attitude, and what guts."

Bailey died just before his 93rd birthday in December 2013 in Trinidad and Tobago. The 'Trinidad Express' called him an icon.

Friday, 7th August 1953

THE CASE OF THE POISONED FOOTBALLER

When Bobby Lulham, the 1948 Kangaroo winger, began to lose his form, nobody could have guessed what was wrong with him. The astonishing truth soon emerged that he had been poisoned by his mother-in-law, whom he had been sleeping with behind his new wife's back.

Born in Newcastle in 1926, Lulham was an exceptional winger, and was soon snapped up by the Balmain Tigers. His debut season in 1947 was highly successful, as his 28 tries made him the competition's top try scorer and helped the club to Grand Final success. In all, he scored 85 tries in 87 games for his club and played ten games for New South Wales, scoring eight tries. He was selected to tour Europe with the 1948-  49 Kangaroos, and made his debut in the third Test against Great Britain. He scored a try in that game but finished on the losing side, before playing in both Tests against France.

Lulham lived with his 21-year-old wife, Judith, in Ryde, when her mother, Veronica Monty, moved in after separating from her husband. It later transpired that Lulham and Veronica had embarked upon a sexual relationship, which was conducted while Judith was at Sunday mass. Court evidence showed that Monty made some warm milk for Lulham and herself as they sat down to talk together on 2nd July 1953. It was alleged that she had attempted to poison him in order to prevent her daughter from finding out about the affair. She maintained that she had intended to take her own life with the poison.

The Australian government had lifted restrictions on thallium sulphate in order to deal with a post-war plague of rats that had affected inner Sydney.

"Suddenly the stark horror hit me. Bobby had been given the poison."

'Thall-rat' was the brand name for the poison, and also those which feasted on the carcasses. Not only was it an effective pest control, it was occasionally used for the wrong reasons, as it was odourless and tasteless.

During a Balmain game against Canterbury on 18th July 1953, Lulham's under-par performance was particularly noticeable, but he assured the club that it was just a dip in form and that his performance level would recover. When he returned home, he needed to call for medical help. After two days in bed, he was admitted to hospital. An anonymous tip-off from a female to the NSWRL doctor Len Greenberg alleged that Lulham's beer had been poisoned by her husband on the day of the Canterbury game. The previous diagnosis had been an ulcer but, with Lulham's hair falling out, the doctors needed little persuasion that thallium had been ingested. He had consumed seven grams. A lethal dosage was considered to be 12.

Interest in the story was immense with various frenzied rumours flying around Sydney. One popular myth was that he had poisoned himself, but to the shock of the general public, his mother-in-law was charged with attempted murder on 7th August 1953 with bail set at £1,000. The prosecutor had claimed that thallium was so easily accessible that she could re-offend. The bail was not paid immediately so Monty spent a night in the cells before leaving the station the next day with her daughter, who lodged the payment. She insisted that the poisoned beverage had been meant for herself, but that Lulham had consumed it without her knowledge. Lulham remained hospitalised, having been at the Royal Prince Alfred Hospital in Camperdown since 21st July.

Amid enormous media coverage, the court case began on 16th November at the Central Criminal Court, heard by Justice Clancy. The number of visitors to the public gallery reportedly exceeded any other trial in Sydney legal history. Monty's solicitor maintained that the prosecution had failed to establish a motive and would not be able to disprove her version of events that the poisoned drink had been an intended suicide bid.

"I bought the poison in town, for what reason I do not know," she testified in court, going on to say that she then decided to take it herself having become depressed. "After this I waited for some reaction, but when none came I did not think the poison was any good. Suddenly the stark horror hit me. Bobby had been given the poison. I did all I could to get him to the doctor. I have never borne any ill-feelings towards Bobby in my life. I consider that I always have and always will … more than like him. There were many things I have done that I know I should not have done. There were many things I said I should not have said, but I want you to believe me when I say, and I say this quite definitely, that I never gave Bobby thallium deliberately." In his evidence, Lulham admitted to three acts of intimacy with his mother-in-law. Sydney was gripped by this real-life soap opera.

Veronica Monty was eventually acquitted of the crime in December 1953. In October 1954 it was revealed that both marriages were to end, with the affair given as the official reason in both cases. Both Judith Lulham and her father, Alfred Monty, were granted their divorces by Judge Wilfred R Dovey, with Judith having named her mother as co-respondent in her divorce proceedings. She remained in the marital home, accompanied by her father, while Lulham and Ms Monty were living at separate addresses and had no contact with each other.

Lulham's health had been damaged to the extent that he could not continue his footballing career. In April 1955, the 48-year-old Mrs Monty shot herself in a North Sydney hotel bedroom where she worked. She had suffered from depression. It was a tragic end to a sad and mysterious case. Lulham died on Christmas Eve in 1986 at the age of 60.

Wednesday, 5th May 1954

A WORLD-RECORD CROWD

When 102,569 people crammed into Odsal Stadium to witness the Challenge Cup Final replay between Warrington and Halifax in 1954, history was made – and it was a miracle that nobody was seriously hurt!

Quite why so many people turned up is something that has never been fully ascertained other than the fact that this was the first time since 1928 that the Cup would be presented in the north, apart from during the Second World War. There were suggestions that the swelled attendance was a protest against London prices, but whatever the reason, Bradford Northern's chairman, Harry Hornby, was delighted. "We have achieved that 100,000 crowd in the north, and it will always be a milestone in the history of the game," he said.

It was the biggest crowd to watch a game of any football code in England since Wembley's first FA Cup Final in 1923 - the White Horse Final. With many others gaining entry unofficially, it is believed that the actual figure numbered around 120,000. Odsal's previous record had been 70,198. Traffic stretched all the way back to Oldham, more than 20 miles away, where police reported it was the busiest they had ever seen the Lancashire town. Near the ground, the authorities did their best to ease congestion with use of walkie-talkies and loud-speaker equipment. The Halifax team needed a police escort just to arrive on time. Many of the crowd only accessed the terraces at half-time, with some not passing through the turnstiles until just before the end of the game. Despite the 7 o'clock kick-off, many Lancashire-based fans didn't get home until 5am.

Police and ambulance workers had their work cut out, although there were no serious incidents. Spectators climbed onto the stadium roof, but were persuaded to descend after loud-speaker appeals. Others pushed down a fence and managed to access the perimeter of the pitch but the police linked arms and kept them at bay. At least 100 people required medical treatment, although not for anything serious. Most had simply fainted or had been

"We have achieved that 100,000 crowd in the north, and it will always be a milestone in the history of the game."

94

injured falling. The stadium announcer even managed to get a message to 14-year-old Timothy Riley, a Warrington supporter, telling him not to drink his flask of tea. His parents, realising that "a dangerous starch preparation" had been used instead of dried milk, telephoned Odsal to get the message to him, and were later relieved to hear that they had been successful.

The original game, which had taken place on 24th April, had finished in a 4-all draw, with Tyssul Griffiths and Harry Bath each kicking two goals at Wembley in front of 81,841 fans. The game remains the only try-less Wembley final. The replay may have taken its place in sporting legend, but how good a spectacle it provided is up for debate. Harold Mather in 'The Manchester Guardian' described it as "a most exciting match", whereas Graham Morris and John Huxley's book 'Wembley Magic', reported that "the match itself lacked life as a real spectacle".

The hero was the Warrington scrum-half Gerry Helme, who collected the Lance Todd Trophy, becoming the first player to win it twice, having previously done so in 1950 when the Wire beat Widnes. Centre Jim Challinor scored a ninth-minute try for Warrington after Bath had fed Gerald Lowe. Griffiths then pulled a couple of points back for Halifax, with a penalty on the stroke of half-time following Dan Naughton being caught offside. The score was 3-2 at half-time. Bath and Griffiths exchanged further penalties before Helme, 12 minutes from time, took the ball 40 yards from the Halifax line, beat three men and dummied winger Stan McCormick before ducking under Griffiths' desperate tackle to slide in at the corner. Bath missed the goal, leaving the score at 8-4. Halifax could still take the lead with a converted try and spent most of the rest of the game deep in Warrington's territory. They thought they had scored in the last minute when halfback Stan Kielty kicked into the in-goal for winger Arthur Daniels, but Warrington's captain and fullback Arthur Frodsham tackled him as he took the ball. Appeals for a try were turned down by referee Gelder, who had also officiated the first encounter.

In the end, Warrington's classier and pacier backs were the difference. Helme and stand-off Ray Price had provided commendable service for their three-quarters Brian Bevan, Challinor, Arnold Stevens and McCormick. Dai Bevan's defence kept Halifax in the game, while their other best performers were in the forwards with Desmond Clarkson, Jack Wilkinson and Derek Schofield playing particularly well, not least Schofield, whose punishing runs provided a constant headache for Warrington's defence.

The two sides also contested the Championship Final three days later, with Warrington coming out on top again, this time by a mere point, 8-7 at Maine Road in front of a crowd of just 36,519, with people apparently fearing another huge crowd and staying away to avoid a potential crush.

The official world-record crowd figure remained unbroken for 45 years until it was beaten in Sydney at Stadium Australia in 1999 by an NRL season-opening double header which attracted 104,583 fans.

WARRINGTON 8 HALIFAX 4

WARRINGTON
1 Eric Frodsham (C)
2 Brian Bevan
3 Jim Challinor
4 Ron Ryder
5 Stan McCormick
6 Ray Price
7 Gerry Helme
8 Dan Naughton
9 Frank Wright
10 Gerald Lowe
11 Harry Bath
12 Austin Heathwood
13 Bob Ryan

Tries: Challinor, Helme
Goals: Bath

HALIFAX
1 Tyssul Griffiths
2 Arthur Daniels
3 Tommy Lynch
4 Billy Mather
5 Dai Bevan
6 Ken Dean
7 Stan Kielty
8 John Thorley
9 Alvin Ackerley (C)
10 Jack Wilkinson
11 Albert Fearnley
12 Derek Schofield
13 Desmond Clarkson

Goals: Griffiths 2

Half-time: 3-2
Referee: Ron Gelder
Crowd: 102,575

GREAT BRITAIN BECOME
THE FIRST WORLD CHAMPIONS

Of the many great stories locked away in Rugby League folklore, the tale of the 1954 World Cup winners takes some beating. A decimated squad, with over 20 withdrawals, had been assembled at the last minute, and they crossed the English Channel with no coach, no balls to train with and seemingly no hope. Yet they wrote themselves into history by returning as the sport's first world champions.

Great Britain had just toured Australia and New Zealand, and the majority of players were not available to go overseas again. The original choice for captain, Willie Horne, had a business to run, as did Halifax's Alvin Ackerley. Billy Boston and Geoff Gunney picked up injuries just before departure. Only Dave Valentine, Gerry Helme and Phil Jackson backed up from the Lions tour in which the Ashes had been lost. Nobody was quite sure whether Jackson would even turn up, but he met his teammates en route having acquired leave from the army. Valentine, the new captain, knew his team's chances had been vastly improved when he saw the Barrow centre standing in the Dover lamplight.

Great Britain also had to make do without a coach. Joe Egan had taken a couple of training sessions in England but the RFL elected to take only a tour manager and masseur. Valentine, therefore, had to oversee the coaching in France. During the first session, in Paris, there were no balls, so the players,

"I don't think that any official rugby team has ever been sent away with so little thought attached to it."

rather comically, had to make do with rolled-up clothes. "I don't think that any official rugby team has ever been sent away ... with so little thought attached to it," said the beleaguered skipper.

Paul Barrière, the president of the French Rugby League, had helped form the International Rugby League Board. In the face of opposition on both sides of the world, he was able to push for a World Cup – 33 years before rugby union did likewise. The Australians needed some persuasion, however, and it was only when the French agreed to cover the costs of the visiting teams that the first Rugby World Cup of either code could go ahead. The tournament was to be played over three weeks and the organisers had displayed no lack of ambition by scheduling matches all over the country in the major stadia of cities like Paris, Lyon, Marseille, Toulouse, Nantes and Bordeaux. The opening game and the final, were to be played at the magnificent Parc des Princes in Paris.

France's poster boy was the great Puig-Aubert. The genius, pastis-loving fullback had crystallised his world-class reputation when France won in Australia in 1951. He scored the World Cup's first points against New Zealand, helping his side to a 22-13 win, which gave the credibility of the tournament, from a local perspective at least, a huge boost.

On the same weekend, Great Britain's new-look side, with nine debutants, beat with surprising ease the tournament favourites Australia, who fielded most of their Ashes winners. Forty years on from Rorke's Drift, they won 28-13, with Jackson and stand-off Gordon Brown each scoring twice. The game marked the debut of a young Mick Sullivan, who would go on to earn a record 46 caps. On the other wing was Scotsman David Rose, who had learned at the last minute that he was to replace Boston when a policeman called at his Jedburgh house late one

---

FRANCE 12 GREAT BRITAIN 16

FRANCE
1 Aubert Puig (C)
2 Raymond Constrastin
3 Jacques Merquey
4 Claude Teisseire
5 Vincent Cantoni
6 Antoine Jiménez
7 Joseph Crespo
8 Joseph Krawzyk
9 Jean Audoubert
10 François Rinaldi
11 Armand Save
12 Jean Pambrun
13 Gilbert Verdié

Tries: Cantoni, Constrastin
Goals: Aubert 3

GREAT BRITAIN
1 Jim Ledgard
2 David Rose
3 Phil Jackson
4 Albert Naughton
5 Mick Sullivan
6 Gordon Brown
7 Gerry Helme
8 John Thorley
9 Sam Smith
10 Robert Coverdale
11 Don Robinson
12 Basil Watts
13 David Valentine (C)

Tries: Brown 2, Helme, Rose
Goals: Ledgard 2

Half-time: 4-8
Referee: Charlie Appleton
Crowd: 30,368

Great Britain's Dave Valentine lifts the 1954 World Cup

night with a message to get to Huddersfield by morning. The glorious chaos of Rose's story – he didn't even have time to get his kit together - summed up one of the most famous months in the sport's history as well as anything else could. He scored in every match. The winners of those opening-weekend fixtures maintained their form throughout with neither losing a match - the group-stage game between the two in Toulouse ended 13-all, in front 37,471 fans - a French record. Only points' difference split Great Britain and France, with the British on top. There had been no final scheduled but, with two teams finishing on the same number of points, it was decided to arrange a play-off to decide the winners. Arranged at two days' notice, it said much for the competence of the organisers and the quality of the tournament that over 30,000 people attended. The decider was also televised live in England via the newly established Eurovision link.

Puig-Aubert kicked an 11th-minute 40-yard penalty but Great Britain grew into the game with Rose and Brown each scoring as they led 8-4 at half-time. France's big moment came early in the second half when Vincent Constrastin's try was converted by Puig to edge them a point ahead. The atmosphere was electric, with the home fans believing their side was about to be crowned world champions. But back came Great Britain and the two-time Lance Todd Trophy winner Helme went in under the posts to leave Jim Ledgard with a simple conversion. Their four-point lead was intact once more and it increased further when Brown scored again. Constratin's second try caused some British hearts to flutter, but they were able to hold on and become the first Rugby League world champions.

With such a young side and all the pre-tournament issues, Great Britain's achievement was absolutely stunning and the players were handsomely rewarded - with a bonus of £10 each! The World Cup has gone on to become a Rugby League icon, with the 15th such tournament scheduled for 2017.

Saturday, 30th March 1957

HAVEN'S CREEPING BARRAGE FAILS

It was Whitehaven's time. Founded in 1948, the Recreation Ground team could only watch with envy as their neighbours Workington Town, founded three years earlier, had swept to league and cup glory in the early 1950s. Haven had a more modest start to their professional life, but when they beat the touring Australians in October 1956 it was clear they had an outstanding team of their own. They subsequently embarked upon a glorious Challenge Cup run into the semi-finals, which had the entire town hooked, but it ended in heartbreak at Odsal with Leeds kicking a late drop goal to deny them their place at Wembley.

Whitehaven fullback John McKeown

Under the astute coaching of the Australian Neville Emery, Haven's heroics had captured the hearts of the whole region and with just five minutes to play against mighty Leeds, the West Cumbrians were 9-8 up. In the days before the limited-tackle rule was introduced, they had held onto the ball for 39 plays – a tactic occasionally referred to as a creeping barrage. If they could maintain possession, a place at Wembley was theirs. Workington had executed the barrage perfectly to close out their Championship semi-final against Wigan six years earlier, but Haven were to fall just short. The crucial moment came when loose forward Geoff Robinson was playing the ball and Joe Anderson, the Leeds prop, nipped around him to secure possession. Whitehaven were adamant that a penalty should have been awarded but the

"Whitehaven's sun had shone brilliantly, but in its setting there was a lasting glory."

referee, Norman Railton from Billinge, disagreed. Soon after, Jeff Stevenson's drop goal from 30 yards sent Leeds to Wembley. Some Haven fans still deny it was a legitimate score, believing that the kick was punted between the posts.

In the first round Whitehaven had been drawn against the Cup holders, St Helens, but with the tie to be played at the Recreation Ground, where Haven's record was outstanding, they knew they could win, and so it proved when Emery's men sent away their illustrious opponents, including Alex Murphy and Alan Prescott, with a 9-8 win in front of a crowd of just under 10,000. Ron McMenemy scored their only try and fullback John McKeown kicked three goals. Hunslet, captained by the great Australian Arthur Clues, were next, and, with home advantage again, Haven dispatched them 7-0 amid a vicious hail storm which left Hunslet's Sam Smith and Brian Shaw suffering from hypothermia at half-time, in need of some revitalising brandy. Syd Lowdon scored Whitehaven's try, with McKeown adding two goals. Robinson, not for the first time, was in superb form at the back of the scrum. Having seen off two excellent sides, Haven enjoyed the fortune of another home draw which saw Widnes travelling north. Once more the majority of the 13,500 crowd experienced a range of emotions as their heroes dug out another slender win with a solitary McKeown goal giving them a 2-0 win.

Whitehaven fans complained when their semi-final tie with Leeds was scheduled for a Yorkshire ground, but the club did their best to negate Leeds' advantage, arranging for the players to stay in Harrogate for three days and prepare thoroughly for the task. Six specially arranged trains took fans to Bradford.

Haven started slowly, perhaps daunted by playing in front of 49,094

LEEDS 10 WHITEHAVEN 9

LEEDS
1 Pat Quinn
2 Delmos Hodkinson
3 Keith McLellan (C)
4 Lewis Jones
5 George Broughton
6 Jack Lendill
7 Jeff Stevenson
8 Joe Anderson
9 Bernard Prior
10 Bill Hopper
11 Bernard Poole
12 Don Robinson
13 Harry Street

Tries: Broughton 2
Goal: Jones
Drop goal: Stevenson

WHITEHAVEN
1 John McKeown
2 Bill Smith
3 Ron McMenemy
4 Syd Lowdon
5 Ron Mullinder
6 Billy Garratt (C)
7 Billy Banks
8 Bobby Vincent
9 John McKinnell
10 Ray Donaldson
11 Steve McCourt
12 Dick Huddart
13 Geoff Robinson

Tries: McMenemy
Goals: McKeown 3

Half-time: 6-4
Referee: Norman Railton
Crowd: 49,094

spectators, as the Leeds winger George Broughton scored twice, although one should have been disallowed as he had touched the corner flag before touching down. The Cumbrians did at least have a couple of penalties on the board from McKeown, who kicked the first and last points of the half. Whitehaven trailed 6-4.

The great Welshman Lewis Jones edged an off-colour Leeds out to an 8-4 lead with a penalty after an infringement by Billy Banks, but Haven would not surrender. McMenemy, signed earlier in the season from Barrow and playing despite a twisted ankle, took Robinson's inside pass to score. They were just a point behind with the conversion to come. With 26 minutes to play, this was the chance to take the lead and see the game out. McKeown's conversion represented the biggest moment in the club's history. From the Odsal touchline it was far from easy, but this was Whitehaven's greatest-ever player. The ball sailed majestically between the posts. Haven looked destined for the Twin Towers. That was the case until Stevenson's heart-breaking late intervention. Even then McKeown had a late chance to win the game, but his halfway-line penalty fell short, as did a drop-goal attempt from near touch.

Walter Thomson's report in the Whitehaven News beautifully described the team's glorious failure. "It was Whitehaven 9, Leeds 8. With five minutes left of this epic Cup semi-final thriller, the sand was running rapidly away with Leeds's hopes. Whitehaven, solid and imperturbable, as their own hills of Cumbrian granite, had possession in their own 25 and the Wembley look written all over their tired but exultant faces. Came tragedy. First the 'robbery', a swift pass back, a swifter drop, and the flying ball soaring high over the chunky Odsal posts carried with it the bitterness of defeat for David, the sweetness of victory for Goliath. Whitehaven's sun had shone brilliantly, but in its setting there was a lasting glory, and much honour."

Leeds went on to win the Cup with a 9-7 win over Barrow with a disputed try helping them no end, while Haven fans old enough to remember have never stopped cursing those last five minutes on that spring afternoon at Odsal.

Saturday, 5th July 1958

THE HERO WITH THE BROKEN ARM

For unlikeliness of victory, the Great Britain performance in the second Ashes Test of 1958 deserves to bracketed with the Rorke's Drift Test match of 1914 when the Lions had stunned the Aussies to win the Ashes, despite being four men short at one point in the second half.

History seemed to repeat itself in Brisbane 44 years later when the British skipper Alan Prescott broke his right arm after just three minutes when tackling Rex Mossop. The red-headed prop astounded everyone by deciding to continue. "I'll play on, tell nobody," he insisted. "I can be of nuisance value. The Australians will have to run round me." The damaged limb dangled uselessly by his side but Prescott remembered the wise words of Jim Sullivan, who had coached him at St Helens. "If you are only on the field getting in the way then someone has to beat you," the great fullback had said. "Always stand and face the opposition."

As well as that catastrophe, the talented stand-off Dave Bolton was forced to leave the field in the first half with a broken collarbone. Injuries were also suffered by Vince Karalius, Eric Fraser and Jim Challinor, all in the first 20 minutes. The latter three also played on, although when Challinor said he needed to leave the field, Prescott, whose captaincy had been criticised after the first Test, was hardly sympathetic: "I've got a broken arm and you want to go off!"

Great Britain had been well off the pace in the first Test but were at least able to welcome back three fine forwards in Brian McTigue, Karalius and Dick Huddart. The presence of loose forward Karalius would at least make things easier for the young scrum half Alex Murphy, who had been outplayed by Keith Holman in the first Test. He more than made up for it at The Gabba.

Before his injury, Challinor had scored the game's opening try in the corner, created by Eric Ashton. Midway through the half, with the side now depleted by injury, Murphy broke from a scrum, fed the great Wigan ball-playing prop McTigue who in turn put the winger Mick Sullivan away for a try. The Lions, against all odds, led 10-2 at the break, but there were much

"I'll play on, tell nobody. I can be of nuisance value. The Australians will have to run round me."

AUSTRALIA 18 GREAT BRITAIN 25

AUSTRALIA
1 Gordon Clifford
2 Ross Kite
3 Greg Hawick
4 Brian Carlson
5 Peter Dimond
6 Tony Brown
7 Keith Holman
8 Brian Davies (C)
9 Ken Kearney
10 Bill Marsh
11 Rex Mossop
12 Norm Provan
13 Kelvin O'Shea

Tries: Marsh, Holman, Carlson, Dimond
Goals: Clifford 3

GREAT BRITAIN
1 Eric Fraser
2 Ike Southward
3 Eric Ashton
4 Jim Challinor
5 Mick Sullivan
6 Dave Bolton
7 Alex Murphy
8 Alan Prescott (C)
9 Tommy Harris
10 Brian McTigue
11 Dick Huddart
12 Johnny Whiteley
13 Vince Karalius

Tries: Southward 2, Challinor, Sullivan, Murphy
Goals: Fraser 5

Half-time: 2-10
Referee: Darcy Lawler
Crowd: 32,965

tougher times ahead for them, not least in a fraught dressing shed at half-time. Firstly, the Australian doctor told Prescott that he simply had to come off the field. "This man cannot continue - it must not be considered," he said, but the tour manager, Tom Mitchell, left the decision to his captain and later recalled: "When the team rose to go out, Alan led them. If he hadn't done so the game was over - the quest for the Ashes was blown away." The doctor called Prescott a Pommy maniac.

Karalius's second-half participation was also in doubt with his back seizing up during the interval. He could only get back to his feet with the aid of Mitchell. "Without him on the field the position was the same as with the captain - certain defeat," said Mitchell. "How he stood up to the first ten minutes I will never know." Taking Bolton's place next to Murphy in the halves, Karalius didn't just get through those first ten minutes – he beat two Australians to play a big hand in Ike Southward's first try on 44 minutes. Britain were 15-2 up. The magnificent Murphy had had a hand in all the tries.

A Billy Marsh try for the Australians reduced the arrears but the Lions, to their eternal credit, continued to attack. Johnny Whiteley and McTigue released the Workington winger Southward who kicked ahead to score his second try. Australia hit back with tries from Brian Carlson and Peter Dimond but neither

Alan Prescott chaired from the field following his heroic performance

was converted and the Lions still held a seven-point advantage. Any realistic hopes of a comeback were snuffed out by the great St Helens duo of Murphy and Karalius, who were having the time of their lives. The diminutive halfback broke free from a scrum and found Karalius, who drew the defence and had the skill to offload to his supporting partner. Murphy raced 30 metres to score under the posts, allowing Eric Fraser to kick his fifth goal. Holman, who had been tormented throughout the game by the magical Murphy, scored a late try and Gordon Clifford's third goal brought the final score to 25-18.

Prescott, the first forward to captain the national team, had played for 77 minutes with a compound fracture of the radius, doing all his tackling with his left shoulder. He had kept an Ashes series alive in the process. His heroics led to him being regarded as one of the bravest players in the game's history and Mitchell fittingly referred to the match as 'Prescott's Epic'.

Ashton was one of many players who was in awe of Prescott's bravery. "I don't know how he did it but he did," he said. "It was a double break from what I could gather afterwards and it finished his career really. Whether it was bravery or bloody madness, I couldn't make my mind up at the time!"

CORRUPTION ALLEGATIONS MAR AUSTRALIAN GRAND FINAL

It goes without saying that referees have got plenty wrong down the years but there has been little evidence of corruption and cheating. Such allegations did emerge after the 1963 Australian Grand Final between St George and Western Suburbs, however, and more than half a century later, it appears that the referee, Darcy Lawler, may have had a case to answer.

Lawler was a high-profile referee who took charge of a vast number of Test matches and Grand Finals in the 1950s and early 1960s. Later referees like Greg Hartley, Barry Gomersall and Bill Harrigan were at the centre of numerous controversies, but none ran as deep as the deciding match of the 1963 season.

One of the Magpies players on that fateful afternoon was Jack Gibson, who was named the coach of the century in 2008. As a player, he was a prop for Easts, Newtown and then Wests, for whom he debuted in 1963. He was also well connected with bookmakers and punters, and had been informed that Lawler, a well-known gambler, stood to gain £600 if Saints won the Grand Final. It was rumoured that bookies, all of whom were operating illegally as sports betting was outlawed in Sydney, had a hold on the referee. It was suggested that he owed them.

In the changing room before the game, Gibson passed the information onto Noel Kelly, the team's hooker, by telling him bluntly: "We can't win. F***ing Lawler has backed them." Kelly said later: "I was shattered and said it couldn't be right. Jack insisted it was right and that he knew the bloke who put the money on." Kelly later told of a meeting he had with a Sydney bookmaker who confirmed that Lawler had been bought. Earlier in the week, Gibson had passed the information on to the Magpies secretary Bill Beaver, who communicated the concerns with the NSWRL. They failed to act and Lawler's appointment remained. St George won 8-3 after benefitting from a penalty count of 18-7. There were a number of contentious decisions. Lawler abruptly retired from the sport, and there was to be no official investigation. Instead, Rugby League was left to deal with speculation and innuendo which ran for decades.

"We can't win. F*ing Lawler has backed them."**

St George won an incredible tally of 11 consecutive Premierships, beginning with in 1956 when they beat Balmain 12-8 - Lawler's second Grand Final. The club remained on its throne, hammering Manly 31-9 in 1957, beating Wests 20-9 in 1958, easing past Manly again in 1959 by 20-0 and thrashing Easts 31-6 in 1960. Each was refereed by Lawler. The run continued as they beat the Magpies 22-0 in 1961, with Lawler the man in the middle again. 1962 saw a much closer decider between the same sides as the Dragons ran out 9-6 winners, with Jack Bradley officiating. And then in 1963 history was made as the same two teams made the final again. Never before or since have the same two sides contested three successive Grand Finals.

The Dragons boasted a plethora of great players, including three of the eight post-war Immortals – fullback Graeme Langlands, centre Reg Gasnier and loose forward Johnny Raper - although Wests had beaten them in all three of their matches in 1963. Interest in the game was enormous and so a record Grand Final crowd of 69,806 was achieved, despite the appalling weather. The Magpies enjoyed promising early possession, keeping the ball mainly in the forwards, but it was the Dragons who scored first when halfback George Evans scored near the right corner. Gasnier was only just off the mark with the conversion, but he soon

ST GEORGE 8
WESTERN SUBURBS 3

ST GEORGE
1 Graeme Langlands
2 Johnny King
3 Reg Gasnier
4 Billy Smith
5 Eddie Lumsden
6 Bruce Pollard
7 George Evans
13 Monty Porter
12 Ian Walsh
11 Kevin Ryan
10 Elton Rasmussen
9 Norm Provan (C)
8 Johnny Raper

Tries: Evans, King
Goal: Gasnier

WESTS
1 Don Parish
2 John Mowbray
3 Bob McGuinness
4 Gil MacDougall
5 Peter Dimond
6 Arthur Summons (C)
7 Don Malone
13 Jack Gibson
12 Noel Kelly
11 Denis Meaney
14 Kel O'Shea
9 John Haynes
8 Kevin Smyth

Try: MacDougall

Half-time: 5-0
Referee: Darcy Lawler
Crowd: 69,806

made up for it with a penalty goal after a Wests offside. Shortly before half time, Magpies winger Peter Dimond was denied a try when he successfully won the race to a kick from Arthur Summons and grounded the ball, only for Lawler to claim he hadn't got it down properly. The half-time score was 5-0.

For the first time since 1958, the Dragons conceded a Grand Final try when Magpies centre Gil MacDougall capitalised on a handling error, but fullback Don Parish missed an extremely simple conversion. MacDougall, the father of future international winger Adam, was later denied a second try with Lawler insisting he hadn't grounded the ball. With 15 minutes left to play, Johnny King, the Dragons winger, scored one of the most controversial tries in Grand Final history, which proved to be the Premiership-clinching score. Wests players claimed he had been tackled as he ran up the touchline. King fell to the floor with an opposition hand on him, but, with Lawler looking directly over the incident, he got up and continued his run to the line. He dived over near the corner for the try, which Gasnier failed to convert.

After King's try it was claimed that Lawler was called a cheat by Wests second row John Hayes. Lawler threatened to send him off if he repeated the slur, only for Gibson to retort: "Send him off and I will rearrange your face on Monday." St George hooker Ian Walsh, who later captained Australia, added fuel to the fire many years later when he said of his relationship with Lawler: "If it was going to be a good day for me he would call me by my Christian name [and] if he called me by my surname it was going to be a tough day at the office."

The 1963 Grand Final was also responsible for the creation of the most enduring image in the history of Rugby League when opposing captains, Norm Provan and Arthur Summons, both splattered in mud, embraced post-match in a moment of mutual respect. The award-winning photo, which was captured by photographer John O'Gready, was called 'The Gladiators' and was published in the 'Sun Herald' newspaper.

The Provan-Summons image has lived on in Grand Finals from 1982 after a new Premiership trophy was modelled on their embrace. There have been several controversial finals since then, but none compare to that rainswept 1963 decider.

BRADFORD NORTHERN ANNOUNCE INTENTION TO QUIT RUGBY LEAGUE

In March 1953 Bradford Northern entertained Huddersfield in the quarter-final of the Challenge Cup, attracting a bumper crowd of 69,429. Just over ten years later, a mere 324 people filtered through the Odsal turnstiles to watch a Division Two fixture against Barrow. A vast number of spectators had gone missing and the club directors finally decided that enough was enough. Halfway through the 1963-64 season, Northern pulled out of the league, 100 years after the formation of the original Bradford club.

In the 1953-54 campaign, when Odsal established a world-record crowd of 102,569 for the Challenge Cup Final replay, Northern's average had fallen by nearly 5,000 to a little over 10,000. The figure continued to fall with every passing season as the pattern mirrored their on-field fortunes. Perhaps also, the departure of great players like Trevor Foster, Joe Phillips and Jack McLean in 1955 and 1956 played a part, and in 1961 the popular, long-serving coach, Dai Rees, was ousted from his position.

A Cup tie at St Helens had been lost 53-6 in 1956. With the decline continuing, Bradford then finished 26th out of 30 in 1960, followed by 24th and then the dreaded last place. When they incurred a club-record 73-5 defeat to Wakefield in the 1960-61 Yorkshire Cup, the 'Telegraph & Argus' produced the scathing headline: "Feeble, Pathetic - Northern just gave it up!" A new league structure was introduced at the start of the 1962-63 campaign, and Northern were consigned to the second division, one of 14 clubs in the lower tier, where they were to come last with just two wins from 26 matches. Odsal's aggregate attendance for the season was just 23,888 - only just over a third of the amount that had turned up to that quarter-final match in 1953. The alarm bells were deafening.

The club stumbled through the first half of the 1963-64 campaign. The nadir was that crowd against Barrow. They played another home fixture, on 7th December against Leigh, which attracted an improved crowd of 841, although it was estimated that the Leyther support accounted for two-thirds of that figure. Bradford lost 33-5, with the South African Enslin Dlambulo scoring the club's final try before the gates of Odsal were padlocked shut, seemingly for good. Four days later, Northern announced that their next game against Oldham had been cancelled and that they intended to have their remaining fixtures suspended. Their bank had withdrawn support and

The legendary Trevor Foster played a huge role in rescuing Bradford Northern

with debts of £8,099, the club was closed down. Their playing record for the 1963-64 season, which included just one win, was expunged from the records.

There were various reasons for the club's demise.

Bradford's directors had relied heavily on income from its pools scheme which had been run by Malcolm Davies, one of the players. He canvassed interest around local pubs, but the club were unhappy with Davies taking a commission so they sold him to Leeds in 1957 for £3,000. Without him, the income was lost. With fans upset at the loss of a popular player, the gate fell by nearly 2,000 for next fixture. Other players to leave Odsal over the next few years included Ken Traill, Jack Scroby, Milan Kosanovic, Derek Davies and Terry Robbins. Club legend Ernest Ward was also treated poorly in the eyes of fans when the club wouldn't offer him a coaching position. He accepted a player-coach role at Castleford, but the club blocked the move. In the end, Ward secured a release after a tribunal and Northern had again come up short in the public-relations stakes.

"Players you'd never heard of would arrive and they'd be straight in the team on the Saturday," recalled the veteran player Len Haley. "It was difficult to see what the management was doing but we never got involved, we just

"The club collapsed. It was unbelievable. Those huge terraces with very few people aboard. It was a minor disaster. All that wonderful talent, wonderful attributes that were connected with Odsal Stadium, all fell away."

got on with playing. They were selling all the players they could get money for. They wanted to sell me to Halifax when I was coming up to ten years' service, and I wouldn't go because I was due a benefit. They said: 'Well if you don't go, we won't play you in the first team.' And for three seasons I was mostly in the second team but I still played 288 times for Bradford." As for the pools scheme, Haley said: "They thought they'd try to run it themselves but they couldn't run the club properly so they weren't going to be able to run the pools. [It] collapsed and that was the final straw that brought the club down."

The club met with the Rugby League management committee in Leeds on 9th January 1964, after which Bill Fallowfield announced that "Bradford Northern FC Ltd notify the League that it will no longer promote Rugby League football. [They] state categorically that it has no intention of continuing as a Rugby League club."

Foster was among the many who were devastated at the club's demise. "The club collapsed. It was unbelievable. Those huge terraces with very few people aboard. It was a minor disaster. All that wonderful talent, wonderful attributes that were connected with Odsal Stadium, all fell away." But the legendary Welshman, along with his former teammate, the New Zealander Joe Phillips, immediately set about rescuing Bradford Northern, rallying the city for the support they needed. They succeeded. On 22nd August 1964, 14,542 fans witnessed the new club's first game against Hull Kingston Rovers. The sport had reverted to one division, and Northern finished in mid-table, winning 15 matches, as well as the pre-season Leeds Sevens tournament. Fourteen months after their re-birth, they beat Hunslet 17-8 at Headingley in the Yorkshire Cup Final. It was a joyous occasion, especially for Foster and Phillips. Northern were back. It was as though they'd never been away.

"Scarcely a day goes past without people stopping me in the street to remind me how we helped save Bradford Northern," Foster remarked in their title-winning year of 1997. "And each time I thank God for giving me the strength and confidence to have had a go. It's the proudest thing I ever did."

THE EMERGENCE OF ARTHUR BEETSON

When the great individual performances are discussed, forwards rarely get a mention. Yet Arthur Beetson, one of Australia's eight Rugby League 'Immortals' produced one of the most breathtaking displays in Test-match history in 1966, when his superlative ball skills, almost unseen at that time in an Australian forward, helped lay on two excellent tries in the early stages of the deciding Ashes Test. There were two other remarkable things about Beetson's performance - it was his international debut and he only played for 40 minutes.

Great Britain had long been producing ball-playing forwards, who could be as valuable as halfbacks. Not so in Australia, though, before Beetson broke the mould. The giant 21-year-old Queenslander was in essence a British-type forward, always keen to promote the football. His emergence went some way to helping Australia wrest control of the international game.

In his debut year with Balmain Tigers in 1966 he impressed enormously, helping them to a place in the Grand Final. There were always question marks over his fitness and weight and so his Test selection was viewed as a risk, not least by Ian Walsh, the St George hooker, who just happened to be Australia's captain. He publicly questioned Beetson's fitness, and he wasn't the only one to do so. Walsh later wrote of his concerns: "I have never known a man to eat so much and still play senior football. He would go right through the menu at every meal. And between meals he would have snacks – going out to a nearby shop and returning with three or four pies, or rolls filled with ham and chicken."

The Lions had won the first Test 17-13 in Sydney, but lost 6-4 in a try-less match in Brisbane to set up the decider. Beetson had missed both through injury. Twelve-thousand miles away, minds were focussed on soccer's World Cup, which would be won at the end of July by England, but Alf Ramsay's boys didn't have to face a force majeure like Arthur Beetson.

A giant of a man with a devilish offload, Beetson could seemingly produce

"I have never known a man to eat so much and still play senior football. He would go right through the menu at every meal."

the unexpected at any time. From his first touch, in the first minute, it was obvious that he was going to be immensely hard for the British pack to handle – but it was his skills, not his raw power, which would steal the headlines. In the days of unlimited tackles, which were soon to end, Australia remained in possession for over four minutes and on the 28th tackle, Beetson's basketball-style pass released winger Ken Irvine for the first try in the 12th minute. 'Artie' had been involved five times in the Australian sequence of tackles, and had always looked to power through a tackle or keep the ball alive. This was turning into an eye-catching debut.

Eleven minutes later, Beetson charged onto Billy Smith's inside pass and stormed through the British defence before surprising everybody by kicking from the halfway line for the other winger, Johnny King, to score. The Lions couldn't believe what they were seeing. Australian forwards had never done this before, but Beetson was ahead of his time.

On 33 minutes, Beetson needed treatment for a leg injury, but was able to resume. At half-time, though, with the score at 8-2, he was withdrawn from the field, with this being the first Anglo-Australian match to have substitutions since 1924. His withdrawal sparked the myth that he was too unfit to carry on – that, at this level, he could only play for 40 minutes. He was christened 'Half-a-game Artie', which stuck for years. His other nickname was 'Meat Pie Artie'. It all added to the Beetson legend. But who cared if he only played for 40 minutes, when he did more than most managed in 80?

The truth was slightly different

AUSTRALIA 19 GREAT BRITAIN 14

AUSTRALIA
1 Les Johns
2 Ken Irvine
3 Peter Dimond
4 Johnny Greaves
5 Johnny King
6 John Gleeson
7 Billy Smith
13 John Wittenberg
12 Ian Walsh (C)
11 Noel Kelly
10 Mick Veivers
9 Arthur Beetson
8 Ron Lynch
Subs:
14 Gary Banks (dnp)
15 Dick Thornett

Tries: Irvine 3, King, Lynch
Goals: Johns 2

GREAT BRITAIN
1 Ken Gowers
3 Bill Burgess
7 Ian Brooke
8 Alan Buckley
10 Geoff Wrigglesworth
11 Alan Hardisty
14 Tommy Bishop
16 Brian Edgar (C)
17 Peter Flanagan
19 Cliff Watson
22 John Mantle
21 Bill Ramsey
25 Dave Robinson
Subs:
- Willie Aspinall (dnp)
23 William Bryant

Tries: Hardisty 2
Goals: Gowers 4

Dismissed: Watson

Half-time: 8-2
Referee: Col Pearce
Crowd: 63,503

as he later explained, starting with why he kicked ahead for King's try when he had broken through the Lions defence. "There has been speculation over the years that I only kicked the ball because I was already 'out of gas'. That's bullshit. I kicked it because I sensed a chance. "By half-time, though, I had just about shot my bolt. I was really doing it tough and in the dressing room I went up to Abdul [Walsh] and said, 'Mate, my shoulder is bloody stuffed.'"

With a formidable platform laid, Beetson's teammates finished the job in the second half, as Australia retained the Ashes they had won in England in 1963. Irvine, who like Beetson was named in Australia's team of the century in 2008, scored two more whilst Ron Lynch, a more-than-capable replacement for the great loose forward Johnny Raper, scored the other try. Alan Hardisty, the stand-off from Castleford, kept things interesting with two tries - one a penalty try - but the Lions always had too big a mountain to climb, especially after Cliff Watson was sent off in the 46th minute for kicking Peter Dimond.

Walsh was chaired around the field by his euphoric teammates as the win marked the first time that Australia had won back-to-back Ashes series. With young men of the calibre of Beetson on the scene, the future looked very rosy for the Green and Golds.

Saturday, 11th May 1968

RUGBY LEAGUE'S MOST FAMOUS MOMENT

It is typical of Rugby League's luck that its most famous moment ultimately did it so much harm. While soccer has revelled for years in Carlos Alberto's breathtaking goal which sealed the 1970 World Cup, rugby union has dined out relentlessly on Gareth Edwards' long-range try for the Barbarians against the All Blacks in 1973, as has cricket with Botham's Ashes in 1981. Rugby league, though, is cursed by Don Fox's incredible missed conversion at the end of the 1968 Challenge Cup Final at Wembley. Seemingly replayed at every opportunity for so many years, such a moment of pure farce firmed up the unjust cloth-cap, knockabout, northern image which Rugby League has always struggled to rid itself of.

When Wakefield's winger Ken Hirst scored Wembley's most bizarre try from Fox's brilliantly disguised blindside kick-off in the last minute of the 1968 Challenge Cup Final, it seemed that Trinity were about to snatch victory, having narrowed the Leeds advantage to 11-10.

All Fox had to do was kick a conversion from in front of the posts to win the Cup.

He missed.

And in an instant he had achieved notorious immortality.

This was no ordinary final, nor was it any ordinary kick. Torrential rain had soaked the pitch and as Fox stood on the waterlogged turf in his soaked, skin-tight jersey, this apparently easy shot at goal was anything but, given the biblical storms which had ruined any chance of a decent game.

Wakefield were seeking their first league-and-cup double, having won the Championship Final a week earlier. Leeds, coached by the pioneering and innovative Roy Francis, who had become Great Britain's first black player in 1947, had taken Wigan apart in their semi-final. The bookmakers couldn't split the sides.

The 'Watersplash Final', as it is fondly remembered, would have been postponed had it been anything other than a televised showpiece occasion which 87,100 people had travelled to. The players slipped and stumbled for

"Aye, son, thi' Dad had a lovely death - he were drowned playing for Leeds in t'Cup final of 1968."

Don Fox slices his last-gasp conversion attempt wide of the Wembley posts

much of the match, with many resembling Bambi on ice. The Leeds hooker Tony Crosby spoke later of his fear of drowning had a scrum collapsed, which appeared to amuse 'The Sunday Times' correspondent, whose match report started: "Aye, son, thi' Dad had a lovely death - he were drowned playing for Leeds in t'Cup final of 1968." The Duke of Kent even needed new socks and shoes after his pre-match walk on the pitch, shaking hands with the players.

The farcical nature of the game was underlined not just in the last try but in the first, as Leeds winger John Atkinson went to field Fox's kick but aquaplaned over the side of the pitch without the ball, allowing Hirst to kick forward and score. Wakefield were 7-4 up after 15 minutes but with thunder, lightning and hailstones now dominating the skyline, there was no further score until the closing stages when the game produced an even crazier moment – a controversial penalty try which incensed Trinity's players and fans, coming in the 68th minute of the 68th Challenge Cup Final in the year '68. A kick from the Leeds half Barry Seabourne stopped dead in a huge puddle. Hirst lost his footing and Atkinson fly-hacked forward. In the scramble for possession the referee, John Hebblethwaite, saw an infringement on the Leeds winger and awarded an obstruction try, which surprised even the Leeds players. Bev Risman's goal put his side 9-7 up. According to Mick Morgan, a non-playing member of the Trinity squad, it was "the worst decision ever in Rugby League."

Risman's 78th-minute penalty edged the score to 11-7, after which came Rugby League's most famous 80 seconds. Fox kicked off hard and low to the blindside. Bernard Watson, the Leeds centre, tried to control the ball but it skewed into the path of Hirst, who hacked it forward. Leeds defenders slipped as they desperately tried to grab possession, allowing Hirst to dive joyously on the ball over the try line, just five crazy seconds after Fox's kick off.

At 11-10, Fox's kick was to become the most famous strike of a ball the code had ever witnessed. Leeds players were too devastated to watch as the Trinity number 10 lined up the do-or-die conversion. "It's not a hard shot, but it's always a hard shot when the match depends on it," Waring told the

Leeds prop Ken Eyre brought down during the 1968 Challenge Cup Final

viewers, and from ten yards, Fox, who had never won the Challenge Cup, sliced the cumbersome wet pudding of a ball horribly wide. "He's a poor lad," Waring noted, poignantly. There was no time for play to resume.

As the prop trudged off the field a broken man - his life never to be the same again - he was interviewed by the BBC's David Coleman, who asked him if the Lance Todd Trophy made up for the miss. "Not really, no" replied a devastated Fox with remarkable restraint. There were suggestions from nearby players that Fox had initially instructed the esteemed reporter as to where he could insert the prestigious award, and that the interview seen by the public was actually take number two.

Fox was the middle of a trio of brothers. Neil, the youngest, remains the sport's all-time leading points' scorer and believes he was fit enough to play in the final, but was overruled by the club. Had he played, he would have been lining up that kick instead of Don. The eldest of the trio, Peter, was the least illustrious player but later found prominence as a coach. Don, initially a halfback, before moving to loose forward and then prop, struggled to recover from the trauma of Wembley 1968, staying out of the limelight after his playing days. An outstanding player, it is deeply unjust that he is remembered solely for one moment of misfortune and despair. It ruined his life. He passed away at the age of 72 in August 2008, having fallen in hospital where he was being treated for depression.

There was also sadness surrounding the story of referee Hebblethwaite, whose wife killed herself eight weeks after the final. The York-based official, who had been forced into mandatory retirement on the basis of his age, did likewise the following April eating a sandwich that he had laced with cyanide.

Don Fox was never the same after his misfortune at Wembley in 1968

LEEDS 11 WAKEFIELD TRINITY 10

LEEDS
1 Bev Risman
2 Alan Smith
3 Syd Hynes
4 Bernard Watson
5 John Atkinson
6 Mick Shoebottom
7 Barry Seabourne
8 Mick Clark (C)
9 Tony Crosby
10 Ken Eyre
11 Bill Ramsey
12 Albert Eyre
13 Ray Batten
Subs:
14 John Langley (dnp)
15 David Hick (dnp)

Try: Atkinson (penalty try)
Goals: Risman 4

WAKEFIELD
1 Gary Cooper
2 Ken Hirst
3 Ian Brooke
4 Gert Coetzer
5 Ken Batty
6 Harold Poynton (C)
7 Ray Owen
8 David Jeanes
9 George Shepherd
10 Don Fox
11 Bob Haigh
12 Matt McLeod
13 David Hawley
Subs:
14 Richard Paley (dnp)
15 Gerry Round (dnp)

Tries: Hirst 2
Goals: Fox 2

Half-time: 4-7
Referee: John Hebblethwaite
Crowd: 87,100

Saturday, 7th November 1970

WORLD CUP FINAL DISGRACE

The 1970 World Cup Final at Headingley is widely regarded as one of the most violent-ever games, played in front of enthralled, but shocked, television audiences in England and Australia, prompting the hysterical headline on the front page of the 'Daily Mail' the following Monday which screamed: "Get these thugs off our TV screens!"

Much of the match went off without incident, with the full-blown violence reserved for the last ten minutes. Australian hooker Ron Turner crudely attempted to trip John Atkinson and while play was on-going, Tony Fisher and John O'Neill were having a dust-up in the background. British stand-off Mick Shoebottom might have decapitated Eric Simms had his swinging arm connected, while Malcolm Reilly missed with a punch at Bob McCarthy. A swinger from Kangaroo sub Ray Branighan aimed at Keith Hepworth also failed to connect. Far uglier was the Australian half Billy Smith kicking Syd Hynes in the back. Great Britain prop Dennis Hartley clumsily went for opposite number Bob O'Reilly off the ball, as another Australian lay prone in the background. O'Reilly, nicknamed 'The Bear', responded a minute later by swinging an arm at Reilly. With so much at stake, the match was descending into chaos.

When some football finally broke out, scrum-half Hepworth stepped past McCarthy and threw a long ball onto which the left winger Atkinson ran at pace and beat the cover to score near the corner. Again fullback Ray Dutton, who had kicked poorly all afternoon, was off target and Australia still led 12-7. With only a couple of minutes left, Great Britain pushed hard for the equalising score, keeping the ball alive, but Hynes was tackled into touch by John Cootes, who just happened to be a Roman Catholic Priest. Hynes responded by fighting with Smith, near the fans, causing numerous players to fly in. Hynes and Smith were sent off.

There was time for one more scrum which Great Britain won against the head, but Reilly's desperate offload went astray. The game ended, but the fighting didn't. Simms offered his hand to Atkinson and received a left jab, although not the mythologised head-butt. Props Cliff Watson and O'Reilly

"Get these thugs off our TV screens!"

exchanged blows as an all-in mêlée erupted. Fisher went in swinging punches and man-of-the-match Bob Fulton went after him. The police were next onto the chaotic scene, as the World Cup Final ended in disgrace.

Ken Arthurson, Australia's manager, described it as "One of the most murderous matches in RL history. The match has become known as the Battle of Leeds - and it was just that. At times there were groups of players fighting 50 metres from where the ball happened to be. It was desperate, dangerous, dastardly stuff. We turned the table on the English that day. This time we kidded them into fighting and they fell for it."

Having won the Ashes in Australia just months earlier, Great Britain had dominated the pool stage of the World Cup, topping the group with three wins. Australia, France and New Zealand managed just one each, but the Australians scraped through on points difference. Great Britain were favourites to be crowned world champions, but it wasn't that simple as Reilly remembered. "We were confident, but in the final we got our tactics wrong," he said. "We tried to physically knock them down but we should have played more football. Tactically we didn't play to our best.

GREAT BRITAIN 7 AUSTRALIA 12

GREAT BRITAIN
1 Ray Dutton
2 Alan Smith
3 Syd Hynes
4 Frank Myler (C)
5 John Atkinson
6 Mick Shoebottom
7 Keith Hepworth
8 Dennis Hartley
9 Tony Fisher
10 Cliff Watson
11 Jimmy Thompson
12 Doug Laughton
13 Mal Reilly
Subs:
14 Chris Hesketh
15 Robert Haigh

Try: Atkinson **Goal:** Dutton
Drop goal: Hynes

Dismissed: Hynes

AUSTRALIA
1 Eric Simms
2 Lionel Williamson
3 John Cootes
4 Paul Sait
5 Mark Harris
6 Bob Fulton
7 Billy Smith
8 John O'Neill
9 Ron Turner
10 Bob O'Reilly
11 Bob McCarthy
12 Ron Costello
13 Ron Coote (C)
Subs:
14 Ray Branighan
15 Elwyn Walters

Tries: Cootes, Williamson
Goals: Simms 2 **Drop goal:** Simms

Dismissed: Smith

Half-time: 4-5
Referee: Fred Lindop
Crowd: 18,776

Australia celebrate winning the 1970 World Cup Final

Maybe there was some complacency due to the Ashes win and the group-stage games."

After a first-minute scrum, Hynes caught Fulton with a swinging arm, causing Paul Sait to run in and offer some retribution. When play restarted, Shoebottom missed with a couple of drop-goal attempts. Dutton soon kicked a goal from a wide position but Hynes' comical attempt at a drop goal didn't get off the ground. Atkinson was tackled into touch near the Australian line, but Great Britain soon lost their lead when Simms potted a simple penalty. At the other end, an attempt from Dutton was abysmal. In the closing stages of the first half, a Great Britain scrum on their own line resulted in Reilly losing the ball in a two-man tackle. Ron Coote picked up and cleverly offloaded to the footballing-priest Cootes, who touched down. Simms missed the goal and at the other end Hynes snapped a drop goal with the last kick of the half. The visitors led 5-4.

Drop-goal attempts from Hynes, Myler and Reilly early in the second half were missed, with the tactic smacking of panic. Australia were more composed and when Fulton moved the ball to the right, McCarthy helped it on for Lionel Williamson to score. Simms converted magnificently and later kicked a drop goal, which was in contrast to Dutton's penalty miss from bang in front. Australia held the lead into the closing stages, resulting in Great Britain desperation, which was the big factor in the outrageous scenes that marred the end of a successful World Cup.

An interesting footnote to the 1970 World Cup is that the original trophy was stolen from the Australian hotel six days before the final, where it had been on display - although due to a sponsorship agreement, a different piece of silverware had been commissioned for the Headingley final. Nevertheless, it was an embarrassing episode for the game and it took 20 years for the iconic trophy to be found when local man Stephen Uttley found it lying in a muddy gutter in Bradford. It was eventually restored and has been presented to the world champions since 2000.

MURPHY RULES THE ROOST AGAIN

Controversy followed Alex Murphy wherever he went.

Whether he was the greatest British player of all time or not is open to debate, but his name is certainly in the top bracket. It is unlikely, though, that Rugby League has seen a cleverer player. His gamesmanship had been the deciding factor in the 1966 Challenge Cup Final, when he ruthlessly exploited a weakness in the offside laws to St Helens' advantage against Wigan. Five years later, as the 32-year-old player-coach of Leigh, opponents Leeds were clear favourites - but never once on the afternoon of 15th May 1971 did the Loiners look like winning the Challenge Cup.

Murphy dominated the build-up, insisting Leigh would win. He then displayed a brilliant game, kicking two drop goals and winning the Lance Todd Trophy as man of the match. He was also involved in possibly the most controversial incident in the history of Wembley Cup Finals when he was accused of faking an injury as the Leeds captain, Syd Hynes, was sent from the field. It was reported that Murphy winked from his stretcher, although he was quick to deny that.

One of the mysteries of the 1971 final is why exactly Leigh were regarded as such underdogs. They had won the 1969-70 Floodlit Trophy, beating Wigan at Central Park, and the 1970-71 Lancashire Cup by getting the better of St Helens at Swinton. If they could beat Wigan and Saints to land trophies, why not Leeds? And as the 1971 league campaign ended, Leigh, in fourth, had finished just one place behind Leeds. Leeds had also suffered the trauma of a terrible injury to Mick Shoebottom, one of their star backs, less than a fortnight before the final.

"Leeds hold all the aces bar Murphy," was The Guardian's headline on the day, although the article stated "There is only one Murphy. A player gifted with aptitude; with skill; with the ability quickly to spot any weakness in opposing ranks; and still, after all his years in the game, with speed off the mark – Murphy has proved a match winner on innumerable big occasions."

There were fun and games on the day before the match began as well. Joe Walsh, Leigh's charismatic winger, was reported to have picked up a watering

"Form horses don't always win."

can and shouted to the Leeds players during the pre-match walkabout: "Here lads. This is the only cup you'll win this weekend!" Another Leigh player joyously observed, "Look at their body language! They are beaten before we start."

Leigh also pulled a fast one with the Rugby Football League by defying an instruction that Kevin Ashcroft's son, Gary, could not be their mascot, as such a practice was not allowed at Wembley. Club officials sneaked the little boy into the dressing rooms in a kit basket before he strode proudly onto the field clutching the hand of club chairman Jack Harding. He was then introduced to the dignitaries, including the Home Secretary, Reginald Maudling, who later presented the Cup to Murphy.

Leeds were without Shoebottom, Ray Batten and Alan Smith. They also had fitness concerns over other players who did take to the field, while Leigh had to do without prop Dave Chisnall, speedster Rod Tickle and scrum-half Tom Canning. Murphy moved into his position, with Tony Barrow coming into the stand-off position and it was Leigh who got off to the better start as prop Jim Fiddler dropped a goal and Stuart Ferguson kicked a penalty. Stan Dorrington was then put away by Murphy to score the game's first try, which Ferguson converted.

Murphy added a drop goal, then worth two points, and Ferguson landed another penalty, opening up a 13-0 half-time lead. No one was taking Leigh lightly now, but those hoping for a Leeds comeback were cheered slightly when John Holmes kicked a penalty on 48 minutes. Back at the other end, Murphy kicked

LEIGH 24 LEEDS 7

LEIGH
1 David Eckersley
2 Stuart Ferguson
3 Stan Dorrington
4 Mike Collins
5 Joe Walsh
6 Tony Barrow
7 Alex Murphy (C)
8 Derek Watts
9 Kevin Ashcroft
10 Jim Fiddler
11 Paul Grimes
12 Geoff Clarkson
13 Paul Smethurst
Subs:
14 Lee Chisnall
15 Roy Lester (dnp)

Tries: Dorrington, Eckersley
Goals: Ferguson 5
Drop goals:
Fiddler, Murphy 2, Eckersley

LEEDS
1 John Holmes
2 John Langley
3 Syd Hynes (C)
4 Ron Cowan
5 John Atkinson
6 Tony Wainwright
7 Barry Seabourne
8 John Burke
9 Tony Fisher
10 Ted Barnard
11 David Hick
12 Bob Haigh
13 Bill Ramsey
Subs:
14 Les Dyl
15 Phil Cookson (dnp)

Try: Wainwright (penalty try)
Goals: Holmes 2

Dismissed: Hynes

Half-time: 13-0
Referee: Billy Thompson
Crowd: 85,514

Alex Murphy holds aloft the Challenge Cup following a memorable Leigh win

another field goal, with Ferguson quickly adding a penalty. The big moment came on 65 minutes. With Murphy lying on the turf, referee Thompson, on the advice of a touch judge, sent Hynes from the field, believing that he had attacked the Leigh talisman. Murphy was carried into the changing room and attended to by a couple of medics, but refused to remove his boots. To Leeds's consternation, he soon returned to the field.

By then, fullback David Eckersley had kicked his side's fourth drop goal and minutes after his captain's return, he crossed for a try, which Ferguson goaled. Leeds did eventually score when stand-off Tony Wainwright was awarded a penalty try, but it was too little too late.

As Leigh celebrated, all Hynes could do was protest his innocence in the face of sporting notoriety. "I tackled Murphy and I thought that was that," he said. "He just fell back and was laughing. I could not believe I had been given my marching orders."

Murphy, typically, wasn't done on the big stage. He surprised everyone by immediately moving to Warrington as player-coach and won another Challenge Cup in 1974 at the ripe old age of 35.

GREAT BRITAIN WIN BACK THE WORLD CUP

Great Britain were crowned champions of the world in 1972, after a thrilling final in Lyon against Australia, when Clive Sullivan's length-of-the-field try provided the sport with one of its most enduring and iconic images.

As was the case in the previous five World Cups, there were just four competing nations. The eventual champions topped the table, having won their round-robin matches against Australia in Perpignan (27-12), France in Grenoble (13-4) and the winless New Zealand in Pau (53-19). Such performances might have been regarded as something of a surprise considering how poor Great Britain had been in 1971. They had lost once to France and twice to New Zealand, who had won a Test series on British soil for the first time since Albert Baskerville's pioneering 1908 All Golds.

As in the inaugural World Cup of 1954, few believed that the British side had a genuine shot at success. "Even our own press said we had no chance, but hoped we gave them a decent game and didn't lose by too big a margin," said the British hooker Mike Stephenson.

Australia were seeking to defend the title they had won two years earlier against Britain at the infamous Battle of Headingley. The make-up of both teams had changed drastically, with Leeds winger John Atkinson being Great Britain's only surviving player. In came men of the calibre of Sullivan, Stephenson, Paul Charlton, Brian Lockwood, Phil Lowe and George Nicholls. They were coached by Jim Challinor, one of the 1958 Lions heroes, and a try scorer in that famous Test in Brisbane. Australia only fielded Bob Fulton and props Bob O'Reilly and John O'Neill from their triumph two years earlier. Fulton, though, was in great form in the 1972 competition, scoring five tries, including a hat-trick in the defeat to Great Britain. On the wing, they chose John Grant, who became the inaugural chairman of the Australian Rugby League Commission in 2011.

The wonderful events of the final have deservedly taken their place in Rugby League folklore, but it was played in front of a tiny crowd of just 4,231. The showpiece match had been scheduled for the Stade Gerland in Lyon,

"Even our own press said we had no chance."

Clive Sullivan receives the World Cup after Great Britain's 1972 victory

which was miles away from the Rugby League heartlands in the south of the country and, with the hosts not in the final, interest in the tournament had waned considerably.

With ten minutes gone, Terry Clawson's penalty just inside the touchline sailed between the posts. At the other end, Australian prop John O'Neill scored the first try of the final, and it was a beauty as he soared down the blind-side, beating Phil Lowe, George Nicholls and Paul Charlton to touch down in the corner. Ray Branighan's toe-ended conversion from the touchline was perfect and the Kangaroos led 5-2. The Australians soon scored what has often been regarded as the greatest disallowed try ever seen. On the 25-yard line, the halfback Dennis Ward hoisted a teasing kick and, from an onside position, the great fullback Graeme 'Changa' Langlands raced through, dived over the line, caught the ball in mid-air and grounded it fairly. But the referee incorrectly disallowed it for offside. It was an incredible effort by a player so good, that after retiring he became one of the first six post-war Immortals in Australia.

Langlands was soon upstaged by Sullivan. With Australia attacking again, Bob O'Reilly's offload to Langlands went astray and Sullivan scooped up the ball. He arced towards touch and straightened up, before scorching up the touchline and planting the ball over the Australian try line for a sensational score. "Everybody's saying 'go, go, go!', and he goes for a try!" was Eddie Waring's call of one of the great moments in British Rugby League.

Great Britain set off on a lap of honour

The half-time score was 5-5 but the Aussies again opened up a five-point gap when Arthur Beetson supported Ward's jinking run and scored, despite Stephenson almost knocking the ball from his grasp over the line. Branighan's goal was simple. Great Britain weren't done yet though, and were just a converted try from taking the game into extra-time. The big moment came when Sullivan's mesmeric footwork caused the Australian defence all manner of problems before he linked with Brian Lockwood who sent Stephenson over the line. Stevo could have gone much closer to the posts, but Clawson, ten metres to the left, made no mistake and took the game to extra-time by locking the scores at 10-10.

Clawson missed with a penalty attempt from a similar distance to his successful shot early in the game, but the Green and Golds were kept at bay, which meant that Great Britain won the World Cup courtesy of the fact they had the best record in the group matches.

A drawn final may have been an unsatisfying way to crown the world champions, but when Sullivan lifted the beautiful trophy, no-one in Great Britain colours cared.

LYON : La Grande-Bretagne tient l'Australie en échec (10-10) et enlève la Coupe du monde de jeu à XIII

Hier après midi, à Lyon, la Grande-Bretagne a enlevé la Coupe du monde de jeu à XIII en tenant l'Australie en échec : 10 à 10. A l'issue du match, le capitaine britannique Clive Sullivan, héros de la rencontre, brandissant la coupe que vient de lui remettre M. Pradel, maire de Lyon, est porté en triomphe par ses coéquipiers.

(Nos informations détaillées en pages sportives)

Great Britain's David Jeanes halted by the Australian defence

GREAT BRITAIN 10 AUSTRALIA 10
(after extra-time)

GREAT BRITAIN
1 Paul Charlton
2 Clive Sullivan (C)
3 Chris Hesketh
4 John Walsh
5 John Atkinson
6 John Holmes
7 Steve Nash
8 Terry Clawson
9 Mike Stephenson
10 David Jeanes
11 Phil Lowe
12 Brian Lockwood
13 George Nicholls
Subs:
14 Dennis O'Neill (dnp)
15 Bob Irving

Tries: Sullivan, Stephenson
Goals: Clawson 2

AUSTRALIA
1 Graeme Langlands (C)
2 John Grant
3 Mark Harris
4 Geoff Starling
5 Ray Branighan
6 Bob Fulton
7 Dennis Ward
8 John O'Neill
9 Elwyn Walters
10 Bob O'Reilly
11 Arthur Beetson
12 Gary Stevens
13 Garry Sullivan
Subs:
14 Stephen Knight (dnp)
15 Fred Jones (dnp)

Tries: Beetson, O'Neill
Goals: Branighan 2

Half-time: 5-5
Referee: Georges Jameau
Crowd: 4,231

Saturday, 20th September 1975

CHANGA'S WHITE BOOTS NIGHTMARE

Kevin Sinfield and Jamie Peacock enjoyed the perfect farewell in 2015 with Leeds Rhinos. So too did the Parramatta pair Ray Price and Mick Cronin in 1986, Penrith's Royce Simmons in 1991, Canberra's Mal Meninga in 1994, Brisbane's Shane Webcke in 2006 and Manly's Steve Menzies in 2012. But not every legend is able to bow out of Rugby League with Grand Final success.

Take Graeme Langlands, for instance.

The former St George fullback is one of the eight Australian Rugby League Immortals, chosen by 'Rugby League Week' magazine to mark the greatest Australian players from 1945. He remains regarded as a champion of the sport. The 1975 Australian Grand Final – the first to be televised in colour - was supposed to be the final game of a magnificent career, but it ended in defeat, embarrassment and utter humiliation to the extent that it is now what Langlands is best remembered for.

Langlands had received a pain-killing injection which hit a nerve and deadened not just the pain in his groin, but his entire leg. Consequently, his performance was a shambles as he could barely walk. St George lost 38-0 - a record Grand Final score. To complete Langlands' nightmare, he wore a pair

"He was a mighty player, a champion who deserved a better ending. It was unfair; the bloody shoes had nothing to do with his game that day. He was simply in pain."

of white boots as part of a sponsorship agreement with Adidas as a favour to the former great winger Ken Irvine, who was promoting the boots. In those days, unlike the NRL and Super League era, every player wore black. A pair of boots of any other colour was regarded as flashy.

The usually great fullback stood out a mile, for both performance and footwear and it couldn't have happened on a worse day. To make matters worse, he was the player-coach of the side. "It was an injection that went wrong," he wrote in his autobiography, 'Larrikin and Saint'. "It wasn't the doctor's fault. The injection went in where the nerves shouldn't have been. They had moved because of all the injuries that I've had around the groin." The planned farewell went so badly that Langlands decided to withdraw his retirement and play on in 1976 – but he lasted just four matches and he retired in April, shortly after the new season had started.

His problems were evident very early in that ill-fated Premiership decider. An attempt to find touch 20 metres away saw the ball land five metres away from his kicking foot before bouncing a couple of times without reaching the touchline. It looked like an infant had kicked the ball.

**EASTERN SUBURBS 38
ST GEORGE 0**

EASTERN SUBURBS
1 Ian Schubert
2 Bruce Pickett
3 John Brass
4 John Rheinberger
5 Bill Mullins
6 John Peard
7 Johnny Mayes
13 Ian McKay
12 Elwyn Walters
11 Grant Hedger
10 Arthur Beetson (C)
9 Ron Coote
8 Kevin Stevens
Subs:
14 Bunny Reilly
15 Des O'Reilly

Tries: Brass 2, Mayes 2, McKay, Beetson, Pickett, Schubert
Goals: Peard 7

ST GEORGE
1 Graeme Langlands (C)
2 Paul Mills
3 Roy Ferguson
4 Ted Goodwin
5 John Chapman
6 John Bailey
7 Billy Smith
13 Henry Tatana
12 Steve Edge
11 Barry Beath
10 Peter Fitzgerald
9 Robert Stone
8 Lindsay Drake
Subs:
14 Bruce Starkey
15 Robert Finch

Half-time: 5-0
Referee: Laurie Bruyeres
Crowd: 63,047

He could barely move and was easily tackled. At half-time, with the score just 5-0, a row broke out with the club's secretary-treasurer, Frank 'Fearless' Facer, over whether the player should return to the field of play. Langlands insisted he would continue, and got his way, but it was during this period that the Dragons crumbled in spectacular fashion. Langlands was eventually substituted on 68 minutes. It was heartbreaking to watch such a legend perform so pathetically.

Langlands had moved from Wollongong to St George in 1963 in order to play at the highest level and won a Grand Final in his first season. He won three more Premierships in the next three years. 1963 also saw him make the first of a then-record 33 New South Wales appearances. A first Test cap also came his way as he enjoyed one of the greatest debut seasons that anyone could remember. He took part in three World Cups - in 1968, 1972 and 1975, captaining Australia in the last two. In the 1972 final, he scored what has been described as the 'greatest try that never was', when he was wrongly given offside after spectacularly catching Dennis Ward's kick. He played in 34 non-World Cup games for Australia as well, and went on three Kangaroo tours. Not only was he a world-class fullback, he was a great centre and a top-class kicker, whether at goal or in play. He enjoyed the most remarkable of Rugby League careers.

Easts' captain was Arthur Beetson, the great ball-playing forward, who is also a member of the Immortals. He wrote of his sympathy for Langlands in his 2004 book. "As far as I'm concerned, Changa is a true Immortal. For all who knew him and saw him, the '75 Grand Final was no more than a sad 'one-off'. He was a mighty player, a champion who deserved a better ending. It was unfair; the bloody shoes had nothing to do with his game that day. He was simply in pain."

Langlands took the boots to England for Australia's remaining games in the 1975 World Cup, even though he didn't play in any of the games. He was captain-coach, but only played in their home matches in June. After training one day near their West Yorkshire base, Langlands tied the boots together and threw them so they lay hanging from a crossbar. He turned his back on them and walked away.

KIWI FURY AS MILLS STAMPS ON GREENGRASS

When debates arise about the worst piece of foul play ever seen on a Rugby League field, many of those old enough to have seen it will invariably plump for an incident involving the Welsh prop Jim Mills and his New Zealand counterpart John Greengrass from 1975, which unfolded in front of a shocked live-television audience.

With two minutes to go in a World Cup match at Swansea, Greengrass took the ball from dummy-half, stepped inside Bill Francis, went past Tony Fisher and then powered through the Welsh captain, David Watkins, and the fearsome Mills to plant the ball down for a late consolation try. With sickening brutality, Mills reacted by standing over his opponent and stamping on his head.

The referee Georges Jameau immediately sent Mills off. A dazed Greengrass was led from the field with a towel pressed to the side of his head and when the towel was removed, a gaping wound was exposed. The victim required 17 stitches above and below his left eye, although Mills initially denied that the incident had been a deliberate act. When Greengrass came into the bar after the game where the players were assembled, all of the Welsh players

Jim Mills

"I've only seen the incident once and I cringed. I can't explain it. Brainstorm, stupidity, moment of madness."

apologised to him, apart from one. Jim Mills.

It was a sad end to a terrific match, with Wales enjoying a superb win. The lead changed hands several times with the spectators thoroughly entertained, although it had been a fractious contest with several skirmishes. Francis scored first when he supported Stuart Gallacher's break but man of the match Tony Coll, the Kiwi second-row forward, got his side on the board with a long-range try. Francis and John Bevan scored further Welsh tries as they opened up a 17-14 half-time lead. Phil Orchard had crossed for New Zealand's try after a brilliant offload from a teenage Kurt Sorensen. Goalkicker Tony Gordon levelled the scores with an early second-half try, but tries from David Willicombe and John Mantle got the Welsh home before Greengrass's late score.

Mills was suspended until 2nd January, although that was far from the end of the story as the fall-out lasted for years. The New Zealand Rugby League banned him from playing Rugby League in their country, although the Rugby Football League in the UK questioned the legitimacy of such a ruling. The argument was to resurface when he was selected by Great Britain to play in the same tournament two years later. "To condone the New Zealand ban on Mills' international appearances would create a totally unacceptable precedent in world Rugby League," said David Howes, the RFL's public-relations officer. "The selection of Mills was purely on merit and not designed to upset or challenge our New Zealand colleagues." Ron McGregor, president of the NZRL, hit

WALES 25 NEW ZEALAND 24

WALES
1 David Watkins (C)
2 Roy Mathias
3 Frank Wilson
4 David Willicombe
5 John Bevan
6 Bill Francis
7 Peter Banner
8 Jim Mills
9 Tony Fisher
10 Mick Murphy
11 John Mantle
12 Stuart Gallacher
13 Brian Gregory
Subs:
14 Glyn Turner (dnp)
15 Clive Jones

Tries:
Francis 2, Bevan, Willicombe, Mantle
Goals: Watkins 5

Dismissed: Mills

NEW ZEALAND
1 Warren Collicoat
2 Phil Orchard
3 Fred Ah Kuoi
4 Dennis Williams (C)
5 Tony Gordon
6 Bob Jarvis
7 John Smith
8 Dane Sorensen
9 Tony Conroy
10 John Greengrass
11 Kurt Sorensen
12 Tony Coll
13 Peter Gurnick
Subs:
14 Bruce Dickison
15 Lindsay Proctor

Tries:
Coll, Orchard, Gordon, Greengrass
Goals: Gordon 5, Collicoat

Half-time: 17-14
Referee: Georges Jameau
Crowd: 2,645

back, saying: "There is no way Mills can play in New Zealand as far as we are concerned. Our decision is quite clear – he is not acceptable on any field in the country." In the end, the embarrassment of all parties was spared when Mills withdrew from the squad to have a hernia operation.

Two years later, in 1979, with Great Britain scheduled to undergo a full Lions tour of the Southern Hemisphere, the argument between the two countries flared up when Mills was again selected. Ron McGregor, the president of the NZRL, said: "Mills has been banned from playing in New Zealand or against any New Zealand side. Ours is a firm decision and one which will not be changed." George Rainey, chairman of the Auckland League, said that the British had shown their "irresponsibility" by picking Mills. "Certainly we feel that to accept such a ban would be to set an unhealthy precedent," was Howes's response. Mills did tour, but the only Test he played was the first Ashes match against Australia.

Surprisingly, the story did have a happy ending. In June 2008, Greengrass telephoned Mills completely out of the blue whilst holidaying with his wife in England. Mills initially hung up, believing it to be a prank call, which prompted Greengrass's wife to text and reassure him they were genuine. "I really appreciate it because that incident has niggled me all my rugby career," said Mills. "I didn't just upset John and New Zealand, I upset a lot of people. You couldn't get a worse incident and to have him come over here and offer the hand of friendship means a lot. It's made me feel a lot better. I've only seen the incident once and I cringed. I can't explain it - brainstorm, stupidity, moment of madness. The only thing I can think of is I blamed myself for him scoring. You think, `Bloody hell, what have I done here?' When you do something like that there's no way back."

Greengrass said: "Back home it's brought up all the time. They talk about the worst incidents in football and that's always shown. I was bitter for a couple of years but it's water under the bridge. Life's too short to hold grudges."

Sunday, 24th April 1977

CHRIS SANDERSON DIES AFTER ON-FIELD INJURY

Eight minutes into the Salford-Leeds league match in April 1977, the 23-year-old Leeds scrum-half, Chris Sanderson, left the field with a head injury. He was accompanied to hospital by his wife of barely six months, Sally. Just before half-time, the terrible news came through that he had died. The game was abandoned.

Sanderson, who had joined the club in 1971 from York Juniors, hadn't always been a regular in the Leeds side, although he did play in the 1975 Challenge Cup semi-final against Warrington and was a substitute in the club's Yorkshire Cup wins of 1975 and 1976. But with Peter Banner having left the club to go to Australia, Sanderson had every chance of playing at Wembley.

Colin Dixon, the Salford player-coach, said: "Every single one of the lads on the field felt shattered. When something like that happened you've got to be out to know what it is like. I went cold when Syd Hynes [the Leeds coach] told me." Six years earlier, Dixon had been the player involved in the incident which ended Mick Shoebottom's career, and briefly paralysed him. "Things seemed to be mending," Dixon continued, "then something like this happens." An official from the Salford club said: "We do not know what happened. He was suddenly noticed on the ground away from the play." The cause of death was not immediately apparent.

The inquest concluded that Sanderson had died after attempting to tackle the Salford player Ken Gill. He had been knocked unconscious after taking a blow to the head. "Truly it was an unfortunate chance, one in many millions," said the coroner, Mr David Blakey, as he recorded a verdict of misadventure. According to the pathologist, Dr Roger Gillett, asphyxiation was the cause of death due to the inhalation of vomit while Sanderson was unconscious.

"Truly it was an unfortunate chance, one in many millions."

136

Eye-witness, Sergeant Denis Harris, said: "They met more or less head-on. I did not see their heads meet but they came face-to-face. I think this is called a smother tackle, which is quite orthodox. It seemed to me that he was trying to get his arms round the other player to try and prevent him from passing the ball."

Gill was in Australia at the time of the inquest, but had prepared a statement which said that he fell to the ground after the collision clutching his face and that he didn't know which part of Sanderson's body had hit him. "It is quite plain on the evidence of all the witnesses that there was nothing particularly violent about this Rugby League football match," continued the coroner. "There are hundreds of tackles in a single game and, over the years, millions of tackles. In these, there are sometimes injuries but no fatalities."

The day after the incident, on the Monday, the Rugby Football League declared the match null and void, not to be replayed. Salford had finished in sixth, and Leeds ninth – which meant they missed out on the Premiership play-offs. David Howes, the public-relations officer for the RFL, said: "This is an exceptional decision because of the nature of the abandonment and the time factor, for the first-round matches in the Premiership play-off are due this weekend. It was felt that it would be insensitive to replay the fixture within 48 hours of Chris Sanderson's tragic death. Another alternative considered, a request by Leeds for the two points to be awarded to them because they were leading 5-2 when the game was abandoned, was not acceptable because only 38 minutes had been played."

On the Tuesday, a testimonial fund was set up to help Sanderson's widow and children. Widnes, who were to be Leeds' opponents at Wembley, sent £50, and a game between Great Britain and Leeds was arranged for May before the team flew to Australia for the World Cup. A crowd of 11,000, the best at Headingley all season, attended the match, raising £7,000 for the fund. Leeds beat Widnes in the Challenge Cup Final and dedicated the win to Chris Sanderson. Sally was the first guest to be invited into the changing-rooms after the game.

Sanderson's name joined the tragic roll-call of Rugby League players who have died from an injury or condition sustained on the field of play in this country. Others include Frank Townsend, a winger who died playing for Featherstone in a match at Wakefield in 1946; Hudson Irving, a Cumbrian who died playing for Halifax against Dewsbury in 1947; David Craven who also died at Thrum Hall, playing for Fax against Workington in 1949; Dennis Norton who suffered chest pains and died 12 days after playing for Castleford against the 1951 New Zealanders; Ralph Slater who died the day after an 'A' team game for Rochdale against Oldham in 1953; John Davies who died of a heart attack after collapsing while playing for Dewsbury against Batley in 1969 and Jeff Whiteside who died of spinal injuries sustained while playing for Swinton's 'A' team against Rochdale in 1976. One of the try-scorers in the first ever Wembley Challenge Cup Final, played in 1929, Wigan's Roy Kinnear, also collapsed and died on the field of play – in a war-time rugby union match played in 1942.

JOHN BURKE BREAKS HIS NECK

A day after his 21st birthday, Workington Town's stand-off, John Burke, fielded a pass from his halfback partner, Arnold 'Boxer' Walker in a home match against Leeds. Typical of the way he looked to play the game, Burke immediately looked for a gap in the defence. He was tackled and landed on the Derwent Park turf. The match was stopped. Something wasn't right. Burke had broken his neck and damaged his spine.

"There was a scrum down and the ball came out. It was going over my head to the centre but I jumped up and caught it," Burke recalled many years later. "I landed back down with the ball and about four or five players landed on top of me. The next thing I know the referee is asking me if I was okay and I couldn't talk. I was taken to hospital at Hensingham and then through to the spinal injury unit at Hexham the next day. At that time when somebody was injured there was no neck brace put on, you were just lifted off the field."

Burke's neck was broken in two places and his spinal cord was trapped which rendered the player paralysed. A two-hour manipulative operation was carried out the following day, but Burke was destined for life in a wheelchair.

"I was in and out of consciousness for a while, and my spinal cord was trapped between vertebrae and then after a few days I came round and was told the extent of my injuries," he said many years later. At the time I was married with a six-month-old daughter and the biggest thing for me was, as I was totally paralysed, I couldn't hold my daughter, which drove me mad. But I got stronger and stronger and now, years later, I feel independent, I can do a lot more for myself. I have an adapted bungalow, which Workington Town helped raise money for through a trust fund."

Burke had made his Wigan debut in January 1977 and remained at the club throughout the year, playing his final match for the club in December at Leeds. In early 1978, he moved to Cumbria for an £11,000 fee and went on to play 16 matches for Town. His favoured position was at fullback, although with Paul Charlton firmly established there, Burke became a very handy stand-off.

"It was horrible," remembered Allan Green, one of 4,006 spectators present. "I was on the Popular Side. Burke was an expensive signing. He had played only a few games for Town, but had shown himself to be a class stand-off. Over the years that I have watched Town he could have been one of their best signings ever. I can see it in my mind still. He was making one of his jinking, darting runs. He was going at speed towards the scoreboard end, between halfway and the 25-yard line. There were a lot of defenders around him. He crashed into a tackle, and was pole-axed instantaneously. Everyone knew it was serious. The game was stopped for a while, and he was stretchered off. Soon everyone knew that he was unlikely to walk again. Workington people were stunned."

Such injuries were rare, although just over three months earlier, the Penrith Panthers prop John Farragher had become a quadriplegic after a scrum collapsed. News of Burke's appalling injury was even reported in the 'Sydney Morning Herald'.

Town immediately set about breaking the record for a Rugby League testimonial fund. Manchester United and Burnley soccer clubs helped with fundraising. Tom Mitchell, the charismatic Town chairman and former Great Britain tour manager raised a four-figure sum doing laps of Derwent Park. A benefit match between the 1979 Great Britain Lions and Widnes was staged at Naughton Park, whilst there were several bucket collections and many other fund-raising activities organised. In total, over £50,000 was raised and it paid for a purpose-built bungalow for Burke, his wife Jackie and young daughter Louise in Bickershaw, halfway between Wigan and Leigh.

Mitchell presented Burke with an England shirt, calling it "the jersey he would surely have gone on to win himself." Years later, the great administrator wrote: "If a young Rugby League player could have been certain of going to the very top of his chosen sport, it was John Burke."

Happily, Burke was never forgotten by the sport he had once graced. Many years later when the Rugby League Benevolent Fund was set up to aid injured players, a donation was made to Burke to pay for an adapted kitchen. "This has been a massive boost for me, and allowed me to have greater freedom within my own home," he said. "It will make a great difference to my quality of life."

It was one of those strange twists of fate that four years after the accident, Walker, by then playing for Whitehaven, went down in a tackle at the Recreation Ground, in a match against Hull Kingston Rovers. 'Boxer', as he was nicknamed' lay on the turf thinking of Burke, believing he had suffered the same fate. Supporters wept as an ambulance came on to the field to take Walker to hospital as the match was abandoned. Some believed he had died, but fortunately, there was no neck break and his career resumed a couple of months later.

Burke was not so fortunate - and likewise Matt King and Alex McKinnon since. King was paralysed in April 2004 playing in an Academy match for London Broncos against Halifax. McKinnon was a Newcastle Knights player in 2014 when he was badly injured in a match against Melbourne Storm. He, too, is now a wheelchair user. Both men, like Burke, have won an abundance of admirers for the way they have dealt with their terrible situations.

"If a young Rugby League player could have been certain of going to the very top of his chosen sport, it was John Burke."

Wednesday, 11th October 1978

NEWTOWN PLAYER IMPRISONED IN BANGKOK HELLHOLE

It is safe to say that the Rugby League community in Sydney was plunged into shock the day an Australian newspaper revealed that a first-grade Rugby League player was to face the death penalty without trial for trafficking a huge quantity of heroin in Thailand.

At the end of the 1978 season, in which Manly had been declared premiers, Paul Hayward, the stand-off half for the Newtown Jets, decided to spend some time in Bangkok. That might seem perfectly run of the mill, but it was a trip which saw his life plummet into chaos as he ended up incarcerated in one of the most inhumane prisons in the world. His life fell apart, and he died shortly after his release.

On 11th October, as the Australian Kangaroos were touring England, police stormed into Hayward's hotel room and found three-million Australian dollars' worth of heroin, which had been purchased for less than $40,000. When the story broke two days later, the sport was rocked, especially with the revelation that he could face the death penalty without trial. "Aussies face firing squad!" screamed the front of Sydney's 'Daily Telegraph'.

"His dramatic arrest just after the 1978 football season is still remembered as the day Rugby League lost its innocence," reflected the 'Courier Mail' many years later.

Hayward played 79 times for the Newtown Jets between 1973 and 1978, scoring 14 tries and 43 goals. He played for Souths as a junior and toured New Zealand with a combined Sydney team in 1976. He was a small, nippy player with a style similar to the future Test half Peter Sterling. Hayward formed a

"Aussies face firing squad!"

promising halfback partnership with Barry Wood, the father of Nathan who later played in Super League for Warrington and Wakefield. Hayward was also a proficient enough boxer to be selected for the 1976 Montreal Summer Olympics, but his Jets contract saw him classed as a professional and he was disqualified.

Hayward's accomplice was Warren Fellows, the son of the 1949 Melbourne Cup-winning jockey, Bill. Both men were 26 and were employed by a notorious member of the criminal underworld, Arthur Stanley 'Neddy' Smith, Hayward's cousin.

Thai narcotics officers found nearly eight and a half kilograms of heroin in a suitcase in Hayward's room. "Insane with fear, I stupidly cling to the hope that they will close the case without looking under the flimsy blue towel that covers the 24 bags of grade-four heroin," wrote Fellows in his 1998 book, 'The Damage Done'. "There is a grotesque silence in the room as the towel is removed. I want to cry but my body is so terrified it cannot manage even so simple a task."

At the police station, Major Vyraj, who led the arrest, instructed Hayward to run for 100 yards before he attempted to shoot him. "If he misses, Paul is free. If he doesn't miss, then he will say that Paul tried to escape," Fellows explained. As the plan was about to be put into action, Fellows bowed to the Thais' demand for him implicate a third man, William Sinclair. Herded by electric cattle prods and in leg chains, the trio were taken to a remand prison. Despite being desperate for food, Fellows was unable to eat the prison food of rice in dirty water. They shared a cell with around 30 others. At least the death-penalty threat had been dropped, although with hindsight, it might have been kinder for Hayward to have been shot.

They were moved to Maha Chai prison until their trial, where sewer rats "as large as small cats" roamed free. They witnessed murders and discovered that Thai prisoners would kill and eat the rats, as well as cockroaches, such was the unpleasantness of the vile prison food.

Their nightmare continued. Fellows was one day forced to stand in human excrement that came up to his chin. As well as selling heroin, guards stole food parcels sent by relatives and ate the contents in front of the prisoners. Another guard, who moonlighted as a taxi driver, raped and beat the sister of an inmate, leaving her clinging onto life. That prisoner, in turn, arranged for friends on the outside to ambush the guard and murder him.

After two and a half years of adjourned trials, Hayward was finally sentenced to 20 years imprisonment on 23rd July 1981. Fellows and Sinclair received 33-year sentences along with a Thai taxi driver who was also implicated. The men were incarcerated in the infamous Bang Kwang prison, nicknamed the Bangkok Hilton.

The horror of Bang Kwang is best demonstrated by a story told in the prologue of Fellows' book. "I was awakened late one night by the screaming of a young French prisoner in the cell next door," he wrote. "The sound of his scream was excruciating. It wasn't just a scream of pain, but of madness too. It was the sort of sound you would never want to hear coming from a human being. I'll never forget it." Fellows persuaded a guard to open his cell door. "He was alone, curled into a ball, facing the corner. His screams didn't stop for the whole time we were there – he seemed totally oblivious of our presence. As soon as we turned him over we could see what was wrong. On his neck, just below the ear, was an enormous lump, about the size of an avocado. It appeared to be moving." A blade was located and the lump sliced open. "Out of the gash spilled hundreds of tiny, worm-like creatures, wriggling and oozing like spaghetti," Fellows continued. According to hospital staff, a cockroach had crawled into his ear, burrowed through to his neck and laid its eggs."

Hayward eventually came through 11 years of misery, surviving a 1985 riot which saw police shoot ten prisoners dead. His parents had died while he was imprisoned, and his third child was born. Without him, the Jets made the 1981 Grand Final and then lost their place in the competition in 1983. He received sporadic visitors, including one from the future Leeds coach Graham Murray and another from a 'Rugby League Week' reporter. He and Fellows were now at the mercy of the drug they had once trafficked, having become addicted to heroin themselves. 'The Canberra Times' reported in 1989 that Hayward had "almost lost his mind through the use of bad drugs." Hayward contracted HIV through contaminated needles. He was released on 7th April 1989.

When they were free men again, Hayward and Fellows met up back in Sydney, with Hayward reportedly struggling to re-adapt to normal life. He died of a drug overdose in his Canterbury house on 9th May 1992 at the age of 39. He was survived by his wife, Gail, and their three children.

STATE OF ORIGIN IS BORN

The biggest phenomenon in Rugby League was born on a cold Tuesday night in Brisbane in July 1980. Its name? State of Origin.

With New South Wales having won 20 consecutive Interstate series against Queensland, it was decided, after incessant persuasion from the Queensland Rugby League, that the third game of the 1980 series would be played under 'origin' rules.

Queenslanders who had previously gone to play in the Sydney competition, as most of their best players had done, had to play for the Blues. But under the new rules, John Lang, Kerry Boustead, Greg Oliphant, Rod Morris, Rod Reddy and Alan Smith were able to return home. This they did along with one of Rugby League's greatest ever players, Arthur Beetson - all donning the maroon jumper for the inaugural State of Origin match. They were joined by a couple of highly promising young players. Centre Mal Meninga was celebrating his 20th birthday, while Wally Lewis wore the number-eight jersey at loose forward.

Queensland simply had to win or the concept may not have continued. Senator Ron McAuliffe, in charge at the QRL, had never stopped pushing the idea, believing it was the only way to breathe life into the state series. When he finally got his way he knew it had to work, telling his players: "The future of the game is in your hands. We have taken this bold step. If we are beaten we cannot retreat to any other position. We must win."

Sydneysiders were cynical about the proposals, with the recently retired Australian captain Bob Fulton calling it "the non-event of the century." There have always been suggestions that New South Wales didn't take the early years as seriously as their opponents but in that first game, their teamsheet was littered with great names, like the classy fullback Graeme Eadie, centres Mick Cronin and Steve Rogers, wingers Chris Anderson and Greg Brentnall, the great halfback Tommy Raudonikis and the fearsome prop Craig Young.

The 33,210 crowd which packed out Lang Park raised the roof when

"The future of the game is in your hands. We have taken this bold step. If we are beaten we cannot retreat to any other position. We must win."

Beetson was introduced to the crowd. "The greatest memory was the noise that erupted at Lang Park when he was introduced when we walked onto the field," said Lewis. "We were told we'd be introduced to the crowd individually. All the players were welcomed onto the field. When it was Arthur's turn, I've never heard a noise to level that sound. I don't think there ever will be another sound to match that one." Beetson was winding down his career with Parramatta, even figuring in their reserve-grade side that season, but his presence galvanised both teammates and supporters alike. The famous Queensland team spirit was born that night.

Beetson was credited with sparking the Origin catchphrase "Mate against mate, state against state" when he was alleged to have hit his Eels teammate Cronin during the match, although the generally accepted version of events has been wildly exaggerated over the years. Nevertheless, the theory was that if Beetson could take out his mate Cronin, then State of Origin should mean the world to every player. It certainly did to the Queenslanders anyway.

It was Brentnall who scored Origin's first ever try in the corner courtesy of Steve Edge's pass which followed Cronin's break, but the Maroons hit back when Chris Close got on the outside of Rogers to send Kerry Boustead to the corner and with Meninga regularly kicking penalties, they led 13-5 midway through the second half. The game-breaking moment came when Close took Meninga's pass 30 metres out. From a standing

QUEENSLAND 20
NEW SOUTH WALES 10

QUEENSLAND
1 Colin Scott
2 Kerry Boustead
3 Mal Meninga
4 Chris Close
5 Brad Backer
6 Alan Smith
7 Greg Oliphant
13 Rod Morris
12 John Lang
11 Arthur Beetson (C)
10 Rohan Hancock
9 Rod Reddy
8 Wally Lewis
Subs:
14 Norm Carr (dnp)
15 Bruce Astill (dnp)

Tries: Boustead, Close
Goals: Meninga 7

NEW SOUTH WALES
1 Graham Eadie
2 Chris Anderson
3 Steve Rogers
4 Mick Cronin
5 Greg Brentnall
6 Alan Thompson
7 Tommy Raudonikis (C)
13 Jim Leis
12 Graeme Wynn
11 Bob Cooper
10 Craig Young
9 Steve Edge
8 Gary Hambly
Subs:
14 Steve Martin
15 Robert Stone

Tries: Raudonikis, Brentnall
Goals: Cronin 2

Half-time: 9-5
Referee: Billy Thompson
Crowd: 33,210

Tempers flare during the first State of Origin game

start, he straightened up and stepped through some flimsy defence to score by the posts, helping him become Origin's first official man of the match. Raudonikis pulled one back for the Blues - again from Edge's pass - but they couldn't prevent their opponents running out 20-10 winners.

Alan Clarkson, from the 'Sydney Morning Herald' concluded: "I was strongly against such a match, but last night's gripping clash showed that such a fixture would be a welcome addition to the League programme."

State of Origin was up and running, but many were still not convinced. The format remained the same in 1981 when the Blues again wrapped up the Interstate Series in just two games, with the dead-rubber played to Origin rules and the Maroons turned around a 15-0 deficit to win 22-15. From 1982 the State of Origin became a best-of-three competition with the Interstate series finally killed off.

Origin has continued to grow with television audiences and attendance figures higher than anybody could have imagined on that wonderful opening night.

Sunday, 14th September 1980

WIGAN STUNNED BY NEWCOMERS FULHAM

In 1980, after 53 years, London finally had another professional Rugby League team. The new club was set up by soccer's Fulham FC and their first match went like a dream as they hammered relegated Wigan in front of nearly 10,000 boisterous fans at their iconic Craven Cottage home. This most pigeon-holed of sports was finally threatening to spread its wings.

Fulham were only voted into the league in June 1980 and had less than three months to assemble a squad. The 46-year-old actor and writer Colin Welland was made a director and was beside himself with joy. "It's the best thing to hit London since McDonald's hamburgers," he said. "For exiles like myself, it's a prayer answered. For union buffs, it's an eye opener. And for all other cockneys, denied so much – decent beer, real fish and chips – it will be a chance to make up a bit of lost ground."

The one-time England centre forward Malcolm MacDonald headed up the club's marketing department and pushed the concept as hard as anybody, helping to ensure that the new venture dominated Rugby League's 1980-81 pre-season. The papers couldn't get enough of the story.

There had been three London clubs before and, if history was any guide, Fulham were going to be up against it. London Highfield lasted just the 1933-34 season and Acton and Willesden managed only the 1935-36 campaign. Streatham and Mitcham fared slightly better, getting beyond their first year, although they were disbanded 26 matches into the 1936-37 season.

Chairman Ernie Clay was optimistic, pointing out that money wasn't an issue and that overheads were comparatively low. "Do you think I spent all this money, time and planning not to make the thing a success?" the northern-born Clay pointed out. Out of 30 clubs, 26 had voted them in, three had abstained and one had failed to turn up.

The key for Fulham was the signing of scrum-half Reggie Bowden from Widnes in the role of player-coach. A veteran of 16 finals, he was a hardened winner; just what the new club needed. He was a character, too. Asked for his thoughts before one Wembley final by the BBC, whilst being massaged

"It's the best thing to hit London since McDonald's hamburgers."

by the Chemics' physio, he quipped: "I prefer the wife." Bowden was joined by several other players from Widnes, who helped give the Fulham line-up a competitive look. Their first signing was Roy Lester who joined on a free transfer from Warrington. They also signed the 18-year-old rugby union winger Adrian Cambriani from Swansea. The squad cost over £150,000 to assemble, but the 'Dad's Army' nickname was already circulating. "Too old", was becoming a regular criticism.

Not everybody was behind them. In mid-August, it was reported that a snooty local residents' association was in the process of taking out an injunction to prevent the venture from going ahead. They aimed to invoke the Lord's Day Observance Act to prevent the Wigan game from taking place. "It is a thorn in our side," said MacDonald, "but hopefully we can overcome it." Thankfully, they did just that, with the injunction thrown out four days before the game.

It may have been Fulham's first match of the season, but it was Wigan's sixth. Having won Lancashire Cup games against Rochdale and Whitehaven, they lost their opening Division Two match at York before getting off the mark with

---

FULHAM 24 WIGAN 5

FULHAM
1 John Risman
2 Adrian Cambriani
3 Mal Aspey
4 Derek Noonan
5 Iain MacCorquodale
6 David Eckersley
7 Reg Bowden (C)
8 Ian van Bellen
9 Tony Karalius
10 Roy Lester
11 Tony Gourley
12 David Allen
13 David Hull
Subs:
14 John Wood
15 Neil Tuffs

Tries: Cambriani 2, Tuffs 2, Allen
Goals: MacCorquodale 4
Drop goal: Eckersley

WIGAN
1 George Fairbairn (C)
2 Dennis Ramsdale
3 Dave Willicombe
4 Steve Davies
5 Jimmy Hornby
6 Bernard Coyle
7 Ness Flowers
8 Jeff Townend
9 John Pendlebury
10 Malcolm Smith
11 Terry Hollingsworth
12 John Clough
13 Dennis Boyd
Subs:
14 Les Bolton
15 Bill Melling

Try: Coyle
Goal: Fairbairn

Half-time: 10-0
Referee: Fred Lindop
Crowd: 9,552

Fulham celebrate a memorable victory against Wigan

a comfortable win at home to Batley. Back in the Cup, they pulled off a superb victory at Widnes, four days before their date in the capital. Widnes, ironically, had been heavily weakened by losing players to Fulham.

Perhaps the Widnesian conquest had taken too much out of Wigan, as they were comprehensively outplayed by Fulham. They must have regretted their request to be the Londoners' first opponents as they shipped in five tries, scoring just one themselves, which came right at the end. They were never in the game from the moment Iain MacCorquodale kicked Fulham into a 2-0 lead. Cambriani soon scored the first try and then came up with another. For that brace, he would become, a week later, the Observer newspaper's sporting personality of the week.

Substitute Neil Tuffs added two more in the second half with David Allen also getting in on the act. MacCorquodale ended the afternoon with four goals and David Eckersley added another point. The atmosphere was almost indescribable. It was a dream come true for many.

The crowd figure was 9,552, which was more than double Fulham FC's last home fixture, against Bradford City. The papers were impressed, too. The Telegraph reported on "Fulham's dream start", while the Mirror wrote "Classy Fulham off to a flier". The Express weighed in with "Fulham's he-men are a hit."

Professional Rugby League was up and running again in the capital and, this time, with solid-looking foundations.

FANS BURN DOWN STADIUM AS PARRAMATTA BREAK DUCK

There are many ways to celebrate winning a Grand Final, especially if it's the first in a club's history, but when Parramatta's fans joyously burned down their stadium it was quite a novelty, even for Rugby League.

Founded in 1947, the Eels had never been more than bridesmaids, but in the early 'eighties had assembled some of the finest talents ever to come through the system of one club. Halfbacks Peter Sterling and Brett Kenny went on to enjoy incredible careers, as did three-quarters Eric Grothe and Steve Ella. With well-established internationals like Mick Cronin and Ray Price also in the side, the Eels were more than competitive, finishing third on the competition ladder in 1981 before taking their place in the first Australian Grand Final to be played on a Sunday. One newspaper cartoonist mischievously sketched a church service with Eels fans on one side, and Jets supporters across the aisle.

The Jets had finished one place above them and had come through three play-off matches to make the final. The second of those, a 20-15 win over Manly, involved one of the most notorious brawls ever seen. The Jets were a match for anybody, and boasted the inaugural New South Wales State of Origin captain, Tommy Raudonikis, at scrum-half. At 31, the charismatic playmaker was still a major force and deep into the 1981 Grand Final, his try helped Newtown into an 11-7 lead. Phil Gould, later a top coach and media personality, had earlier set up a try for centre Brian Hetherington, with a sumptuous short ball.

Parramatta's hero was Kenny. He scored two tries, including one in the final moment down the left side line where his magnificent dummy made a fool of Jets' fullback Phil Sigsworth. Bob 'The Bear' O'Reilly's offloading game was also instrumental in the Eels' comeback. In 2008, as part of the sport's centenary celebrations, O'Reilly was retrospectively awarded the Clive Churchill Medal as man of the match.

The Eels were presented with the huge J.J. Giltinan Shield and conducted their lap of honour, after which many of the fans headed back to the Parramatta Leagues Club, an entertainment venue situated near their famous

"Ding dong the witch is dead!"

149

old stadium, the Cumberland Oval. The ground, which had originally been built for local cricket, was now ramshackle. It was barely capable of housing the huge crowds that the club had recently attracted.

A few articles in the local press suggested that an upgrading of facilities may be possible. Perhaps that gave jubilant fans an idea because, with the Leagues Club full, many spilled into the stadium. One such supporter was Bryce Eulenstein, a writer for 'Rugby League World' magazine between 2007 and 2009. "Arriving at the Leagues Club, we noticed some commotion at the Oval, and a small plume of smoke developing above the grandstand," he said. "We wandered over and walked into history. There were groups of people in various parts of the ground who were quite simply going berserk. The old seats around the oval were being ripped up. The fences were pushed down, the fittings removed from the dressing rooms and the walls smashed. Water sprayed out from broken pipes, and whatever could be found was either looted or destroyed. People were using the timber from the seats and fences to start fires, some of which ignited parts of the grandstand. Amidst these scenes, people simply sat quietly in the grandstand and reflected upon the moment. My most vivid memory was the destruction of the scoreboard. Set on a ten-foot brick base, the scoreboard was of fibro construction. A group of youths were plundering the scoreboard like a gang of Mongol hoards in a fit of rage. Beneath them, another enraged gang decided to pile timber up against the brick pedestal and set fire to it. The gang on the top continued their raging

---

PARRAMATTA EELS 20
NEWTOWN JETS 11

PARRAMATTA
1 Steve McKenzie
2 Graeme Atkins
3 Mick Cronin
4 Steve Ella
5 Eric Grothe
6 Brett Kenny
7 Peter Sterling
13 Bob O'Reilly
12 Steve Edge (C)
11 Ron Hilditch
10 Kevin Stevens
9 John Muggleton
8 Ray Price
Subs
14 Steve Sharp
18 Paul Taylor

Tries: Kenny 2, Atkins, Ella
Goals: Cronin 4

NEWTOWN
1 Phil Sigsworth
2 John Ferguson
3 Mick Ryan
4 Brian Hetherington
5 Ray Blacklock
6 Paul Morris
7 Tommy Raudonikis (C)
13 Craig Ellis
12 Barry Jensen
11 Steve Blyth
10 Phil Gould
9 Michael Pitman
8 Graeme O'Grady
Subs
26 Geoff Bugden
16 Jim Walters
14 Ken Wilson
20 Shane McKellar

Tries: Hetherington, Raudonikis, O'Grady **Goal:** Morris

Half-time: 7-6
Referee: Greg Hartley
Crowd: 57,333

Parramatta fans survey the scene after the 1981 Grand Final

destruction. Then, one by one, they stopped, looked at each other, and said "Oh shit!" as the flames started licking at their shoes. Suddenly the shouts of fury turned into meek cries for help. They eventually escaped harm, which is more than can be said for the scoreboard. The destruction of Cumberland Oval was complete and much to the joy of Eels fans everywhere, it had to be completely rebuilt."

Back in the Leagues Club, the fans demanded to hear from their coach, Jack Gibson. He eventually emerged, producing just six words: "Ding dong, the witch is dead!"

Homeless for four years, Parramatta were forced to share Belmore Sports Ground with big rivals Canterbury. They won two more titles in that time before the new Parramatta Stadium opened in 1986. They went on to win their fourth Premiership in six seasons, this time against their former landlords, the Bulldogs.

BRADFORD STAGE WALK OFF

When Brian Noble scored a second-minute try in Bradford Northern's Premiership quarter-final match at Hull Kingston Rovers in May 1982, following a brilliant bust by a 21-year-old Ellery Hanley, there was little hint of the drama to follow. By the 56th minute, six players had been sent off, and the visiting team decided they had had enough. Northern's captain, Jeff Grayshon, who had just been dismissed by referee Robin Whitfield, was followed from the field by the rest of his team and they didn't return. Whitfield, who admitted he sensed something wasn't right at kick-off, awarded the game to Rovers.

Never in the modern era had Rugby League seen anything like it, although in 1947 Dewsbury also staged a walk-off having had three players sent off in a game against Wakefield. In Australia in 1970, North Sydney players walked from the field in a round-one match against Canterbury, but returned to finish the match. "During half-time we discussed walking off," said Noble, "because we were getting violently battered. I couldn't button my shirt up after the game because I'd been on the receiving end of some rough stuff. I spent the night in Hull General Infirmary. Chris Parrott got poleaxed before half-time as well. The referee wasn't protecting the team. So we agreed that if anyone else gets taken out, we'll just walk off, but I'm not sure that it was Jeff Grayshon who led the players off – that became the story. I think it was Phil Sanderson."

In spite of the outcome, most of the rough stuff came from the home side, with several punches thrown in the tackle. Paul Harkin appeared to stamp on an opponent and Steve Crooks felled Parrott with a terrible high tackle. "You've got to shift him for that", a spectator behind the commentator was heard to shout. "Their game is just harassment," complained Bradford's Alan Redfearn, the co-commentator. Parrott had to be withdrawn. John Millington then launched a head-butt in a scrum. The penalty count was totting up, eight to three in Northern's favour.

The first pair to be sent off were Rovers' Millington and Bradford's Gary

"During half-time we discussed walking off because we were getting violently battered."

van Bellen for fighting in the 21st minute, straight after the head-butt. Fourteen minutes later they were followed by Steve Hartley and Dean Carroll – again one from each team – also for fighting, although a minute earlier Hartley had been accused of standing on Carroll's head. It was now 11 against 11, but had Whitfield dealt with the perpetrators of the initial offences, Northern would have had a two-man advantage. Four minutes before half-time Bradford's Ian Ellis became the fifth player to go, for a late tackle on Harkin. Redfearn accepted that the decision was correct, but squarely blamed Whitfield for the disintegration of the match.

Enjoying the wind advantage, Rovers were now in command with tries from Phil Hogan and Kevin Watson along with three goals from the Great Britain fullback, George Fairbairn, following Noble's opener. They led 12-5 at the break. Ian Robinson's dummy-half try, which Fairbairn converted, opened the second-half scoring, although Noble scored his second for Northern on 52 minutes to reduce the arrears to 17-8. Minutes later, frustrated by a knock-on decision against his side, Grayshon appeared to throw the ball at the referee from half a yard behind

---

HULL KINGSTON ROVERS 17
BRADFORD NORTHERN 8

HULL KR
1 George Fairbairn
2 David Laws
3 John Lydiat
4 Ian Robinson
5 Ged Dunn
6 Steve Hartley
7 Paul Harkin
8 John Millington
9 David Watkinson
10 Steve Crooks
11 Phil Hogan
12 Kevin Watson
13 David Hall (C)
Subs:
14 Tracey Lazenby (dnp)
15 Ray Price

Tries: Hogan, Watson, Robinson
Goals: Fairbairn 4

Dismissed: Millington, Hartley

BRADFORD
1 Keith Mumby
2 David Barends
3 Ellery Hanley
4 Alan Parker
5 David Smith
6 Dean Carroll
7 Andrew Robinson
8 Jeff Grayshon (C)
9 Brian Noble
10 Gary van Bellen
11 Chris Parrott
12 Ian Ellis
13 Graham Idle
Subs:
14 Kevin Morgan (dnp)
15 Phil Sanderson

Tries: Noble 2 **Goal:** Carroll

Dismissed:
van Bellen, Carroll, Ellis, Grayshon

Half-time: 12-5
Referee: Robin Whitfield
Crowd: 9,130

him, and became the sixth player to be sent off on this incredible afternoon. This is when the players left the field. Rovers' players stayed on the halfway line, confused. "No one knew what to do," said Noble. "Ok, so we're walking off! In the changing room there were lots of people coming in asking what was happening. People were really nervous saying should we go back out. I was young so I just followed everyone else."

The next day Bradford's chairman Ronnie Firth issued a statement suggesting that his players didn't return to the field for reasons of self-protection. He was censured by the Rugby Football League as part of the club's punishment along with the players on duty, and Northern were banned from the 1982-83 Challenge Cup, John Player Trophy and Premiership. The club was also fined,

Jeff Grayshon was one of six players dismissed during a fiery fixture

with Grayshon suspended until September. Firth claimed to be appalled and successfully challenged the punishment. Northern were re-instated into the three competitions for the 1982-83 season, with the punishment suspended. Grayshon's ban was reduced to five matches on appeal. He appealed that as well, but lost.

On the same day in the same competition, another unusual game took place when recently crowned league champions Leigh and Warrington played out a 1-1 draw, with Steve Donlan and Bob Eccles exchanging drop goals, but nothing could touch the drama of what happened on that incredible Bank Holiday Monday at Craven Park in 1982.

Saturday, 30th October 1982

INVINCIBLE!

S ometimes a champion team sets the bar so high that nobody can quite believe what they have just witnessed. In soccer's 1970 World Cup Final, Pele's great Brazil team demolished Italy 4-1 and set a benchmark against which all future greatness could be measured. Twelve years later, the same thing happened in Rugby League when the Australian tourists, retrospectively nicknamed 'The Invincibles', produced a seminal 80 minutes of Rugby League perfection in the first Ashes Test match at Hull. Their performance would become the stuff of legend.

The 15th Kangaroos are synonymous with brilliant football played at a breath-taking speed, backed up by levels of fitness and athleticism that were way beyond the British game in 1982. The warning signs had been there, but had largely been ignored. The Lions had endured a disastrous tour of the Southern Hemisphere in 1979, losing the first Ashes Test 35-0 en route to being whitewashed, but with British thinking centred more around optimism than reality, few seemed to see the dangers. Even in Australia, the former St George hooker Ian Walsh was scathing of his country's selectors, believing that too many young players had been overlooked, but the Australian players had been hardened by the new State of Origin concept and were light years ahead of their British counterparts in nearly every facet of the game.

Shellshocked Great Britain players and fans reflect on Australian dominance

The Kangaroos swept through the tour, winning all of their matches and hammering most of their opponents. The game in which they made the most impact was at Boothferry Park when they were responsible for a truly remarkable moment in international Rugby League history, in a game played before a capacity crowd with thousands more locked out. Alarm bells should have sounded when Frank Stanton named his team because Australia were good enough to leave out the tour vice-captain and Queensland skipper, Wally Lewis, along with Canterbury's great halfback, Steve Mortimer.

Great Britain's humiliation could have been far greater had they not been awarded 21 of the 28 penalties awarded. From the second of those, in the second minute, they took a two-point lead with a successful shot at goal by the debutant Lee Crooks, although Mal Meninga tied the scores four minutes later. In hindsight, it was a surprise that it took 21 minutes for the Kangaroos to score a try. When the giant Meninga handed off Les Dyl to score in the right-hand corner, it looked so simple. He took the conversion himself, but missed. Australia added just one more try in the first half, when Wayne Pearce assisted Les Boyd with an inside pass following a break from the genius halfback Peter Sterling. It was only 10-4 at the break, but the difference in quality between the sides was easily apparent.

The tourists were imperious after the interval, although the first try of the half was gifted to them as the barnstorming wing Eric Grothe swooped on a dropped ball to run 40 metres to score, despite an admirable

GREAT BRITAIN 4 AUSTRALIA 40

GREAT BRITAIN
1 George Fairbairn
2 Des Drummond
3 Eric Hughes
4 Les Dyl
5 Steve Evans
6 John Woods
7 Steve Nash (C)
8 Jeff Grayshon
9 David Ward
10 Trevor Skerrett
11 Les Gorley
12 Lee Crooks
13 Steve Norton
Subs:
14 Ken Kelly (dnp)
15 David Heron

Goals: Crooks 2

Sin Bin: Ward

AUSTRALIA
1 Greg Brentnall
5 Kerry Boustead
3 Mal Meninga
4 Steve Rogers
2 Eric Grothe
6 Brett Kenny
7 Peter Sterling
8 Craig Young
9 Max Krilich (C)
10 Les Boyd
11 Wayne Pearce
12 Rod Reddy
13 Ray Price
Subs:
14 Steve Ella (dnp)
15 John Muggleton (dnp)

Tries: Meninga, Boyd, Grothe, Price, Boustead, Kenny, Pearce, Reddy
Goals: Meninga 8

Sin Bin: Krilich

Half-time: 4-10
Referee: Julien Rascagnères
Crowd: 26,771

Australia's Eric Grothe rounds Great Britain's Des Drummond

attempt on him by the British fullback, George Fairbairn. Meninga's side-line goal twisted the knife further.

The hookers, David Ward and Max Krilich, were each sin-binned for five minutes before Australia broke clear again. Des Drummond brought down the marauding stand-off, Brett Kenny, but later in the set, the all-action lock forward, Ray Price, strolled over by the posts after taking Sterling's clever flick. Minutes later, Kerry Boustead scored near the corner after Kenny and centre Steve Rogers had opened up the defence. Meninga again kicked a beauty from a wide position.

The next two tries perfectly encapsulated the yawning chasm between the two nations. Pearce stormed onto a short ball, scattered two defenders and offloaded beautifully to Kenny, who burned off the cover from 30 metres out for a glorious score which Meninga goaled. Australia led 30-4 with 22 minutes still left. Soon after, following a rare British attack, the Kangaroos broke free with more stunning football. Krilich offloaded to Craig Young in his own half. The prop carried the ball into the British half, drew Fairbairn and sent the supporting Pearce to the posts from 40 metres.

A further wonderful long-distance move failed to come to fruition thanks to Drummond's superb cover tackle on Grothe, but Rod Reddy was the next scorer in the last minute when he ran a great line, hit Sterling's short ball and scored ten metres to the left of the posts. Meninga's goal was greeted by the final hooter and one of the most compelling exhibitions of complete Rugby League play was brought to an end.

"There's no answer to that," was all a bemused Britain coach Johnny Whiteley could say. No-one else during that glorious 22-match tour had any answers either.

"There's no answer to that!"

Tuesday, 22nd February 1983

GRANADA CAPTURES CLASSIC ALEX MURPHY RANT

At five past midnight on 22nd February 1983, there was little on offer for late-night television viewers in the north-west. The two BBC channels had shut down for the night, and there were 20 minutes left of a film called 'The Eleventh Hour' on the new Channel Four. Rugby League fans and curious channel hoppers, meanwhile, were about to be confronted by the head coach of Wigan, almost purple with rage at his team's ineptitude. To give the story another dimension, it just happened to be the man widely regarded as the greatest player of all time. It was, of course, the inimitable Alexander James Murphy.

Introduced by Richard Madeley, who went on to bigger – but not necessarily better – things with ITV, the programme cut straight to Murphy's pre-match talk as he addressed his players in the wake of their disappointing midweek Challenge Cup exit at the hands of Castleford. Such access to the sanctity of the changing-rooms was exciting new territory for the sport.

"Now listen," he started, menacingly. "You know what happened on Wednesday. You know what the problem was - too many players not competing. Now look, we can't make excuses for our performance. On the day we wasn't good enough. Colin [Whitfield] I want a better performance from you today. You know what the problem is. You're putting your head down every time you've got a problem. I want your head up in the air, and I want you running with the ball. They'll come out to knock you down. They'll come out and try to dust you. I don't want any silly penalties. Discipline! I know you don't like it - we've got to do it. And we do have a problem. We've got to win today. There'll be a lot of knockers on the terrace, and rightly so because they're disappointed they're not going to Wembley. We've got to pick ourselves up today. We've got to get up off the floor and we've got to give it back to them spectators. They pay our wages. Without them we're knackered. Your money – one hundred and sixty quid. Now you don't deserve that but that's what you're getting. If we win today and next week, we'll win the league. Let's go out today and win it. Come on. Best of luck!"

Things didn't quite go to plan for Murphy who, in 1983, was a highly-

"If you don't want to train, f*** off somewhere else!"

renowned young figure in the coaching world. He had led Leigh to the league championship in a memorable four-horse race in 1982, and was subsequently appointed to the Wigan head-coaching job. This was his first season at Central Park and he had started well, winning the John Player Trophy Final and competing strongly all season in the league, although four days earlier they had lost that cup tie to Castleford. With only the league to play for, Wigan chose the worst time possible to suffer their first home defeat of the season as Hull Kingston Rovers were far too good for them, winning 21-5. Whitfield had scored the Riversiders' only try. Murphy was incandescent with rage, and the cameras memorably captured his fury after the game, and beamed it to the region just over 24 hours later.

"Is anybody proud of that out there?" he asked the players rhetorically after hanging up his sheepskin coat to reveal resplendent blazer and flannels. "Can we honestly say, is that the best we can do? Fifth in the league, could have gone second! I've told you – you're good players when you do it all the time," he continued as players swigged from beer bottles. "And I'm having no more doctor's notes neither, and excuses. You train here now from now on. If you don't want to train, fuck off somewhere else!"

At this point, a hand covered the lens, albeit only for a couple of seconds. Murphy continued. "David [Stephenson], you're going to train three times a week and if you don't train three nights a week, you're going on the list. You're a mile overweight and you're looking for excuses all the time. Right? I'm telling you to your face, I'm not telling you behind your back. You get down here Tuesday, every single one of you. If you don't [want to do anything about it], you know where my office is. I accept letters. We've a week to get it right, and we're gonna get it right. Widnes at home and I want no absentees. Life's got to go on you know. It doesn't finish, like, because we've lost two games. It doesn't finish because we've been knocked out of the Challenge Cup. We've worked hard all season."

An embarrassed looking club chairman, Maurice Lindsay, shuffled into the dressing room, also in a sheepskin coat. "Be bloody proud of yourself," Murphy went on. "Be men!"

The programme returned to the studio, where Madeley was covering his eyes. He removed his hand, looked up and whistled. No words were needed. Nearly 20 years later, a late-night programme called 'Rugby League Raw' delivered such material on a regular basis, but in 1983 such a broadcast was unheard of.

Murphy spoke of the incident in his 2000 autobiography, 'Saint and Sinner'. "Worst of all was not only had I let myself be depicted as some raging dressing-room bully, but I had to apologise to my mother for the language I had used," he wrote. "I knew she would be horrified. Words that sound perfectly normal in the aftermath of a tough, physical game of rugby, when everybody is entitled to blow a fuse, are hardly the sort of thing you would like to hear in your living room over your evening meal. And nobody would like his mother to hear it."

Monday, 2nd May 1983

KEVIN HUMPHREYS RESIGNS IN DISGRACE AS NSWRL CHIEF

Between 1973 and 1983, the seventh president of the New South Wales Rugby League, Kevin Humphreys, had perhaps been the sport's most powerful and influential man since its inception in Australia. Then his world came crashing down. He resigned in disgrace just five days shy of his tenth anniversary in the job. An episode of the 'Four Corners' investigative programme called 'The Big League' was aired by the ABC network. Both Rugby League and the government of New South Wales were thrown into turmoil by the startling revelations of corruption.

In his decade at the helm, Humphreys had been responsible for implementing a modernisation strategy which had transformed Australian Rugby League. He negotiated substantial television and sponsorship deals, oversaw the introduction of State of Origin, stamped out the on-field thuggery which had blighted the game in the 1970s and brought unprecedented levels of business nous and professionalism to the governing body.

The story began in 1977 when Humphreys was acquitted of misappropriating $52,519 from the Balmain Leagues Club. The 'Four Corners' programme presented evidence that showed the trial had been a miscarriage of justice with the New South Wales government allegedly intervening to have him cleared. It was also suggested that officials were taking monies from clubs and international matches, while sub-standard facilities remained a feature of the game.

At 6.20pm on Monday, 2nd May 1983, two days after the programme was aired, Humphreys resigned his post at the NSWRL, becoming the first president of the organisation to stand down in more than half a century. "The demise of Kevin Humphreys may be the biggest story EVER to break in the history of Australian Rugby League," concluded 'Open Rugby' magazine.

Unlike many senior administrators of today, Humphreys had played the sport at the highest level. He figured in 39 matches for Balmain between 1953 and 1956, scoring nine tries. He went on to become club secretary in 1965 and

"The demise of Kevin Humphreys may be the biggest story EVER to break in the history of Australian Rugby League."

was propelled to the roles of NSWRL president and ARL chairman following his predecessor Bill Buckley's death in 1973. The appointment was welcomed throughout the sport. 'Rugby League Week' initially spoke of Humphreys heading up a Rugby League revolution: "The 'young bloods' headed by the dynamic Kevin Humphreys swept into office in NSW this weekend and launched a campaign which will see Rugby League spiral to dizzy heights." Those other 'young bloods' were Manly's Ken Arthurson, Canterbury's Peter Moore, Souths' Charlie Gibson and Cronulla's Bob Abbott. The group became known as 'The Cartel' in the media and it proved to be a wonderfully successful combination.

Three years later, Humphreys became the first full-time executive director of the NSWRL. He went from strength to strength, helping the sport prepare to face a changing world. Playing standards rocketed, with the Australian Test team now kings of the international scene. The game became a hit on colour television. State of Origin was born, quickly becoming a phenomenon. Winfield began a lucrative sponsorship of the Sydney competition, which soon expanded with new clubs like Canberra Raiders and Illawarra Steelers introduced to the Premiership.

The programme's main allegation was that the NSW government had intervened to pervert the course of justice in Humphreys' 1977 trial, and so the subsequent fallout involved much more than the resignation of Kevin Humphreys. The formation of a Royal Commission led to the imprisonment of the former New South Wales chief stipendiary magistrate Murray Farquhar and also the standing down of NSW Premier Neville Wran - although he was later exonerated of any wrongdoing. It was revealed that from 31st July 1974, Humphreys began to "fraudulently take and apply for his own use and benefit" money from a cash float held by the club. By 11th August 1975, he had left eight vouchers for $19,940. On 18th February 1976, club auditors discovered that $30,579 was missing and not covered by vouchers. Humphreys told the auditor that "he loaned this to a friend who was in financial trouble," but later admitted to the Commission that he had lost the money gambling. Within ten days he had borrowed $52,000 from three well-known Rugby League figures - the great coach Jack Gibson, Arthurson and the former Kangaroos coach Norm 'Latchem' Robinson – as well as a company director called Geoffrey Willian Gardiner. Humphreys deposited the four cheques into the club's bank account on 4th and 8th March 1976.

On the 24th of that month, 'The Sun', an Australian newspaper, revealed that the Balmain Leagues Club accounts showed an unauthorised loan of $19,000. Humphreys claimed it was used for Rugby League matters, and that it had been repaid, but the case was placed in the hands of the Fraud Squad. The final report recommended nine charges of financial misappropriation against the NSWRL president. Humphreys faced up to 15 years in prison, but at some point between November 1976 and August 1977, somebody with access to the police file leaked it to his legal team. There were also suggestions that Wran had ordered that the charges against Humphreys be dropped.

After Humphreys announced his resignation in 1983, he shared a beer with his close friend Arthurson and told him, "You know I feel bloody awful about the problems I've caused my family and obviously about the damage I've done to myself … but the worst thing is I've been an instrument of causing discredit to the game … and that's the last thing I would ever have wanted to do."

Tom Bellew succeeded Humphreys at the NSWRL with Arthurson taking over his job at the ARL. In 1986, Arthurson took over from Bellew at the NSWRL as well. Despite the scale and the hysteria of the 'Four Corners' scandal, Rugby League simply moved on, building upon Humphreys' successes and putting the scandal behind them.

The Royal Commission was referred to as a watershed in the history of public corruption in New South Wales. As well as the imprisonment of Farquhar and Wran standing down from the NSW Premiership, Humphreys was ordered to face the same charges on which he had been acquitted six years earlier. Found guilty of fraud and theft, he was fined $4,000 and given a two-year good-behaviour bond.

The whole unfortunate episode represented an unprecedented fall from grace for one of the best administrators in the game's history. Humphreys died in 2010, having just turned 80.

Saturday, 7th May 1983

FEATHERSTONE STUN THE CHAMPIONS AT WEMBLEY

Featherstone Rovers fans will never forget the day they stunned Hull FC at Wembley in 1983. Bookmakers had stopped taking bets on the newly-crowned league champions Hull, while Featherstone had finished just one place above the dreaded relegation zone.

Things were very different for Rovers in the State Express Challenge Cup as they swept aside Batley, Salford and St Helens to set up a meeting with Bradford in the semi-final at Headingley, a match best remembered for Ellery Hanley's extraordinary 90-metre try, which turned out to be in vain for the beaten Northern side. Rovers eventually prevailed 11-6 with John Gilbert, John Marsden and Terry Hudson crossing the try line. Hudson's form throughout the Cup matches had been excellent and he was to play a significant part at Wembley.

It wasn't just the rugby club in Featherstone which had endured

Featherstone's Steve Quinn lifts the Challenge Cup

difficult times. The final was played amid a backdrop of industrial disharmony, with the town struggling badly in the teeth of a recession which saw thousands of miners in the local area lose their jobs. Getting to Wembley wouldn't put bread on the table of those families, but it was a welcome distraction for many, even if they didn't expect their team to win.

"I think the floodgates will open."

163

The Airlie Birds had beaten Blackpool, Wakefield and Warrington before turning over Castleford in the semi-final when Kiwi superstar James Leuluai scored a try almost as good as Hanley's, as he produced at least four sidesteps to score from over 40 yards.

"We were supremely confident that we would win," Hull's Lee Crooks reflected in his 2011 autobiography. "And why shouldn't we be? With only Featherstone to beat, the double was inevitable. We even started betting with each other on which of us would win the Lance Todd Trophy. In hindsight, it's clear our mental approach wasn't right. We were ripe for an upset."

Hull, whose players had strutted around during the pre-match walkabout in hideous lime-green suits, yellow ties and white shoes, enjoyed two sets of six deep in Rovers' territory in the opening minutes of the final, which culminated in an unsuccessful drop-goal attempt by Crooks. The fact that Featherstone's defence had seen them off would have substantially boosted the confidence of the West Yorkshiremen, and that was underlined further in the seventh minute of the match.

Featherstone won a differential penalty for a scrum infringement. Unable to kick for goal, Steve Quinn kicked for touch and on the first tackle Hudson's delayed pass enabled David Hobbs to beat Leuluai to the corner - a dream start for Featherstone, even though Quinn missed the tough conversion.

Hull were rattled. Charlie Stone lost the ball in his own half, but was reprieved when Hudson's attempted drop was charged down by Trevor Skerrett. Things went from bad

FEATHERSTONE ROVERS 14
HULL FC 12

FEATHERSTONE
1 Nigel Barker
2 John Marsden
3 Steve Quinn
4 John Gilbert
5 Ken Kellett
6 Alan Banks
7 Terry Hudson (C)
8 Mick Gibbins
9 Ray Handscombe
10 Steve Hankins
11 David Hobbs
12 Tim Slatter
13 Peter Smith
Subs:
14 Paul Lyman
15 Gary Siddall

Tries: Hobbs 2
Goals: Quinn 4

Sin bin: Hudson

HULL
1 Gary Kemble
2 Dane O'Hara
3 Steve Evans
4 James Leuluai
5 Paul Prendiville
6 David Topliss (C)
7 Kevin Harkin
8 Trevor Skerrett
9 Keith Bridges
10 Charlie Stone
11 Paul Rose
12 Lee Crooks
13 Steve Norton
Subs:
14 Terry Day
15 Mick Crane

Tries: Crooks (penalty try), Leuluai
Goals: Crooks 3

Sin bin: Rose

Half-time: 5-0
Referee: Robin Whitfield
Crowd: 84,969

to worse for Hull as they lost scrum-half Kevin Harkin to a head injury as he dived for a loose ball at Hudson's feet. Within minutes, Crooks missed another shot at goal; this time a penalty attempt. "Normally he'd back-heel those over," observed the great Alex Murphy on commentary duties. Before too long, he missed another.

Hull's Kiwi fullback Gary Kemble had to be at his best to produce a try-saving tackle on the Rovers stand-off, Alan Banks, but he conceded a penalty in the process which Quinn kicked to put his side 5-0 up. The 21-year-old Hobbs, meanwhile, remained a big threat when in possession. Five minutes before half-time, Featherstone lost their centre John Gilbert as a result of a Paul Rose high tackle. He was replaced by the 17-year-old Paul Lyman, while Rose became the first player to be sin-binned in a Wembley final. Hull had endured a disastrous half, but at least it was only 5-0.

The match turned in Hull's favour early in the second half, with Mick Crane now filling in for Harkin, instead of David Topliss. Two minutes into the half, Crooks was awarded a penalty try when referee Robin Whitfield adjudged that Hobbs had impeded him as he chased his own kick. It was the first penalty try in a Wembley Cup Final. Crooks goaled his own try to level the score. When Leuluai scored under the posts in the 54th minute from Rose's clever offload, Crooks converted that too. The game had turned on its head, with the favourites now 10-5 up. "I think the floodgates will open," declared Murphy. How wrong he was.

Halfway through an incident-packed second half, Hudson was sin-binned for kicking Topliss and Crooks extended the lead to 12-5. Surely the game was up for Featherstone – but, amazingly, they were still able to mount a comeback. Quinn kicked a wide penalty before Hobbs sent the Rovers fans crazy by scoring his second try which followed a scrum win against the head. Quinn added the goal. At 12-all, it was shaping up to be one of the best Cup Finals in years. There were just six minutes left. The 21-year-old Hobbs was having a storming game.

As a replay seemed likely for the second year in a row, Hobbs knocked over what seemed to be the winning drop goal with three minutes left, only for Whitfield to disallow it on the basis that it flicked off Skerrett on the way through; such were the rules back in 1983. It mattered not, as, almost immediately, Hull prop Charlie Stone was ruled to have headbutted Peter Smith. From 20 yards, Quinn, who passed away in April 2016, hit the target with the penalty to win the Cup for Rovers.

The pre-tournament 33/1 outsiders had pulled off the biggest Wembley upset since 15th-placed Widnes beat league leaders St Helens in 1930. Hobbs, for his two tries and a fantastic all-round display, won the Lance Todd Trophy as the game's outstanding player. He had also been rated at 33/1 to win the prestigious award. Rovers coach Allan Agar, who even turned out for cash-strapped Carlisle against St Helens in the first round because they still held his playing registration, was subsequently named the 1983 Man of Steel, as he was deemed to have had the biggest impact on the game in that particular season. He remains the only coach to win the award.

Friday, 18th November 1983

WALLY LEWIS IS COMING!

When Rugby League's international transfer ban was lifted after six years in September 1983, English clubs treated themselves to some of the finest talents. Over the next year, Hull FC signed Peter Sterling, St Helens flew over Mal Meninga, Wigan won the prize scalp of Brett Kenny and Leeds picked up the great winger Eric Grothe. All were members of the great 1982 Kangaroos squad.

Easily the biggest signing, however, was pulled off by Division One cellar-dwellers Wakefield Trinity, who shocked everyone by announcing the capture of the iconic Queensland captain, Wally Lewis. The signing was announced in the papers on 18th November. "The surprise in soccer could have been no greater if Diego Maradona had joined Notts County," was Paul Fitzpatrick's pithy summary in 'The Guardian', and it hit the nail on the head. This was the most stunning transfer deal in years.

The Australia stand-off had toured with his state in late 1983 in a three-match sojourn, in which they lost narrowly to Hull Kingston Rovers, but hammered Wigan and Leeds. With King Wally on their doorstep, Trinity saw their chance and pounced, although all Lewis wanted to do initially was get rid of them. "When the first offer of about £150 a game was made to me, I rejected it. When the calls continued I carried on knocking them back. I then thought the only way I'd get rid of them was to suggest a huge amount. So I did and they agreed. Then I said they'd have to bring my brother too and they were ok with that so I thought there's no getting out of this!" Lewis was paid £1000 per match, with the money not paid by the club, but by a benefactor. The deal made him the highest-paid player of all time.

Lewis flew out of Brisbane airport on 2nd December and made his Trinity bow just two days later in a home match with Hull, for whom Sterling was also making his first appearance. With the halfbacks from Australia's last Test win on display, Wakefield's crowd was more than twice that of usual and the club's biggest in ten years. The current editor of 'Rugby League Express', Martyn Sadler, remembers the game well. "With his first touch of the ball Wally made a break and fed [his brother] Scott, who dashed down the left wing to score the opening try of the game. At that moment we knew that we were in for some thrills." But Trinity faded, with Sterling at his imperious best, and Hull won 32-16.

Debutants Wally Lewis (Wakefield) and Peter Sterling (Hull FC) in action in December 1983

Lewis faced other problems, with many of his teammates refusing to warm to him on account of his astronomical wage. "It wasn't the friendliest of welcomes for me because the Wakefield players had heard what I was earning," he said. "The only friendly blokes at first were the coach Derek Turner and Brian Briggs, who I was staying with, as well as Barry Hough, the benefactor who was paying my wages. The captain Nigel Stephenson shook hands with me but not too many others did and that carried on for a while because they thought the club were paying me a massive amount of money. In the end, I told them that I'd had a gutful of them and that the club weren't paying me one cent, which was true because Barry Hough was putting up the money."

"The surprise in soccer could have been no greater if Diego Maradona had joined Notts County."

Lewis also confirmed the truth in the anecdote of the player who spent an entire match taunting him over his wage. "He kept saying, after hitting me, 'How are you feeling thousand-pounds-a-match man?' It went on and on. Late on, he got me across the nose and said it again so I said, 'about £900 pounds better off than you, you Pommy bastard!'"

Sadler has no difficulty in recalling Lewis's ten games for the club he supports. "His fourth game was at Castleford on Boxing Day morning, and legend has it that Wally arrived breathless and a little intoxicated from an all-night party in Hull on Christmas Day. Wakefield coach Derek Turner had been cursing Wally in the dressing-room before the game, and had already given Wally's number six shirt to a young replacement. But the King arrived just in time, grabbed the shirt, and sweated off the beer with a faultless performance. Raymond Fletcher, writing in the 'Yorkshire Post' the next day, revealed that Wally had taken something like 57 passes, but was only tackled three times in the entire game, although Castleford still managed to win 24-8, with Wally having some trouble in motivating the other Wakefield players, who were said to be jealous of the amount of dosh he was receiving."

Lewis saved his best performance for a home match with St Helens during which he scored a hat-trick of tries, but his time at the club wasn't all sweetness and light. He was sent off, somewhat controversially, at Leeds, which was one of five games in which he ended up on the losing side. His final Trinity appearance was a Challenge Cup tie at Halifax, who advertised on Yorkshire TV urging fans to come and, "See the great Wally Lewis." Wakefield won 19-7 with Wally crossing for two tries. His time was soon up. Without him, Wakefield went out of the Cup at home to Division Two side York and were relegated to the second division after losing their remaining eight league matches. Lewis went on to be crowned the first winner of the Golden Boot as the world's best player for his 1984 performances, and it all began for him in Wakefield.

There was regular speculation that Lewis may one day return, and supporters began a fanzine rather optimistically entitled 'Wally Lewis is Coming'. But it didn't happen. The Australian genius played only ten games for the club, losing five, but he is remembered as fondly as any of the fine legends the club has ever produced.

KENNY AND STERLING
LIGHT UP WEMBLEY

For however long the great Rugby League matches are discussed, the 1985 Challenge Cup Final, the 50th played at Wembley, will feature prominently; and deservedly so, for it was one of the most extraordinary afternoons in the sport's proud history. It featured a compelling face-off between Wigan's Brett Kenny and Hull's Peter Sterling, who, for Parramatta Eels, New South Wales and Australia, were perhaps the greatest halfback pairing the game has ever produced.

Wigan held the upper hand going into the Wembley final. They had twice thrashed the Black and Whites in the fortnight prior to the game - 40-4 in the league, with Kenny scoring twice, and 46-12 in the first round of the Premiership Trophy. However, with men like Sterling, Lee Crooks, Steve 'Knocker' Norton and a wonderful quartet of Kiwis - Gary Kemble, James Leuluai, Dane O'Hara and Fred Ah Kuoi - in their backline, no-one was writing off Hull FC. There were ten overseas players in the game – a Cup Final record.

The game was preceded by a parade of 49 legends - one player from each of the previous Wembley finals, dating back to 1929. Not surprisingly, the biggest cheer was saved for the iconic Wigan hero Billy Boston. There were 11 Lance Todd winners in the parade.

Hull took an early 6-0 lead with a Lee Crooks penalty and a Kevin James try which was set up by a Sterling runaround and Kemble's inside pass to the try scorer. Kenny wasn't to be outdone by his international teammate. He produced a first-half performance which went a long way to securing him the Lance Todd Trophy as man of the match, playing a major role in all three of Wigan's first-half tries. For their first try, he kept the ball alive on the last tackle for Ian Potter, whose long pass allowed John 'Chicka' Ferguson, who had flown in from Australia for the final, to finish superbly. The Australian genius then scored a spectacular long-range try himself, ghosting between two defenders on halfway and beating Kemble with a beautifully precise, curving run to the corner. Then, as if his world-class status needed any further underlining, his long pass to David Stephenson a minute before half-

**"If you weren't a Rugby League fan before that,
I'd be very surprised if you weren't now."**

time, saw the centre free Henderson Gill for a superb 75-metre try up the touchline with Sterling and Kemble trying in vain to halt him. All three were stunning scores.

The day before the match, Wigan were booted off the Wembley pitch when trying to organise a training session during the traditional Wembley walkabout, but it obviously wasn't needed. They were in complete charge when Kenny set up another try at the start of the second half, producing a clever dummy which foxed the Hull defence, allowing him to send a jubilant Shaun Edwards to the line. Next it was Sterling who stepped up. Two minutes later he broke through 30 metres out and offloaded out of the tackle on the try line for the supporting Steve Evans to score.

Wigan finally scored a try without Kenny's assistance when Sterling's pass went to ground on the halfway line and Ferguson swooped to run in his second try. At 28-12, Hull's quest for their first win underneath the Twin Towers looked to be in tatters as they needed three converted tries to win.

With Great Britain's young centre Garry Schofield, surprisingly benched by coach Arthur Bunting, now on the field, Hull came roaring back. Norton sent Paul Rose away close to the line, and the second row's offload allowed Leuluai to score. Sterling then put the other substitute, Gary Divorty, over for a try and things were suddenly a lot more interesting. From the resultant Wigan kick-off, in the 76th minute, Leuluai, playing his first game in three weeks, broke through and scored an incredible try which, for sheer breathtaking quality, was

WIGAN 28 HULL FC 24

WIGAN
1 Shaun Edwards
2 John Ferguson
3 David Stephenson
4 Steve Donlan
5 Henderson Gill
6 Brett Kenny
7 Mike Ford
8 Neil Courteney
9 Nicky Kiss
10 Brian Case
11 Graeme West (C)
12 Brian Dunn
13 Ian Potter
Subs:
14 Nick du Toit
15 Danny Campbell

Tries: Ferguson 2, Kenny, Gill, Edwards
Goals: Gill 3, Stephenson

HULL
1 Gary Kemble
2 Kevin James
3 Steve Evans
4 James Leuluai
5 Dane O'Hara
6 Fred Ah Kuoi
7 Peter Sterling
8 Lee Crooks (C)
9 Shaun Patrick
10 Neil Puckering
11 John Muggleton
12 Paul Rose
13 Steve Norton
Subs:
14 Garry Schofield
15 Gary Divorty

Tries: James, Evans, Leuluai 2, Divorty
Goals: Crooks 2

Half-time: 16-8
Referee: Ronnie Campbell
Crowd: 97,801

Wigan's Brett Kenny makes a break as Hull FC's Peter Sterling looks on

almost up there with his try against Castleford in the 1983 semi-final. "The game now is alive!" shrieked Ray French on commentary duties. "What more could we want?" The try reduced the arrears to just four points, but Wigan were able to cling on, allowing their Kiwi skipper Graeme West to lead his team up the Wembley steps and lift the Cup.

Sterling was magnanimous in defeat, and glowing in his praise for his close friend. "It was Brett who proved the real difference," he said. "I coped with the loss a lot better because I just had incredible admiration for him. And if you're going to get beat, you might as well get beat by one of the champions of the game."

The triumph was Wigan's seventh under the Twin Towers, a joint record. Hull had still never won at the famous stadium - something they eventually put right in 2016.

Nearly 100,000 people, and millions more on television, had witnessed the most stunning of Wembley occasions, which has remained the benchmark for great Rugby League matches. "If you weren't a Rugby League fan before that," said the 'Grandstand' presenter Des Lynam, "I'd be very surprised if you weren't now."

Saturday, 2nd November 1985

SCHOFIELD'S FOUR TRIES KEEPS TEST SERIES ALIVE

Five years without a Test victory over Australia or New Zealand was beginning to grate. Something special was needed to break Great Britain's run of woe and, on 2nd November 1985, Garry Schofield's superb exhibition of masterful support play saw him score all four of Great Britain's tries as they won the second Test match at Wigan to keep alive their best-of-three series with the Kiwis.

It was a particularly impressive result given how well New Zealand had played over the previous few years. In 1983 they had beaten the Australians in Brisbane to share a two-match series. In 1984 they whitewashed the British Lions. A year later they lost a thrilling series to Australia by two matches to one, narrowly losing twice, before hammering them 18-0 in the last game. Crammed full of world-class players, their team was a force to be reckoned with.

The Maurice Bamford-coached Great Britain had lost a gripping first Test 24-22 against the 1985 Kiwis with a disputed late try getting the tourists over the line. Schofield, who had only recently returned from a spell in Australia's Winfield Cup with Balmain Tigers, hadn't played well and came in for criticism in the media, although he more than made up for it at Central Park a week later.

Those predicting a British win might have expected it to be close, as the first Test had been. Instead, Great Britain swept aside their Southern Hemisphere opponents with consummate ease. Stand-off Tony Myler and captain Harry Pinner at loose forward were in majestic form, underlining their growing reputations as two of the best ballplayers in the world. The Kiwis were rocked by the loss of their influential captain, Mark Graham, on the morning of the game, as well as his fellow second-rower Owen Wright. They were replaced by Graeme West, who had captained Wigan to Challenge Cup glory six months earlier, and Sam Stewart who later played for London Crusaders and Hull Kingston Rovers. The only change to the Great Britain starting line-up was the introduction of prop Jeff Grayshon who, at 36, was chosen for the first time in three years to replace Lee Crooks. This bold selection more than paid off. Shaun Edwards and Chris Burton replaced David Hulme and Chris Arkwright on the two-man bench.

The home side started poorly when Joe Lydon spilled Gary Kemble's aimless bomb near the halfway line in the first minute, but the talented utility back made amends in the eighth minute by opening the scoring with a penalty goal. Olsen Filipaina, the talismanic Kiwi stand-off, who had so memorably got the better of the Australian captain Wally Lewis in the recent trans-Tasman encounters, levelled the scores at 2-2 after 12 minutes. A few minutes later, Ellery Hanley engineered a gap from a scrum-base move, which Schofield exploited beautifully by beating Gary Kemble, Hugh McGahan and Dane O'Hara to the try line. Lydon failed to convert from out wide but made up for it with a penalty shortly after. This was a promising start, and it didn't take long for Schofield to strike again. On the half-hour mark, the big number 10, John Fieldhouse, broke through West on halfway and offloaded to

---

GREAT BRITAIN 25
NEW ZEALAND 8

GREAT BRITAIN
1 Mick Burke
2 Des Drummond
3 Garry Schofield
4 Ellery Hanley
5 Joe Lydon
6 Tony Myler
7 Deryck Fox
8 Jeff Grayshon
9 David Watkinson
10 John Fieldhouse
11 Andy Goodway
12 Ian Potter
13 Harry Pinner (C)
Subs:
14 Shaun Edwards
15 Chris Burton

Tries: Schofield 4
Goals: Lydon 4
Drop goal: Pinner

NEW ZEALAND
1 Gary Kemble
2 Dean Bell
3 James Leuluai
4 Gary Prohm
5 Dane O'Hara
6 Olsen Filipaina (C)
7 Clayton Friend
8 Kurt Sorensen
9 Howie Tamati
10 Dane Sorensen
11 Graeme West
12 Sam Stewart
13 Hugh McGahan
Subs:
14 Fred Ah Kuoi
15 Ricky Cowan

Try: Bell
Goals: Filipaina 2

Half-time: 12-2
Referee: Barry Gomersall
Crowd: 15,506

the supporting 20-year-old, who hared away to score his second. Although Lydon missed another tough conversion, the hosts had a commanding ten-point lead. Fieldhouse was having a storming game and when the tricky Kiwi half, Clayton Friend, broke free, it was the red-headed prop who brought him down.

It only took a couple of minutes of second-half play before Schofield had completed his hat-trick. Pinner's short ball sent Ian Potter free and his sublime offload was met by the supporting Myler. The redoubtable Widnes stand-off beat Stewart, drew two more tacklers and offloaded to Schofield who scored under the posts. With Lydon converting, Great Britain had an impregnable 18-2 lead and the supporters inside Central Park were buoyant. Great Britain hadn't played like this for years.

Dean Bell got the only Kiwi try a few minutes later when he shrugged off a weak tackle by Edwards. Pinner then added a field goal and with four minutes remaining, another break by the captain released Hanley whose pass gave Schofield his fourth try, to cap an incredible individual performance.

"Scoring four tries in a Test match against a team as good as New Zealand was an absolute dream," said Schofield. "I hadn't played very well in the first Test and the media were on my back. People said I was tired because I'd not long been back from my stint in the Winfield Cup with Balmain, but I knew that was a load of rubbish." The Hull centre had enjoyed a memorable debut season in 1983-84, culminating in him becoming the youngest British Lion at the age of 18. His second season didn't go quite so smoothly, and he found himself dropped from the Hull starting line-up for the classic Wembley final against Wigan. But champions bounce back and his extraordinary feat against the Kiwis equalled the Great Britain record for tries in a match set by Jimmy Leytham in 1910 against Australia, Billy Boston in 1954 against New Zealand and Alex Murphy in 1959 against France. More importantly this compelling Test series was still alive and was due to be decided at Elland Road in the third match seven days later.

By the conclusion of this wonderful series, the two nations could not be separated. A late Lee Crooks penalty earned Great Britain a 6-all draw in a game remembered for being one of the most violent of the decade. It was watched on the BBC by nine million people.

Schofield's tries kick-started a memorable ten years for Great Britain which saw them overtake the New Zealanders and push Australia so close in three Ashes series and two World Cup Finals.

"Scoring four tries in a Test match against a team as good as New Zealand was an absolute dream."

Saturday, 9th July 1988

FIRST BRITISH WIN OVER AUSTRALIA IN TEN YEARS

❝ It started when [Andy] Greg drove the ball up from dummy half and evaded four Aussies with his nuggety strength. He ducked under a few swinging arms, drew fullback Garry Jack, and gave me the ball. I was still on our 25-yard line, but I knew I still had the fitness and strength, and I just went for it. Wally Lewis and Wayne Pearce, two of the greatest players ever to wear the green and gold, were chasing me down but I did have the step on them and I knew Martin Offiah was supporting me. I could hear him at the side of me, shouting 'Just give me the ball!' But I could see Lewis giving up as I glanced behind, after trying to pull Martin back, and then out of the corner of my right eye I could see that I could hold off Pearce as well. Thinking 'If I'm going to run all this way, I may as well score' I just pinned my ears back and made it to the sticks - a special moment."

These are the words of the late Mike Gregory, describing his greatest moment as a Rugby League player in his highly acclaimed autobiography, 'Biting Back'. Even though they describe in great detail one of the modern era's most famous moments, they do not even begin to illustrate just what an unlikely win Great Britain pulled off on 9th July 1988 at the new Sydney Football Stadium in the third game of the Ashes series. Great Britain hadn't beaten Australia since 1978. Thereafter they had been hammered on a regular basis, although a much-improved performance in the third Test of 1986 gave hope to a few. However, when Joe Lydon, Andy Goodway, Steve Hampson and Des Drummond failed to make the tour for one reason or another, it was just the start of the selection difficulties that coach Malcolm Reilly would face in the coming months.

Things got worse when the tour started. Shaun Edwards lasted barely a handful of minutes before he had to fly home. He was to be joined on the sideline by Garry Schofield, Lee Crooks, Andy Platt, Paul Medley and Paul Dixon. Just when it seemed that things couldn't get any worse, Kevin Beardmore and Richard Eyres pulled out of the side 24 hours before the third Test with injuries. Paul Hulme was forced to play hooker for the first time in his life, in the most daunting of circumstances. Andy Gregory was also

"If I'm going to run all this way, I may as well score."

injured, but was determined to play. He later admitted to calming his nerves by enjoying a couple of pints of Guinness the night before.

The Ashes had already been lost in the most disappointing fashion with a game to spare. Tour matches were also lost against Northern Division, Manly and a President's XIII in Canberra just four days before the third Test. Great Britain weren't given a chance of winning the last Test but somehow, they pulled it off. David Howes, the tour's business manager, immediately compared the unlikely triumph to the Rorke's Drift Test of 1914.

In front of swathes of empty seats, such was the lack of interest in what was predicted to be a one-sided game, Great Britain made a fantastic start. Phil Ford had a try contentiously disallowed, but Martin Offiah soon crossed near the left corner after a classy Andy Gregory-Kevin Ward run-around had opened up the Australian defence. Later in the half, Ford surged onto Andy Gregory's pass to weave in and out of numerous defenders and score by the side of the posts. The tourists led 10-0 at half-time, a scoreline which didn't reflect their domination as Offiah and Ward had gone close to further scores.

Lewis narrowed the gap minutes into the second half, scoring by the posts with a great show of strength. British winger Henderson Gill then scored his first try after winning the race to an Andy Gregory grubber kick. Slammin' Sam Backo soon marked his Australian Test debut with a try, goaled by Michael O'Connor, as the deficit was reduced to 16-12, before Great Britain produced two of the most famous tries in Test-football

AUSTRALIA 12 GREAT BRITAIN 26

AUSTRALIA
1 Garry Jack
2 Andrew Ettingshausen
3 Michael O'Connor
4 Peter Jackson
5 Tony Currie
6 Wally Lewis (C)
7 Peter Sterling
8 Martin Bella
9 Greg Conescu
10 Sam Backo
11 Paul Vautin
12 Wally Fullerton-Smith
13 Wayne Pearce
Subs:
14 Gary Belcher
15 Bob Lindner

Tries: Lewis, Backo
Goals: O'Connor 2

GREAT BRITAIN
1 Phil Ford
2 Henderson Gill
3 David Stephenson
4 Paul Loughlin
5 Martin Offiah
6 David Hulme
7 Andy Gregory
8 Kevin Ward
9 Paul Hulme
10 Hugh Waddell
11 Roy Powell
12 Mike Gregory
13 Ellery Hanley (C)
Subs:
14 Darren Wright (dnp)
15 Brian Case

Tries: Offiah, Ford, Gill 2, Gregory
Goals: Loughlin 3

Half-time: 0-10
Referee: Francis Desplas
Crowd: 15,994

Henderson Gill and Phil Ford jump for joy after a Lions try

Mike Gregory, Phil Ford and Martin Offiah celebrate Great Britain's memorable Sydney win

history to seal the match in glorious fashion.

First, Paul Loughlin dummied to kick in his own 20, before beating five defenders and sending Gill to the corner, memorably celebrated with "a bit of a boogie", in the words of Darrell Eastlake, the Channel Nine commentator, to leave Australia with too much to do. Gill's try and celebration gave British Rugby League its most famous moment in years.

Mike Gregory then capped a famous afternoon with his incredible try. Great Britain had stunned absolutely everybody, not least those watching back home, with a thoroughly unexpected 26-12 triumph. It had taken them ten years, but, despite numerous handicaps, Great Britain had finally beaten the old enemy again.

WIDNES BEAT WIGAN IN WINNER-TAKES-ALL DECIDER

It was a dream for the neutral when the two teams at the top of the first division met in the final match of the 1988-89 season to decide the outcome of the league championship. Widnes and Wigan duly served up a classic.

The Chemics went into the match on 39 points, with Wigan on 38. Widnes needed to avoid defeat but went into the match without their genius stand-off Tony Myler. They were also out of form, having recently succumbed to Bradford and Hull, before scraping past Hull Kingston Rovers and Castleford. Wigan had to do without Great Britain halfbacks Shaun Edwards and Andy Gregory. Ged Byrne became a makeshift scrum-half, but they were on a three-month winning run, having beaten St Helens 14-7 at Central Park four days earlier. Few could confidently pick a winner.

After a minute's silence for the victims of the Hillsborough Disaster the day before, the home side got off to an awful start when Andy Currier put the kick-off out on the full. Joe Lydon's penalty set up an immediate attack for Wigan, from which Andy Platt dummied his way over through some weak defence. The ball had been in play for just 19 seconds, with only one tackle having been completed. Lydon converted and the visitors were 6-0 up. Jonathan Davies, who had been a Rugby League player for just three months, pushed a simple penalty shot horribly wide. Two minutes later, he was well off target again, albeit with a much harder attempt. Stand-off David Hulme was then carried off injured. This was all in the first seven minutes, and it made for a nightmare start for Widnes.

Just when they needed divine intervention, it was provided by their brilliant winger Martin Offiah. He took Alan Tait's inside pass just inside Wigan's quarter and accelerated to the corner with a swerving run, beating Steve Hampson's tackle in the process. Few could have supplied that sort of finish. Davies again failed with the boot.

Widnes soon fell for another sucker punch, with Andy Goodway shrugging off Offiah's flimsy attempted tackle to score ten metres to the right of the posts. Lydon's conversion nudged his team 12-4 ahead. Widnes supporters knew Offiah's brilliance could win them the title. They also knew

"The whole of Widnes goes absolutely potty!"

his defence could hand it to Wigan.

The Chemics hit back with some wonderful handling which led to a slightly fortuitous try just before half time. Emosi Koloto's deft touch sent fellow second-rower Mike O'Neill free. He lost possession as he ran into Wigan's quarter but Wright kicked it on for the ever-opportunistic Offiah to touch down. Davies goaled and the deficit was down to two at half time.

After a difficult half, Widnes would have been delighted to trail by such a slender margin. They started the second half spring heeled. Offiah was denied a hat-trick by an awkwardly bouncing ball before Kurt Sorensen stormed onto Phil McKenzie's dummy-half pass for the game's next try. Davies converted. For the first time, Widnes led. Naughton Park was louder than ever.

In the next set, Offiah brought the house down with an unbelievable try. He took Joe Grima's looping offload on halfway, and weaved in-field past two men, before beating Hampson with a devastating arc to the corner. "The whole of Widnes goes absolutely potty!" shrieked the commentator John Helm. Widnes were rampant now. The marvellous Koloto broke through and Richie Eyres offloaded to David Hulme, who strolled in under the posts. Davies's goal put Widnes three scores ahead. Koloto was deservedly sent off for a rash high tackle on Ian Potter. The same referee, John Holdsworth, had sent off Eyres in the recent Challenge Cup semi-final against Saints, and it had cost them the game. So when Ellery Hanley pulled a try back from close range, Widnes fans were panicking. At 26-18, Wigan needed two more tries in ten minutes.

WIDNES 32 WIGAN 18

WIDNES
1 Alan Tait
2 Jonathan Davies
3 Andy Currier
4 Darren Wright
5 Martin Offiah
6 David Hulme
7 Paul Hulme
8 Kurt Sorensen (C)
9 Phil McKenzie
10 Joe Grima
11 Mike O'Neill
12 Emosi Koloto
13 Richie Eyres
Subs:
14 Barry Dowd
15 David Smith (dnp)

Tries: Offiah 3, Sorensen, P Hulme, McKenzie
Goals: Davies 4

WIGAN
1 Steve Hampson
2 Tony Iro
3 Dean Bell
4 Joe Lydon
5 Mark Preston
6 Ellery Hanley (C)
7 Ged Byrne
8 Ian Lucas
9 Nicky Kiss
10 Adrian Shelford
11 Andy Platt
12 Ian Potter
13 Andy Goodway
Subs:
14 Martin Dermott
15 Denis Betts

Tries: Platt, Goodway, Hanley
Goals: Lydon 3

Half-time: 10-12
Referee: John Holdsworth
Crowd: 17,323

Widnes duo Kurt Sorensen and Martin Offiah show off the Championship trophy

Any possible comeback was snuffed out by the magnificent McKenzie, who had controlled the second half with his incisive work from acting half. A dummy close to the Wigan line bought him a try which precipitated a mini pitch invasion. Davies kicked his fourth goal and the hooter sounded a few minutes later. The Chemics had won both the match and the title.

Widnes went on to win the Premiership Trophy, a one-off European Championship, the Charity Shield and the World Club Challenge against Canberra Raiders. Wigan managed to console themselves with a brilliant Challenge Cup triumph, famously beating St Helens 27-0 at Wembley.

WALLY LEWIS SACKED AS BRISBANE BRONCOS CAPTAIN

If any club knew how to make headlines, it was Brisbane Broncos in their early years. From their 1988 debut in the Winfield Cup, they were the sport's glamour club and a journalist's dream.

The captain, Wally Lewis, arguably Rugby League's greatest-ever player, always seemed to be in the news. Worshipped in Queensland, hated south of the border, everybody had an opinion on the Australian Rugby League skipper. He was almost as controversial as he was brilliant. He was the megastar of 1980s Rugby League and the first winner of the Golden Boot as the world's best player.

Broncos coach Wayne Bennett may not have been quite as newsworthy at the time, but he is now regarded by many as the best coach in the history of the game. His stature in Rugby League has always been colossal. He might be monosyllabic in interviews, but he has been at the centre of numerous high-profile stories down the years.

By far and away the biggest Broncos story of them all, not surprisingly, featured both men. It came in 1989 when the coach did the unthinkable and took the captaincy away from Queensland's footballing god at the conclusion of their second season in the Winfield Cup. It was a sensation. The media were hysterical. Fans were devastated. Lewis was humiliated. It proved to be the beginning of the end of his magnificent career. Bennett insisted it was for the best in the long term. In hindsight, it was the moment he stamped his mark on a club that he subsequently led to numerous glories.

Lewis was the only realistic candidate to captain the Broncos when they were formed. In their first match he was at his imperious best, leading them to a 44-10 drubbing of champions Manly in round one of the 1988 Winfield Cup. A year later, he produced a captaincy masterclass in game two of State of Origin when he led a patched-up Queensland to an improbable triumph in Sydney, despite injuries forcing Allan Langer, Mal Meninga, Michael Hancock and Paul Vautin off the field, while Bob Lindner played on with a fractured fibula. Lewis's glorious try became an iconic moment of 1980s

"We were unanimous about it. He wasn't bigger than the club."

181

Rugby League as he steered the Maroons to a 16-12 win. It was Queensland's Rorke's Drift. King Wally, as he was known throughout Australia, was as big as Rugby League itself. He was the captain of club, state and country and those positions seemed set in stone.

But the inescapable truth was that the Broncos weren't firing. They had failed to make the top-five play-offs in 1988 and 1989 and Bennett knew that something had to change. On the penultimate Friday of September in 1989, Lewis attended a meeting with Bennett and was hit with the news immediately. "I'm taking the captaincy off you," said Bennett to an unprepared Lewis, who remained silent for 15 seconds.

"I suppose you'd like to know why," enquired the coach, before he began listing the reasons. Wally was away too much on representative duty. He was unapproachable and didn't mix well. He didn't have a good relationship with the younger players. His time-keeping was an issue. He was too focused on his own numerous commitments away from the club. Lewis tried to reason with his boss, but to no avail. The meeting ended after 20 minutes.

According to Adrian McGregor, Lewis's biographer, "the captaincy was more than a title to him, it was his role, it defined him and much in his life flowed from it. He had captained Queensland since 1981, Australia since 1984."

"We were focused on getting things right," Bennett told 'Rugby League World' magazine many years later. "Put all the ducks in order and then you can start to fire your bullets and that was part of that process. Wally was a great player, a huge headline player and we had to expect the worse but we were unanimous about it. He wasn't bigger than the club."

One of the first people to find out was Lewis's close friend David Fordham, with whom he worked at Channel Ten. "He had tears in his eyes and an emotion I'd never seen on his face before," he said.

John Ribot, the club's general manager and teammate of Lewis for state and country, tried to persuade Lewis to announce that he had resigned the captaincy. "Get stuffed!" was the deposed skipper's eloquent reply. Ribot assured Lewis he was still wanted at the Broncos.

Lewis and his family went to Los Angeles before newspapers broke the story on 15th October. Journalists tracked down his hotel and jammed the switchboard. The beleaguered receptionist at the Vagabond motel in San Francisco asked him "Who the hell *are* you?" The world share markets had just collapsed, but the 'Sunday Mail' broadsheet in Brisbane still led with the Wally Lewis bombshell.

At 5.05pm that day, an earthquake measuring 6.9 on the Richter scale struck San Francisco as the Lewises were in their room. Sixty-seven people were killed. The motel was badly damaged, as was the room, but they escaped unhurt. The family returned home to face the media circus and to get on with the rest of his career.

Such a trauma may have provided some perspective, but Lewis remained angry at Bennett's decision for many years. He was still a great player, as he had recently proved for Queensland, but the following season was to be his

last year at the Broncos. He was then controversially axed from the Kangaroos squad, despite claiming he had proved his fitness after injury. He spent two seasons at Gold Coast before retiring in 1992.

In 2008 some closure to the episode was finally achieved when Lewis admitted that Bennett's decision had been correct. "There have certainly been some tough times - for me and for several other players - when we didn't agree with him and the decisions he made," he said. "But, looking back, you have to admit while the decisions he has made you may not have agreed with at the time, they probably were for the long-term benefit of the Broncos. They have become such a wonderful and powerful club. They are respected throughout the world and he is a big reason for that."

Without their talisman, the Broncos thrived and went on to win the Grand Final in 1992 and 1993.

BALMAIN HEARTS BROKEN IN THE LAST MINUTE

Canberra Raiders and Balmain Tigers produced the most thrilling of Rugby League finals in 1989, which saw the Winfield Cup leave Sydney for the first time. It was one of the most gripping and compelling afternoons in the 81-year history of Rugby League in Australia.

The Tigers were chasing their first Premiership since 1969. Canberra, who had entered the league in 1982, were looking for a maiden success. The sides had lost the two previous finals: the Raiders to Manly in 1987 and Balmain to Canterbury a year later; the game in which the Tigers' superstar import Ellery Hanley had been cynically taken out of the game by Terry Lamb.

The Green Machine boasted international talent like Bradley Clyde - who, at 19, would win the first of his two Clive Churchill Medals as man of the match - Gary Belcher, Laurie Daley, Ricky Stuart, Steve Walters and the captain Mal Meninga, who had recovered from a broken arm sustained earlier in the season and who tearfully called the win the best moment of his life. The multi-talented Balmain side included Garry Jack, Steve Roach, Gary Freeman, Benny Elias and Paul Sironen. From Great Britain they had imported centre Andy Currier and Shaun Edwards, who was named substitute. They were captained by the Australian Test loose forward, Wayne Pearce.

The Tigers took the lead when the prolific Currier kicked a simple penalty. The Balmain winger James Grant then intercepted a terrible offload from the Kiwi forward Brent Todd to score the first try. Currier's conversion attempt was a shocker, but the Tigers were 6-0 up. The Raiders hit back with some thrilling ball movement, but were kept them at bay. Walters was tackled a couple of inches short, but they had to make do with a Meninga penalty. Soon after, Matthew Wood was denied a try by a copy-book cover tackle by Garry Jack at fullback for the Tigers.

Just before half-time, Sironen put his side firmly in control. A speculative hack forward from Currier foxed Belcher and Grant was first to the loose ball. He found Currier, who linked with Sironen and the giant forward stormed 20 metres to the posts. It felt like such a significant score, one which seemed likely to prove a Premiership winner, especially when Currier tagged on the

"The best moment of my life."

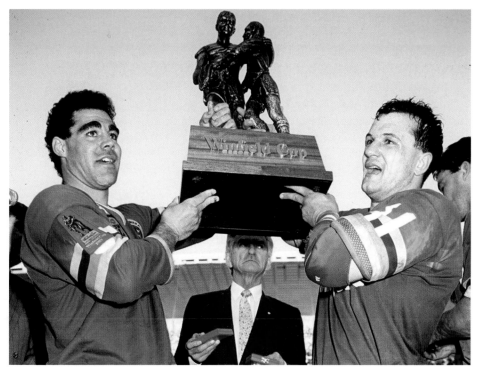

Mal Meninga and Dean Lance celebrate Canberra's Grand Final win

simple goal. It was 12-2 at half time.

Three minutes into the second half, Wood was again a whisker away from scoring in the corner, only to be denied by Pearce. Twelve minutes later the Tigers' dam finally burst when Gary Belcher crossed, with the supreme handling of Canberra finally proving too much. Meninga's goal reduced the gap to four points. Balmain searched for the game-breaking try, but in the final 20 minutes a series of incidents occurred, which combined to take the game away from them. Just past the hour mark, they spread the ball to the left and it seemed certain that Michael Neil would score, but Meninga saved the day with a sensational ankle tap, which kept his side in the contest. The Tigers instantly moved the ball right but Pearce's error wasted a big overlap.

In a much-criticised decision, Tigers coach Warren Ryan then withdrew the highly influential Roach and Sironen. The big prop had earlier been scythed down by a Dean Lance tackle which is remembered almost as much as any of the tries in this magnificent game. But the criticism was unfair as Kevin Hardwick had been introduced in such circumstances right through the season, especially when they were defending a lead. Ryan's magnificent coaching career never recovered.

Balmain did win a penalty for offside which Currier converted with ten minutes left. The gap between the sides was still just a converted try. Time seemed to stand still when Elias rattled the crossbar with a drop goal which would have given his side an unassailable lead. The noise reverberated around the stadium. Freeman was five metres offside yet the referee Bill Harrigan, shaken by the pressure, admitted later that had the Kiwi halfback collected the rebound and scored, he would have erroneously awarded the try.

What followed was one of the iconic moments of Grand Final history. The Raiders threw the ball from side to side. Chris O'Sullivan put up a bomb. It was collected by Daley, whose basketball pass found John 'Chicka' Ferguson in the last minute of the game. The former Wigan winger stepped inside three defenders to score one of the great Grand Final tries a few metres to the left of the posts. With seconds remaining, Meninga kicked the goal to take the game to extra-time at 14-all.

In the third minute, Jack uncharacteristically dropped a high ball under no pressure. O'Sullivan kicked a drop goal straight from a scrum. There was plenty of football to be played, but it proved to be a psychological blow to the Tigers, who were now behind for the first time.

With just minutes remaining, the substitute forward Steve Jackson took Meninga's off load and beat five defenders to score his first senior try. It was a surreal moment which sparked hysteria in the capital. The destination of the Winfield Cup was finally decided.

The Rugby League public sympathised with the Tigers but the Raiders had been the better side. Their gloriously expansive football was a welcome antidote to the defensive mindset which had been prevalent in the mid-1980s. They successfully defended their title in 1990 and won it again in 1994 in Meninga's final game for the club.

CANBERRA RAIDERS 19
BALMAIN TIGERS 14
(after extra-time)

CANBERRA
1 Gary Belcher
2 Matthew Wood
3 Mal Meninga (C)
4 Laurie Daley
5 John Ferguson
6 Chris O'Sullivan
7 Ricky Stuart
8 Brent Todd
9 Steve Walters
10 Glenn Lazarus
11 Dean Lance
12 Gary Coyne
13 Bradley Clyde
Subs:
14 Kevin Walters
15 Steve Jackson
16 Paul Martin

Tries: Belcher, Ferguson, Jackson
Goals: Meninga 3 **Drop goal:** O'Sullivan

BALMAIN
1 Garry Jack
2 Steve O'Brien
3 Tim Brasher
4 Andy Currier
5 James Grant
6 Michael Neil
7 Gary Freeman
8 Steve Roach
9 Benny Elias
10 Steve Edmed
11 Paul Sironen
12 Bruce McGuire
13 Wayne Pearce (C)
Subs:
14 Kevin Hardwick
15 Shaun Edwards
16 Michael Pobjie

Tries: Grant, Sironen
Goals: Currier 3

Half-time: 2-12
Referee: Bill Harrigan
Crowd: 40,500

Saturday, 10th November 1990

GREAT BRITAIN LEFT DEVASTATED BY MAL MENINGA

One of the great Test matches in Rugby League's glorious international history took place at Old Trafford in November 1990 as Great Britain were beaten 14-10 right at the death by Mal Meninga's heartbreaking try in front of 46,615 spectators.

Mal Reilly's men had beaten the Kangaroos 19-12 at Wembley a couple of weeks earlier and stood on the verge of winning the Ashes for the first time in 20 years. For much of this pulsating second Test it looked like they would be good enough to do that.

The Aussies responded to that first-Test loss by making a raft of changes. The great Brisbane halfback Allan Langer was dropped, with Ricky Stuart moving from six to seven. Cliff Lyons, the brilliant stand-off from the Manly Sea Eagles club, came in to partner him. Laurie Daley and Dale Shearer came into the three-quarter line for Mark McGaw and Michael Hancock. Benny Elias came in for Kerrod Walters at hooker, whilst Glenn Lazarus and Brad Mackay replaced Martin Bella and John Cartwright in their pack. For Great Britain, Andy Platt replaced Roy Powell with Paul Dixon moving into the second row.

Halfway through the first half, after a typically intense beginning, Shearer, the Kangaroo left wing, scored the game's first try from Lyons' short ball. The prolific Queensland winger beat Ellery Hanley's despairing dive to get to the line. Meninga was off target with both the conversion attempt and a 30-metre penalty. His toe-ended style didn't always look the smoothest. Paul Eastwood did get his side on the board with a penalty, leaving the half-time score 4-2 to the tourists.

Garry Schofield, who had enjoyed a magnificent tour of New Zealand in the summer and who, along with Hanley, had played a huge part in Great Britain's win at Wembley, saved a try with a great tackle on his former Balmain teammate Benny Elias. At the other end, Schofield engineered his side's first try with a marvellous dummy and offload for his Leeds club mate Dixon. The same combination had broken the line in the first half but

"Had we gone 12-10 up, we'd have grown an extra leg and won the Ashes."

Dixon failed to get the ball down. This time his try helped put his side into a 52nd-minute 6-4 lead, although Eastwood's conversion attempt was unsuccessful. With Schofield's control of the game growing as the minutes ticked down, the omens looked more than promising for Great Britain.

Australia's response was spectacular as Lyons posted one of the great Ashes tries four minutes later. He finished off a breathtaking move which saw the ball passed a dozen times. The final pass was a beauty as Meninga set Andrew Ettingshausen free down the right and he chipped infield for Lyons to score next to the posts. Meninga's goal put the tourists 10-6 ahead.

On 70 minutes came the moment that made every British Rugby League fan believe that the Ashes were finally coming home. A menacing Stuart crossed the halfway line and attempted a long pass to the right to set his three-quarter line free. Instead, the British substitute Paul Loughlin snaked out his long arm and brought the ball in before streaking away to the try line to level the scores. From pretty much the same spot as earlier, Eastwood this time sent the conversion wide of the other post.

"Had we gone 12-10 up, we'd have grown an extra leg and won the Ashes in my opinion," coach Malcolm Reilly lamented years later.

As the clock ticked down, a draw seemed likely, but in the dying embers of the match Stuart stepped past Lee Jackson's attempted tackle in the shadow of his own posts and set off downfield. He was supported by Meninga, who impeded Carl Gibson off the ball and took the ball ten metres from the line to score the try which

GREAT BRITAIN 10 AUSTRALIA 14

GREAT BRITAIN
1 Steve Hampson
2 Paul Eastwood
3 Daryl Powell
4 Carl Gibson
5 Martin Offiah
6 Garry Schofield
7 Andy Gregory
8 Karl Harrison
9 Lee Jackson
10 Andy Platt
11 Denis Betts
12 Paul Dixon
13 Ellery Hanley (C)
Subs:
14 David Hulme (dnp)
15 Kevin Ward
16 Paul Loughlin
17 Roy Powell (dnp)

Tries: Dixon, Loughlin
Goal: Eastwood

AUSTRALIA
1 Gary Belcher
2 Andrew Ettingshausen
3 Mal Meninga (C)
4 Laurie Daley
5 Dale Shearer
6 Cliff Lyons
7 Ricky Stuart
8 Steve Roach
9 Benny Elias
10 Glenn Lazarus
11 Paul Sironen
12 Bob Lindner
13 Brad Mackay
Subs:
14 Greg Alexander (dnp)
15 Des Hasler (dnp)
16 Mark Sargent (dnp)
17 John Cartwright (dnp)

Tries: Shearer, Lyons, Meninga
Goal: Meninga

Half-time: 2-4
Referee: Alain Sablayrolles
Crowd: 46,615

Great Britain's Daryl Powell in action at Old Trafford during the Lions' heartbreaking loss

devastated the British team. Martin Offiah had left the field injured. Had he been out there, he would have had the pace to get back and stop the try.

Had the game finished 10-all, the Ashes would have still been alive. It is something of a myth which has developed over the years that Great Britain lost the Ashes when Meninga scored, but it was a series-changing moment and one from which the British players took a long time to recover. Andy Gregory, the diminutive British half, was distraught. "That was the nearest we got to winning the Ashes," he said. "I sat in the changing rooms afterwards and just thought that sport was supposed to be enjoyable. It was the lowest I'd ever been in my life."

Meninga, on the other hand, had just experienced a career high. "It was the prime moment of his Rugby League career," said his predecessor as captain, Wally Lewis. The great centre helped the Kangaroos seal the series against a shattered Great Britain side, with a 14-0 triumph at Elland Road.

FORMER WORLD CUP FINALIST ARRESTED

It has always been difficult for a retired player to cope with life after football. Some stay within the game, some move into an alternative profession and there are those who invest their career earnings by starting up a business. Whichever option is chosen, though, it's wise not to follow the example of Garry Sullivan, who had played for Australia in the 1972 World Cup Final.

Between 1985 and 1991, the softly-spoken Sullivan and his stepfather made over three-million Australian dollars from a spate of armed robberies. Their arrest in October 1991 made for stunning news given Sullivan's successful footballing career.

It is an unfortunate quirk of fate that two players from the Newtown Jets club in the 1970s were, independently, to become notorious criminals. Paul Hayward had only recently been released from a Bangkok jail for heroin trafficking when his former teammate was arrested.

Sullivan played country football for Kurri Kurri, and was proficient enough to be included in their team of the century when it was named in 2008. He moved into first grade with Newtown Jets in 1970 and later that year toured Europe in Australia's World Cup campaign, although he wasn't selected for the final. In 1972 he played in both of Australia's Tests with New Zealand and in three matches at loose forward in the World Cup in France, including the final. He also played three games for New South Wales in 1972 and 1973. His first-grade career ended in 1975 and he moved into coaching in Newcastle, leading Maitland to the 1977 Newcastle District Grand Final. Thereafter, as far as Rugby League supporters were concerned, Sullivan disappeared from the game. He was last heard of running a martial-arts school in Queensland.

Ten years later, in May 1985, fueled by crippling gambling habits, he and

Bill Orchard, his stepfather, stole $28,000 at gunpoint from the ANZ bank at Sunnybank, a suburb in Brisbane. A month later they made off with $91,000 from the Westpac bank at Palm Beach. Their new career was up and running. By the end of the year, they had netted a further quarter of a million dollars from two more jobs. In April 1987 an attack on an armoured security van bagged the pair $316,000 and in 1988 they returned to Sunnybank to target another van, this time walking off with $420,000.

Two years later, in a different suburb called Sunnybank Hills, Sullivan and Orchard went a step further. Sullivan climbed onto the roof of the van and poured petrol through the vents, threatening to set it alight unless money was surrendered. Two guards were beaten up and a third, William Shanks, was forced to hand over $694,000. As the two thieves sped away, Shanks shot repeatedly at the back of the car but the pair managed to escape. Another man, a previously prolific armed robber called Bernie Matthews, was wrongly arrested for this crime and imprisoned.

Sullivan and Orchard continued their spree, but in March 1991 the end was in sight. Orchard was photographed buying a van which was used in a robbery four days later at Kuraby, another Brisbane suburb. The police traced the vehicle back to the dealership and were able to circulate the photograph throughout Australia. Five months later, Orchard splashed out on a $62,000 cabin cruiser from his proceeds of a $500,000 robbery committed at Loganholme. A sales representative at the boat company recognised Orchard from the picture and notified the police. The net was tightening.

On 25th October 1991 the pair drove to Indooroopilly in Brisbane and took $116,000 from two security guards who were due to fill an ATM at Suncorp bank. They returned to the Gold Coast where they were arrested the next morning, and charged with 14 armed robberies over six and a half years. Eighteen revolvers, four shot guns and around $160,000 was found at their houses.

On 16th December, Sullivan, 44, and Orchard, 54, were imprisoned for 20 years having been likened in court to the perpetrators of the Great Train Robbery. They had admitted that they were gambling addicts who had squandered their ill-gotten gains on horseracing with single bets of up to $100,000. Prosecutor Jeff Hunter told the court it was "banditry on a scale that has not before been seen in Queensland." Sullivan even escaped from Borallon prison in December 1993 and was on the run for two years before he was arrested for stealing a toothbrush in Adelaide.

When Sullivan was imprisoned, Matthews was granted a release and cleared of the 1990 hold-up at Sunnybank Hills, but he reoffended and later befriended the former footballer in prison. The two of them played touch football for the Over Fifties, losing in the final of the Borallon Jail Cup in 1999 to a team called the Young Bloods. For Sullivan, it was a far cry from playing in a World Cup Final.

"Banditry on a scale that has not before been seen in Queensland."

Sunday, 21st June 1992

BEN ALEXANDER KILLED IN CAR CRASH

The Australian Rugby League team were in camp in Coogee preparing for the second Ashes Test match against Great Britain in June 1992 when the captain Mal Meninga took a phone call. It was appalling news. He was asked to tell Brad Fittler that his best friend, Ben Alexander, had been killed in a car crash. A devastated Fittler withdrew from the Australian side and returned to Penrith, the club that the young pair played for. Alexander was the younger brother of the club captain, Greg.

The Panthers were Rugby League's reigning premiers having so memorably beaten Meninga's star-studded Canberra Raiders the previous September to win their first Grand Final. On the night of the accident, the players had been awarded their Premiership jackets by the coach, Phil Gould. Earlier in the day, the 20-year-old hooker Alexander had led the reserve-grade side to a 25-6 win over Easts, kicking a drop goal.

A night of celebration turned to tragedy when his Honda Prelude went through a red light in the Sydney suburb of Colyton at 10.20pm, hitting another vehicle and spinning out of control before striking a telegraph pole. Alexander was killed instantly. His teammates in the car Glen Liddiard, Luke Goodwin and Scott Murray escaped relatively unhurt, although the latter was hospitalised with a broken jaw. It later emerged that Alexander was nearly three times over the legal drink-drive limit, and he wasn't wearing a seat belt.

"When Mal passed on the news I shook my head and went and sat and in a corner and cried. I bawled and bawled. I felt very bewildered and very alone," Fittler recalled years later. "I loved you then and I love you now," he said poignantly of Alexander. Fittler also admitted to having occasionally driven when over the limit and that he had once caused an accident, breaking his nose in the process.

The tragedy devastated the close-knit, community-driven Panthers. The club was further affected with those close to Alexander struggling to come to terms with the news. Greg Alexander missed a significant chunk of the second half of the season, going to Greece to try to come to terms with the events. When he did play he was considerably underweight. The team lost their way badly, with Liddiard walking out on his contract. They failed to make the semi-finals.

Mark Geyer, Alexander's brother-in-law, had enjoyed a breakthrough

"I loved you then and I love you now."

year in 1991, establishing himself as one of the world's best forwards. He never played again for the Panthers, tearing up his contract as he succumbed to the twin temptations of recreational drugs and alcohol. An injury sustained in another car crash meant that he had to cancel a lucrative short-term deal with Leeds. He joined Balmain in 1993, but when they cancelled his contract for disciplinary reasons, he ended up playing bush football for Umina. "I proceeded to go off the rails in Umina," he said. "I was on the drink every day. I was abusing drugs - marijuana - and then before going on the drink at night would be some speed. I would dissolve it into my beer. I'd get paid by Umina on a Sunday and by Tuesday I would be broke because of drugs. I was using the excuse that it was my way to mourn. I realise now that it was a cop-out because Ben would never have wanted me to go down that track. I was using that as a pretty poor excuse. Even though I was shattered by Ben's passing I should have, in his memory, got on with things." In 2016 he recalled: "It set the whole district spiralling out of control. We weren't ready to deal with the grief of the death of Ben. We all went our separate ways and I've got no doubt we would have been a dynasty team if we'd stuck together and tragedy didn't strike. But it is what it is. Ben would have turned 45 yesterday and we remember him as fondly as ever. We love him and we miss him."

Fittler ended a turbulent 1992 with a World Cup winner's medal at Wembley, but the Alexanders found themselves in court two years after the accident. Ben's four siblings, along with Geyer, were charged with assaulting Ben's ex-girlfriend who, in turn, was accused of taunting the family over the death in an ugly row which had broken out in a Penrith hotel in February 1993, and which had caused Ben's mother to pass out. The family were acquitted in April 1994.

A week after Alexander's death, and just three days after a highly emotional funeral during which Greg delivered an achingly poignant eulogy, the Panthers' first-grade side scored a memorable 18-10 win over Wests. The club had actually considered forfeiting the match, along with their Under-21 and reserve-team matches. The latter two lost without scoring a single point, but the Winfield Cup side, without Greg Alexander and Geyer, and with Fittler coming off the bench, triumphed after tries from fullback Andrew Leeds and winger Graham Mackay. "It's a very tough football club to go through the week we've been through and come out with a performance like that today," said Gould.

The Panthers had been one of the favourites to win the 1992 Winfield Cup, but they finished in ninth place, four positions shy of the last play-off berth after enduring a disastrous year. The Ben Alexander tragedy had shaken the club to its foundations, and it took them years to recover.

THE PERFECT HALF OF RUGBY LEAGUE

This book remembers some famous British wins on Australian soil. Some of those, including 1914, 1958 and 1988, saw the Lions defying a firm underdog status to triumph against the odds in the most difficult and unexpected circumstances. Great Britain's win in Melbourne 1992 was indeed incredible, but for a different reason. This time it was the sheer margin of victory. The half-time score was 22-0 to Garry Schofield's magnificent Lions, and they ended up with a record 33-10 triumph.

Coached by Malcolm Reilly, who, in just four years, had proved himself to be the best Great Britain coach in decades, the Lions headed for the Southern Hemisphere in a confident mood. Under Reilly they had won the final Test in 1988, had come so close to a drawn series with the Kangaroos in 1990 and had won two Test series, both against the odds, against New Zealand.

They had another reason to be optimistic – Ellery Hanley was on the plane. After fitness concerns, the great loose forward would be taking his place in the side. This was surely now Great Britain's best chance in years to return home with the Ashes, but things are rarely so simple and the Lions lost the first Test 22-6 in Sydney without ever looking like challenging the Aussies. Hanley hadn't played by this point and his tour would last only nine minutes as he limped out of a tour match with Newcastle Knights. He had never been fully fit and, with hindsight, his selection had been unwise.

The captaincy was handed to Schofield, a totally different character. With the sagas over his predecessor's fitness and unwillingness to communicate with the media gone, the atmosphere in the camp appeared to change, although few outside the Lions' camp may have noticed.

Australian journalists, as one might expect, gave the tourists little chance, with the following published in the 'Sydney Morning Herald' the day before the second Test: "The Lions have not developed the sophisticated defensive strategies of top Sydney clubs in terms of their positional play at marker or on the fringes of the rucks. The British approach to fielding a team to beat Australia is like someone trying to mend a leaky roof: plug a hole in one place and a leak will appear somewhere else." Bob Fulton, the Australia coach, also

"Same again, lads."

seemed to be of the opinion that his side's opponents weren't up to the task, singling out the tough-tackling and big-hearted Wigan forward Billy McGinty who had been called into the side. "He'll tackle." he said, "But will he leave a hole somewhere else? He'll hunt up around the marker area, but will he be on the ground when needed out wide?" Canberra Raiders' Gary Coyne, who had played for Australia a year earlier, was also scathing of the Lions' chances. "The Poms showed nothing in the first Test to suggest there is a great deal of improvement left," he wrote in his newspaper column. "In Melbourne tonight Australia are going to be too big, too fast and far too disciplined for the Brits,"

As expected, the Green and Golds boasted some magnificent talent like Mal Meninga and Laurie Daley in the centres, Andrew Ettingshausen at the back, Allan Langer at halfback, and a smattering of world-class forwards like Glenn Lazarus, Steve Walters, Paul Sironen and Bradley Clyde. Great Britain were no mugs either, no matter what the Australian media thought. Hanley's injury meant that all six starting forwards came from the champion Wigan club and, with numerous match winners in the backs, the Lions were always capable of competing with their more illustrious opponents. Tries from Phil Clarke, Paul Newlove and Schofield more than underlined that and, along with five goals from Paul Eastwood, the sides turned around with the Lions boasting an astonishing 22-0 lead.

Schofield later revealed that Reilly's half-time talk consisted of just three words; "same again, lads!" Although they weren't able to win

AUSTRALIA 10 GREAT BRITAIN 33

AUSTRALIA
1 Andrew Ettingshausen
2 Rod Wishart
3 Mal Meninga (C)
4 Laurie Daley
5 Michael Hancock
6 Peter Jackson
7 Allan Langer
8 Paul Harragon
9 Steve Walters
10 David Gillespie
11 Paul Sironen
12 Bob Lindner
13 Bradey Clyde
Subs:
14 Brad Mackay
15 Glenn Lazarus
16 Chris Johns
17 Kevin Walters

Tries: Johns, Lindner **Goal:** Meninga

GREAT BRITAIN
1 Graham Steadman
2 Paul Eastwood
3 Daryl Powell
4 Paul Newlove
5 Martin Offiah
6 Garry Schofield (C)
7 Shaun Edwards
8 Kelvin Skerrett
9 Martin Dermott
10 Andy Platt
11 Denis Betts
12 Billy McGinty
13 Phil Clarke
Subs:
14 Gary Connolly
15 Paul Hulme
16 Joe Lydon
17 Karl Harrison

Tries: Clarke, Newlove, Offiah, Schofield, Steadman
Goals: Eastwood 6 **Drop goal:** Schofield.

Half-time: 0-22
Referee: Dennis Hale
Crowd: 31,005

Martin Dermott, Joe Lydon and Daryl Powell celebrate Great Britain's sensational victory against Australia in Melbourne

Great Britain's Kelvin Skerrett tries to break free

the second period by the same margin as the first, another two tries were enough to see them record a comfortable win. Tries by Bob Lindner and Chris Johns caused a few British hearts to flutter, but the magnificence of Graham Steadman's and Martin Offiah's tries provided the cherry on the most palatable of cakes.

Australia retained the Ashes with a 16-10 win in Brisbane in the third Test before the Lions won their two-Test series with New Zealand on aggregate. Great Britain could again hold their own with the best in the world, and their fabulous win in Melbourne was a once-in-a-generation achievement.

PILGRIM'S PROGRESS
HALTED BY UNION HYPOCRISY

Ninety-three years after rugby's great schism, relations between the codes were still strained, something which was no better underlined than when the Rugby Football Union took the extraordinary decision to issue a 12-month ban to a player who had played a solitary match for the Leeds Rugby League reserve team, without receiving anything more than moderate travelling expenses. Such was the outrage at the decision that a parliamentary motion was tabled in the House of Commons, with the RFU widely derided for their antiquated stance.

The player in question was the Wasps fullback Steve Pilgrim who had been named in an England development squad for the 1995 union World Cup. He had also played for the England 'B' team. Struggling to make ends meet, the 25-year-old was keen to maximise his earnings' potential and arranged a trial with the Loiners, hoping it would lead to a permanent deal and a change of codes. It was usually the case that such players would go under the pseudonym "A N Other" in a trial match in order to escape sanctions from union, which was still applying its amateur ideologies, but only when it suited them.

The Pilgrim case came soon after the South African Albertus Einslin rejected a move to Wakefield Trinity because he was offered match payments of £200 to £400 and a job with a £30,000 salary to stay in the 15-man code.

The Wakefield MP, David Hinchcliffe, revealed that he had seen a report from the Welsh Rugby Union which disclosed that two players had received considerable recompense for participating in the South African RFU's centenary celebrations. He said: "There are developments behind the scenes to test whether the current discrimination affecting players like Pilgrim would be legal if taken to civil court, as union is quite obviously a professional sport. Hopefully the latest issues will bring the matter to a head."

"What is disturbing is the hypocrisy which allows the RFU to turn a blind eye of Nelsonian proportions to the cash economy in their own game, while banning a player for the heinous crime of appearing - unpaid - on the same field as honest professionals."

The Rugby Football League's public-affairs executive, David Howes, was just as appalled, and sympathised with the ostracised fullback. "He should consult his MP and strike back through the European courts," he said. "It's a constraint on basic human freedom." 'League Express' summed up the situation in their 'Upfront' column the following Monday: "What is disturbing is the hypocrisy which allows the RFU to turn a blind eye of Nelsonian proportions to the cash economy in their own game, while banning a player for the heinous crime of appearing – unpaid – on the same field as honest professionals."

Cross-code legend Jonathan Davies was another unhappy at union's stance. "Ask if they'd ban [England centre Jeremy] Guscott if he had gone on trial," said Davies, then at Widnes. "They would have turned a blind eye because they couldn't afford to lose him." Even Pilgrim's Wasps coach Rob Smith was scathing of the ban. "To me it's a fairly straightforward issue … if he had played in a trial for a professional soccer or cricket team there would be no problem – we are being prejudiced against just one sport."

Pilgrim was outed by an over-enthusiastic stand-in journalist at a local newspaper the day after scoring a try and kicking three goals at Headingley in front of 2,800 people in a 30-10 win over Wakefield in the Alliance league. He was handed his punishment two days after the game on the basis that he had been found to have contravened the following rule of the International Board Regulation: "No person shall play in a trial or play with a non-amateur club organisation involved in the playing of any other type of rugby football."

"If he has not taken any money and does not go ahead with any Rugby League ambitions, he can apply for reinstatement as an amateur rugby union player in one year," confirmed the RFU secretary, Dudley Wood. But Wood's predecessor, Sir Peter Yarranton, now chairman of the Sports Council, spoke out against the ban. "In view of the fact that Pilgrim has not been paid, we feel there was a degree of unfairness in his situation," he said. "I am unhappy about the manner in which this is being interpreted."

Leeds were also scathing, with coach Doug Laughton remarking: "There will be 10 or 15 players at Cardiff Arms Park who have earned a lot more from rugby than Steve Pilgrim." Although the Loiners didn't offer the player the contract he wanted, the player did make one first-team appearance, away at Widnes in a league defeat in mid-March. He still didn't receive a wage. He also played a game for Halifax but was substituted after 29 minutes at Castleford. He didn't play at the top level again in Rugby League.

Pilgrim served his ban and returned to Wasps. In September 1995, rugby union finally came clean and turned professional. Players have since been free to switch between the two sports.

Relations between the two codes have never since been particularly cordial, but they have thawed considerably. Wigan and Bath played two challenge matches in 1996, whilst the former entered the Middlesex Sevens in the same year and won it in grand style – a feat which Bradford Bulls emulated in 2002. And, in what would have once been an unthinkable move, Rugby League was even played at Twickenham in 2000 when England met Australia in the World Cup.

Little of this was any consolation to poor Steve Pilgrim, whose punishment said far more about the hypocrites imposing it than it did about him.

WIGAN WORLD CHAMPIONS AGAIN!

// On top of the world! Wigan stun the Aussies!" hollered the front page of 'League Express' as the Riversiders served up one of the greatest wins in their incredible history by defeating the Brisbane Broncos at the ANZ Stadium to be crowned champions of the world on the first day of June in 1994.

Wayne Bennett's Broncos had dominated the Rugby League scene down under for two years, winning Premierships in 1992 and 1993, by beating the Brian Smith-coached St George Dragons in both finals. Wigan had ruled British Rugby League for far longer. By the summer of 1994 they had amassed seven consecutive Challenge Cups and five straight league titles, as well as numerous other trophies.

The sides had faced each other before, in the 1992 World Club Challenge, with the Broncos winning 22-8 at Central Park. Two years later, few gave Wigan a chance as they travelled down under without the Auckland Warriors-bound Dean Bell and Andy Platt. A broken jaw suffered in the Premiership Final win over Castleford also ruled out their enforcer Kelvin Skerrett, so Wigan would be facing the might of the Broncos with just one recognised prop - the one-cap Neil Cowie, who had signed from Rochdale Hornets less than three years earlier. Va'aiga Tuigamala, Wigan's new three-quarter from New Zealand rugby union, was even tried in the front row in training before they plumped for the fringe second-rower Billy McGinty to fill in as an emergency prop.

The club had relieved John Dorahy from the coaching duties after the Challenge Cup Final win over Leeds, with former captain Graeme West taking the team to Brisbane in a caretaker capacity. The World Club Challenge was West's fourth game in charge, and it saw him win his second trophy.

Even with some notable absentees, Wigan still boasted a galaxy of stars. Great Britain's Martin Offiah and Jason Robinson filled the wing spots, with fellow internationals Gary Connolly and Shaun Edwards joining them in the backs behind a star-studded back row of Denis Betts, Andy Farrell and Phil Clarke. The Broncos, despite being in a run of indifferent form which

"We've come all the way to Australia and they've still got excuses. I find that mystifying."

saw them languish in mid-table, were still able to boast the brilliant Wendell Sailor and Steve Renouf in the outside backs, with Kevin Walters and Allan Langer in the halves, and Glenn Lazarus and Kerrod Walters in a world-class front row, together with others who had amassed numerous caps and Origin appearances.

Just a few days earlier, eight of their players had been buoyed by Queensland's incredible last-gasp win over New South Wales in the first game of the new series. But in front of 54,220 at Brisbane's home ground, Wigan scored first when Betts did tremendously well to ground the ball following a kick from his skipper Edwards. The metronomic Frano Botica duly kicked the goal and the English side were 6-0 up after seven minutes.

McGinty, who had just agreed to sign for newly promoted Workington Town, enjoyed a barnstorming opening 20 minutes, reviving memories of his Test performance in Melbourne two years earlier. And when Barrie-Jon Mather ghosted through in the 16th minute and turned Sailor inside out to double the lead, Wigan were in dreamland. Botica's goal put them 12-0 up. Sailor did pull back four points with an excellent blindside run which saw him beat Offiah to cut the deficit to 12-4 at the break, but Robinson's 22-metre try less than three minutes into the second half, following Mick Hancock's error, left the Broncos struggling.

Fortuitous tries by Hancock and Julian O'Neill, both in the left corner with over a quarter of the match still to play, had Wigan sweating. But some magnificent defence either side of a 69th-minute penalty goal from

BRISBANE BRONCOS 14 WIGAN 20

BRISBANE
1 Willie Carne
2 Wendell Sailor
3 Steve Renouf
4 Chris Johns
5 Michael Hancock
6 Kevin Walters
7 Allan Langer (C)
8 Glenn Lazarus
9 Kerrod Walters
10 Andrew Gee
11 Mark Hohn
12 Alan Cann
13 Julian O'Neill
Subs:
14 John Plath
15 Peter Ryan
16 Brett Galea
17 Chris McKenna

Tries: Sailor, Hancock, O'Neill
Goal: O'Neill

WIGAN
1 Gary Connolly
2 Jason Robinson
3 Sam Panapa
4 Barrie-Jon Mather
5 Martin Offiah
6 Frano Botica
7 Shaun Edwards (C)
8 Neil Cowie
9 Martin Dermott
10 Billy McGinty
11 Denis Betts
12 Andy Farrell
13 Phil Clarke
Subs:
14 Va'aiga Tuigamala (dnp)
15 Martin Hall
16 Paul Atcheson
17 Mick Cassidy

Tries: Betts, Mather, Robinson
Goals: Botica 4

Half-time: 4-12
Referee: Greg McCallum
Crowd: 54,220

Jason Robinson is followed over the Brisbane tryline by the jubilant Martin Hall

Botica, awarded when Betts was impeded off the ball, carried them over the line. In particular, Connolly was superb at the back, saving three tries. Against all odds, Wigan regained the trophy which they had won in 1987 and 1991.

Among a plethora of excuses offered by the Australian media, Bennett was gracious enough to recognise Wigan's effort in defence. "I couldn't fault our blokes for effort," he said. "But again mistakes proved costly. Wigan saved a lot of tries."

Man of the match Edwards was understandably jubilant but aimed a dig at the Australian whingers. "When Australian teams come to England for the World Challenge game, they have lots of excuses about having been out celebrating since winning the Premiership," he said. "We've come all the way to Australia and they've still got excuses. I find that mystifying. They're now talking about being tired from State of Origin matches and having played last Friday night. Their schedule of matches over here is nothing like ours."

English sides have won a dozen World Club Challenges since its inception, with 11 on home soil, but none of them top the day Wigan lifted the trophy in the Broncos' back yard. It was the perfect end to a season which had yielded four trophies, but had been more than difficult at times. On the journey home, one player decided to match the scale of the victory with a stunning achievement of his own, and was so inebriated that he had to be taken off the plane in a wheelchair, claiming he had just broken the world record for the number of cans of lager consumed on an Anglo-Australian flight.

Saturday, 22nd October 1994

BRITAIN BEAT KANGAROOS DESPITE CAPTAIN'S RED CARD

Rugby League teams so rarely win after a man has been sent off, but on 22nd October 1994, Great Britain pulled off one of their most celebrated wins as they beat Australia at Wembley after captain Shaun Edwards had been dismissed for a first-half high tackle.

Having emerged from the 1990 and 1992 Ashes series with much credit, Great Britain fancied their chances of finally getting the better of the Kangaroos. A first-up win was most welcome, although they had triumphed in the first Test in 1990, only to lose the series.

Ellery Hanley, still a Leeds player, had taken over as coach from the Newcastle Knights-bound Malcolm Reilly, although he elected not to pick himself. Edwards replaced Hanley's club mate Garry Schofield as captain. Still two short of Mick Sullivan's record of 46 Great Britain caps, Schofield was surprisingly dropped from the 17. Paul Newlove was injured so Alan Hunte lined up in the centres, while firebrand Barrie McDermott, who had infamously taken out Paul Sironen a fortnight earlier in Wigan's game against the Kangaroos, made the bench.

The tourists had won their opening five tour matches beating Cumbria 52-8, Leeds 48-6, Wigan 30-20 (in a game billed as the fourth Test and televised live by the BBC), Castleford 38-12 and Halifax, who produced a sterling effort to hold the Green and Golds to a credible 26-12 score line. The big news with their selection was Allan Langer pipping Ricky Stuart to the number-seven jersey, as he had done in 1990. The Canberra half had to settle for a place on the bench. Wendell Sailor, the young Brisbane Bronco, was selected on the wing.

Cliff Richard entertained the crowd, labelling Rugby League "The rock and roll of sport," before the players contested a scoreless 25 minutes. Edwards then stiff-armed a rampaging Bradley Clyde who had stepped inside the Wigan halfback, looking to score the game's first try. The Australian referee Graham Annesley showed the British skipper the red card, and as he walked forlornly to the sheds, his side's hopes of winning seemingly disappearing with him.

Desperate for his team to win without him, Edwards found an unusual way of passing the time. "I couldn't watch the game," he said. "I was sat outside Wembley smoking a cigarette and I don't even smoke! I'd got a

Great Britain fullback Jonathan Davies beats his opposite number Brett Mullins to score a thrilling Wembley try

cigarette off someone and I was a bag of nerves."

Jonathan Davies, playing in what would prove to be his final Great Britain match, came to his captain's rescue. After nudging his side ahead with a penalty goal, he conjured up one of the great Test-match tries. Taking the ball on the halfway line from Denis Betts, he broke through the Australian defensive line and brilliantly exploited the fact that Brett Mullins, the Kangaroo custodian, had unwisely got involved in some argy-bargy with Alan Hunte at the previous play the ball. Davies took the recovering Mullins on the outside and dived in at the corner to score a thrilling try. The Welshman missed the goal but Wembley was buzzing. Great Britain had a foothold; something to build on. There was hope again after the sending-off. The second half was tight, with Great Britain's defence proficient enough to hold out Australia, although the Kangaroos offered less than expected.

In repelling one attack, Davies sustained a shoulder injury which would rule him out for the series. The British defence was immense, something which was beautifully summarised by the inimitable Colin Welland in 'The Observer' 24 hours later. "The second half saw Antipodean fury hurled at the British defence. Time after time it was thrown back in their faces. Sironen, sent clear beneath the posts, was bringing the celebratory XXXX to his lips when Connolly, substituting at fullback for the now injured Davies, threw his mother's council house at him and the day was saved."

The Kangaroos finally broke through with less than ten minutes

GREAT BRITAIN 8 AUSTRALIA 4

GREAT BRITAIN
1 Jonathan Davies
2 Jason Robinson
3 Gary Connolly
4 Alan Hunte
5 Martin Offiah
6 Daryl Powell
7 Shaun Edwards (C)
8 Karl Harrison
9 Lee Jackson
10 Chris Joynt
11 Denis Betts
12 Andy Farrell
13 Phil Clarke
Subs:
14 Bobbie Goulding
15 Barrie McDermott
16 Allan Bateman
17 Mick Cassidy

Try: Davies **Goals:** Davies, Goulding

Dismissed: Edwards

AUSTRALIA
1 Brett Mullins
2 Andrew Ettingshausen
3 Mal Meninga (C)
4 Steve Renouf
5 Wendell Sailor
6 Laurie Daley
7 Allan Langer
8 Ian Roberts
9 Steve Walters
10 Paul Harragon
11 Paul Sironen
12 Bradley Clyde
13 Brad Fittler
Subs:
14 Ricky Stuart
15 Tim Brasher (dnp)
16 Dean Pay
17 David Furner

Try: Renouf

Half-time: 6-0
Referee: Graham Annesley
Crowd: 57,034

Shaun Edwards catches Bradley Clyde high, a challenge that lead to his dismissal

left when Steve Renouf scored out wide, as he had done in the closing stages of the 1992 World Cup final to devastating effect. With the chance to level the scores, substitute David Furner missed the tricky conversion, and Britain wrapped up the victory with a late penalty from substitute Bobbie Goulding, who had done so much to steady the ship after the dismissal of Edwards.

To beat Australia despite being a man short for 55 minutes was a magnificent achievement, but Great Britain were unable to capitalise and lost the series by two matches to one. The period of time that had elapsed since their last Ashes triumph had now grown to 24 years.

"Sironen, sent clear beneath the posts, was bringing the celebratory XXXX to his lips when Connolly, substituting at full back for the now injured Davies, threw his mother's council house at him and the day was saved."

FIRST SHOTS OF THE SUPER LEAGUE WAR ARE FIRED

The morning newspapers in Australia on the first day of April in 1995 blew Rugby League apart. The first shots in what was to become the Super League War had been fired, and the messy fallout would last for two-and-a-half ruinous years.

Sydney's 'Daily Telegraph' reported that some of the biggest stars of the game, including Laurie Daley, Bradley Clyde, Allan Langer, Steve Renouf and Andrew Ettingshausen had signed mega-bucks contracts to play in a new competition. It was believed that around 80 players had already jumped ship, having furtively signed contracts with Rupert Murdoch's News Corporation. This was cloak-and-dagger stuff.

It was reported that the current premiers, Canberra Raiders, along with Brisbane Broncos and new clubs North Queensland Cowboys and Auckland Warriors, would be throwing their lot in with the Rupert Murdoch-backed plans. The role of the Broncos surprised nobody. They had been fierce critics of the Australian Rugby League governing body since their 1988 introduction to the competition. They were widely seen as the agitators.

The ARL's chief executive, Ken Arthurson, was stunned. He wrote in his 1997 autobiography, "We were on our knees. This dreadful deed, this disgraceful corporate raid – the signing of our players in stealth and the dark of night – had knocked the stuffing out of us."

Backed by another media magnate, Kerry Packer, who just happened to be the richest man in Australia, the ARL launched a fightback. Arthurson's club, Manly, as well as Sydney City and South Sydney would be remaining loyal. But they needed to pin down players. And lots of them. At this point, the only one who was definitely going to remain loyal to the ARL was Brad Fittler.

Rugby League was in turmoil.

The Super League War was all about pay-television rights. Since the first regular broadcasts of the sport in Australia in the 1970s, television coverage

"This dreadful deed, this disgraceful corporate raid - the signing of our players in stealth and the dark of night - knocked the stuffing out of us."

Ken Arthurson, the ARL's chief executive, was stunned by events in April 1995

of the sport had been enormously successful. Channel Ten took over the rights from Channel Seven in 1983 but hit financial difficulties and filed for receivership seven years later. Kerry Packer's Channel Nine ensured that the game was not left stranded without television presence and Arthurson described Packer as a 'true friend of Rugby League'. The deal was renewed in 1993 with rights for pay-TV, which didn't exist in Australia at the time, bolted on. But Murdoch was aware of their true worth because a year earlier, his Sky Sports organisation had purchased the rights to soccer's Premier League in England for over £300 million. Having also bought the rights to American's National Football League, Murdoch wanted Rugby League too. News International had already been angered by the ARL's refusal to allow one of its subsidiaries, Ansett Airlines, to take over from Winfield as the game's leading sponsor, and when the governing body stood firm over pay-TV, war was waged.

Back in November 1994, Super League rumours had led Arthurson to invite all 20 Winfield Cup clubs to sign ARL loyalty agreements, which they did. They made a further commitment in February, but many of them would still renege by signing with Murdoch.

With former Kangaroo winger John Ribot and Murdoch's son Lachlan spearheading the Super League campaign, the rebels, in trying to entice players, painted a picture of their global Star League, as it was first known, wiping the floor with a tired Australian Rugby League body which had failed to move with the times. In reality, League had been as popular as ever in 1994 and much of the Super League rhetoric was pure hyperbole. There was even talk of cracking the Chinese market and of Barcelona and Milan hopping on board.

What Super League did have was money. And plenty of it. Bradley Clyde, Laurie Daley and Ricky Stuart were handed astronomical contracts worth $700,000 a season with a $100,000 signing-on fee. Fringe players were bumped up to six-figure salaries. It was fill-your-boots time for the players, and the ARL had to fight fire with fire to prevent every player and club in the competition from heading to Super League.

It was believed over that first weekend that Newcastle Knights would be one of the many clubs to turn their backs on the ARL. In the end, and crucial to the outcome of the war, the Knights remained loyal. Paul Harragon, their captain, signed a huge deal with Arthurson's men and ensured that ARL chiefs came to the city to talk to the players. Origin coach Phil Gould, along with Bob Fulton, one of Arthurson's trusted henchmen, delivered speeches and also outed chief executive, Brad Mellen, as a Super League sympathiser. The Knights squad, which included a young Andrew Johns, signed ARL contracts that night while Mellen resigned and joined the Super League organisation. A club official told Matthew Johns: "You've just fucked the club!"

Arthurson responded to the dramatic April Fools' Day news, which he later called a Pearl Harbour attack, by threatening to kick Canberra, Cronulla and Canterbury out of the 1995 competition. His 40-year friendship with Canterbury legend Peter 'Bullfrog' Moore was over. Super League players were told they couldn't play in October's World Cup or the forthcoming State of Origin series, which prompted Wayne Bennett to walk away from the Queensland job. Radio coverage of the Saturday-afternoon game between Norths and Auckland was continually interrupted by news bulletins breaking the latest stories. The game was in shock. It felt like nothing would be the same again.

The war had begun. In order to gain an advantage, Murdoch looked in England's direction, but there were to be well over two years of court battles, hatred and acrimony to follow.

THE EUROPEAN SUPER LEAGUE ANNOUNCEMENT

For those old enough to remember, British Rugby League's 'J. F. Kennedy' moment came in April 1995 when news broke that Super League, summer rugby and mergers were to be the way forward. The announcement sent shockwaves through the game.

It had been reported three days earlier that something was brewing behind the scenes, but few expected the loose ends to be tied up so quickly and few knew exactly what was coming. Nobody could have foreseen how dramatic the announcement from Wigan's Central Park on that spring Saturday would be.

After 100 years of winter Rugby League, the sport's chief executive, Maurice Lindsay, revealed that the game would become a summer sport. This was an issue that had been debated for years; decades in fact, and plenty were in favour, including apparently, most of the players.

The new Super League would comprise 14 teams. Wigan, St Helens, Leeds, Bradford Northern and Halifax were safe and would enter in their own right. They were to be joined by London Broncos, who were to be fast-tracked from the second division, as well as new clubs Paris St Germain and Toulouse. Six new ventures were to be formed from the merging of 15 existing professional clubs. This is where the fun started.

Workington Town, Whitehaven, Barrow and Carlisle Border Raiders would join forces under the 'Cumbria' banner. Wakefield Trinity, Castleford and Featherstone Rovers would become 'Calder'. Salford and Oldham would merge and be known as 'Manchester', despite neither actually being in Manchester. Widnes and Warrington would now be called 'Cheshire'. Doncaster and Sheffield Eagles would amalgamate and be known as 'South Yorkshire' and, perhaps least surprisingly of all, Hull FC and Hull Kingston Rovers would see the birth of a club called 'Humberside'.

There would be no promotion and relegation for the first two seasons, and an interim competition was to be staged between August 1995 and January 1996, to include a World Cup. The clubs voted through the changes although

"Could it be that the game in England has become a weapon to be used in an Australian civil war?"

Keighley, who were to be denied promotion, and Widnes were two of many to express unhappiness.

To say all hell broke loose would be an understatement, even though Rupert Murdoch's News International would at least be injecting £77 million into the British game over the next five years. Super League clubs were due to receive over £1 million a year with first-division clubs receiving a one-off payment of £100,000.

Incandescent fans protested at the Easter derbies the following weekend when the memorable "Fev is Fev, Cas is Cas, Stick your merger up your ass!" banner was spotted. They were determined at least to help maintain their own unique identities even if that meant dining away from the top table. A turbulent mix of chaos, anger and excitement engulfed the English game for weeks with a variety of rumours circulating. Many were stunned that Lindsay had agreed to the deal so quickly, although he insisted that the offer might not have remained had he dithered.

The announcement meant that Great Britain, as well as New Zealand, had effectively sided with Murdoch in the Australian Super League War and not with the governing body, the Australian Rugby League. The ARL's chief, Ken Arthurson, labelled Lindsay 'treacherous and dishonest'. Even the top clubs were not happy. The Leeds executive, Alf Davies, said: "[The money] won't go very far. If we make the wrong decision then the game could be finished in a short space of time." 'The Observer' newspaper commented, "Remarkably, some clubs – notably the once-proud outfits of Wakefield, Featherstone and Hull KR – have virtually voted themselves out of existence."

There was such anger that BBC1 produced a one-off programme with various figures, including Lindsay, to discuss the news with a live link to baying fans at Keighley. "I think after 100 years," he said, "everybody knows we're still struggling. We haven't really made the advancement we should have done. If you have a look at the FA Premier League, they took a similar decision just two or three years ago and they're really leaping ahead – new stadiums, new excitement – and whether you like soccer or you don't, you have to admire the concept as a truly successful one. We think our game is tremendous. Everyone who watches our game is in love with it, but for some reason we can't get it watched by millions. This gives us the opportunity to put the game on a firm footing financially. It also gives us the opportunity to expand totally in a way we've wanted to do for 100 years but haven't been able to."

The presenter Charlie Lambert asked Sky Sports' Eddie Hemmings: "Could it be that the game in England has become a weapon to be used in an Australian civil war?" Hemmings' response was rather unconvincing. "I think the Australian civil war, if the information I'm receiving from down under is correct, will soon be over," he said. It would go on for another two-and-a-half years.

On the subject of summer rugby, the veteran BBC commentator, Ray French noted, "I'm not really convinced that people are going to flock in droves when it's high temperatures and Blackpool, Southport or Alton Towers call."

Maurice Lindsay and Mal Meninga promote the arrival of Super League in Europe

Kevin Ashcroft, the former Great Britain hooker, was worried for the lower-division sides. "As far as the first division," he said, "they get a £100,000 pay off. That is going to be the death knell for that division. There's no way they're going to be able to compete. The gap is going to grow wider."

The final format for the inaugural Super League season was eventually altered with mergers scrapped, but the shock of that amazing announcement at Wigan, which changed the face of Rugby League forever, will never be forgotten.

Friday, 8th October 1995

IAN ROBERTS CONFIRMS RUMOURS HE IS GAY

It wasn't until 1984 that the state of New South Wales decriminalised homosexuality. Attitudes in sport lagged even further behind society in general, with Rugby League remaining a bastion of heterosexual ruggedness. At the time, a 19-year-old South Sydney junior called Ian Roberts was standing on the verge of a great career. He was gay, but in the ultra-macho world of the Winfield Cup, he had no intention of revealing that little secret any time soon.

Rumours of his sexuality would rage for the majority of his career. In 1989 a popular gossip column in the 'Sun Herald' newspaper reported that Roberts frequented gay establishments, and so the homophobic taunts from opposing fans were further cranked up. It was by now known among most of the players at Redfern that he was gay and coach George Piggins raised the rumours with Roberts that he was a regular on Sydney's gay scene. The big prop insisted he was only there for the music. That sort of uncomfortable conversation was reminiscent of the Nottingham Forest manager Brian Clough and his struggling big-money striker Justin Fashanu in the early 1980s. Fortunately those in Rugby League who knew Roberts' secret behaved far more appropriately than the horribly bigoted Clough, and Roberts' eventual coming-out was a far happier experience that Fashanu's, whose career and life were destroyed.

Midway through 1990, Roberts left Souths for Manly and with talk of his sexuality more common in League's inner circles, it was inevitable that there would be even more taunts from the opposition. "Don't let that bastard bleed on us," one North Sydney player shouted. Insults like 'faggot' and 'poof' were commonplace. His parents, in the stands, had to put up with rampant homophobia for years. His partner Shane, meanwhile, dressed up on matchdays as the club's mascot, Igor!

With the rumours showing no signs of abating, a speaker in a public debate at the Gay and Lesbian Rights Lobby tried to out Roberts in a high-profile speech. He was under further pressure to come out from many who believed that a high-profile role model would help the millions struggling with such a secret.

Roberts, meanwhile, was struggling with tragedy in his personal life, as he explained in a television interview with Peter Sterling in 2016. "Aaron

214

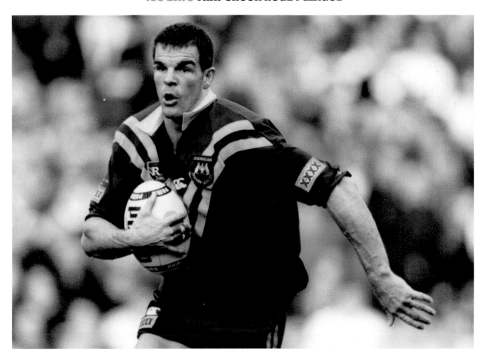

Lowe was a young friend of mine who was murdered," he recalled. "He was someone I really cared about. It still upsets me to talk about it. When the police came to see me about Aaron, I felt incredibly ashamed. I'd been more concerned about my Rugby League career and what the general public would think of me than stepping up and doing the right thing by that child. Aaron was only 15 when he was murdered. He stayed with me and my partner for a year and I'd known him since he was nine. We got him off the street and looked after him. We got him back on the rails. He was back at school and had been with us for six or seven months. To go to that point and think of my career when that boy was murdered, left dead in a ditch, it crushes me."

In 1994 Roberts posed naked for a new gay magazine, 'Blue', and although the pictures unsurprisingly caused a furore among a hysterical media, there was still no official confirmation of his sexuality. The pictures were published while Roberts was in England with the Kangaroos and while there was casual homophobia among his teammates, Terry Hill, his Manly clubmate and roommate, did his best to shield him from it. Paul Freeman, Roberts' biographer, points out, however, that all of the Kangaroo selectors knew he was gay and he was still selected to tour. At least he didn't become another Len Smith. "The people [Roberts] respected in the game were good men, egalitarian in the true League spirit," Freeman wrote.

"Roberts is not the first gay footballer, but he is the first with the courage to live it openly, and to hell with what anyone thinks."

When he was ready, Ian Roberts chose to tell his story in a magazine called 'New Weekly' with the feature entitled 'A man and his match'. The response, on the whole, was more positive than negative. Peter Fitzsimons, writing in the 'Sydney Morning Herald', said that "Roberts is not the first gay footballer, but he is the first with the courage to live it openly, and to hell with what anyone thinks. Surely the wretched schoolyard taunt of 'yer a poofta' has lost an awful lot of sting already."

On the other hand, England, the country of Roberts' birth, was again embarrassed by its tabloid newspapers, which were only too keen to plunge to new depths where taste was concerned. "One of the roughest toughest Aussies ever to rip the Poms apart has admitted he's a poofter," wrote one, while another went with the ridiculously offensive "Bugger me, what have we queer?"

Roberts knew he had made the right decision. "There was a lot of relief for other people," he told Sterling. "My parents had stopped going to games because of what was being shouted out by crowds. They understood why I had to come out. Everyone at Manly knew I was gay so there was no issue. It made things much easier for me personally."

Roberts also had to contend with numerous vitriol-filled letters, as his 1997 biography 'Finding Out' detailed. A former Queensland player who claimed to have played against Clive Churchill wrote upon hearing the news: "What a disappointment that is to myself and sons. Having had a brush with this so-called lifestyle, or deathstyle, it left me feeling dirty and unclean. Homosexuality is a carrier of disease, death, violence, murder, and lacks compassion, it incites jealousy and is an abomination to God."

The hate mail didn't ease up. "I am writing to you both as a friend and under the compulsion of the Holy Spirit of God to warn you of the results you will experience if you continue to live as a homosexual," read one letter. "You are going to become a very ill young man and will eventually die as a result of it." Another said: "Your despicable lifestyle choice has made my son decide to join your lot and I fear more than anything that he is lost to me and to decent living and God forever." There was also this threat: "If it's the last thing I do, you are done for," as well as "You are not even an animal. Your parents will disown you and you will die alone soon. AIDS will finish you in hell."

That anybody should have had to contend with such a stream of poison is appalling, but Ian Roberts is a trailblazer and when, in 2015, the Batley Bulldogs captain, Keegan Hirst, came out, via the front page of a Sunday newspaper, the response was overwhelmingly positive from players and fans alike on social media – and even, for once, in the tabloids.

Mercifully, a lot has changed in 20 years, and Ian Roberts has played no small part in that. Since his playing career ended, he has successfully tackled his illiteracy and mental-health issues, and has starred in over 25 films despite suffering from partial brain damage as a result of on-field injuries. He is a fine role model to many.

Sunday, 11th February 1996

WIGAN FINALLY DEFEATED IN THE CHALLENGE CUP

After eight successive Wembley triumphs, Wigan's astonishing Challenge Cup run eventually came crashing to their bootlaces at The Willows in February 1996 when they succumbed to Salford, a lower-division team.

The Cherry and Whites hadn't lost a Cup tie since February 1987 when Oldham beat them at Watersheddings. On that occasion, a late Paddy Kirwan try and Ray Ashton goal handed the Roughyeds an unlikely 10-8 win. After that, Wigan went on to emerge unbeaten in their next 43 ties, with Shaun Edwards playing in every one.

Having finished top of the Centenary Championship in January 1996, their sixth league title in a row, and having beaten a resurgent St Helens side in a humdinger of a Regal Trophy Final, Wigan were tipped to be far too strong for lower-division Salford in this fifth-round Challenge Cup match. The BBC seemed to agree, passing up the opportunity to televise the match, choosing instead to screen a routine Leeds win away at Warrington.

The Reds, who were the newly crowned Division One champions for the 1995-96 Centenary Season, boasted a strong Wigan influence. They were coached by Central Park legend Andy Gregory and fielded other ex-Wiganers in Steve Hampson, Scott Naylor and Sam Panapa. Gregory was confident enough to predict his team would come up trumps and they did just that, in wonderful fashion.

Welsh prop David Young, who would be named man of the match, opened the scoring in the fourth minute by touching down Mark Lee's grubber and Naylor doubled the lead just before the half-hour mark. This was more than even the most optimistic Reds supporter could have ever expected. Va'aiga Tuigamala, the Samoan colossus, on whom Wigan had spent a fortune in 1993, pulled one back just before half-time, but they still trailled 14-4. Memories were evoked of the fifth round in 1994 at The Boulevard when Hull FC led 21-2, but Wigan stormed back with 20 unanswered points to squeeze home by a solitary point.

Wigan fans were praying for another such collapse and, with Salford being a lower-division team, all was perhaps not lost just yet, but the hosts produced a gargantuan effort in the second half to send shockwaves through the world of Rugby League. Naylor got his second try with the help of Paul

Forber and after a Martin Offiah try for Wigan, Scott Martin sealed the match with ten minutes left. Even at 26-10, the score flattered Wigan, with Salford having a trio of tries disallowed. Tuigamala's late try didn't cause too much consternation for those on the terraces, where the celebrations were already underway. There was only time for the hooter to signal the greatest scenes in the modern era of the stadium for the majority of the 10,048 spectators.

"We've worked hard all season and this is one of my finest moments. Everybody kept talking about this Wigan run but it had to come to an end sometime," said Gregory, who was part of the first five of those eight Cup-winning sides.

"The Pope was still a Catholic, ducks could still swim and it still went dark on the night of Sunday, 11th February," wrote Paul Wilson in his 1996 book 'The Best Years of our Lives', "but by the time the first stars began to twinkle, Wigan were out of the competition they had dominated for the past eight years." The quote summed up the shock reverberating around the sport. The unthinkable had happened.

Hampson, in particular, enjoyed the victory. He had been released by Wigan in 1992 just short of a well-deserved testimonial, which he was now denied. On his lap of honour, he sought out the Wigan chairman Jack Robinson in the stands, and shouted to his former boss: "You didn't want me, did you, Jack? You thought I was finished didn't you?" Former Wigan chairman Maurice Lindsay was one of many who saw this jaw-dropping incident. "It was an eerie moment," he said. "Hampo wasn't just jeering at

SALFORD REDS 26 WIGAN 16

SALFORD
1 Steve Hampson
2 Nathan McAvoy
3 Scott Naylor
4 Scott Martin
5 Darren Rogers
6 Steve Blakeley
7 Mark Lee
8 David Young (C)
9 Peter Edwards
10 Cliff Eccles
11 Paul Forber
12 Lokeni Savelio
13 Sam Panapa
Subs:
14 Ali Davys (dnp)
15 Andy Burgess

Tries: Naylor 2, Martin, Young
Goals: Blakeley 5

WIGAN
1 Gary Connolly
2 Jason Robinson
3 Va'aiga Tuigamala
4 Kris Radlinski
5 Martin Offiah
6 Henry Paul
7 Shaun Edwards (C)
8 Neil Cowie
9 Martin Hall
10 Terry O'Connor
11 Scott Quinnell
12 Simon Haughton
13 Andrew Farrell
Subs:
14 Andrew Craig
15 Kelvin Skerrett

Tries: Tuigamala 2, Offiah
Goals: Farrell, Paul

Half-time: 14-4
Referee: David Campbell
Crowd: 10,048

Scott Naylor leads the Salford celebrations

Scott Martin takes on Wigan's Simon Haughton and Henry Paul

Andy Gregory, a key Wigan player for many years, shouts instructions to his Salford players

Jack. His face was contorted with anger. There were tears in his eyes and he was almost bawling."

The defeat led to an astonishing episode involving Robinson and the 'Wigan Observer' which claimed, correctly, that a number of Wigan players had partied to excess in Tenerife in the lead-up to the match, but they mistakenly included Neil Cowie as one of the revelers. He had been elsewhere. It was alleged that Wigan tried to sue the newspaper on the grounds that they had missed out on a hefty transfer fee for Cowie from Leeds, who had apparently pulled out of the deal upon reading the story. Robinson was charged with conspiracy to defraud and tried, but cleared over a year later.

As for the repercussions of the defeat at Salford, it marked the beginning of the end of Wigan's incredible ten-year domination of British Rugby League. They had to wait until 2002 to get their hands on the famous trophy again.

"The Pope was still a Catholic, ducks could still swim and it still went dark on the night of Sunday, 11th February, but by the time the first stars began to twinkle, Wigan were out of the competition they had dominated for the past eight years."

SUPER LEAGUE'S GLORIOUS BEGINNING

A year of arguing was finally over. Super League was here, and so was summer rugby, along with video referees, squad numbers, pre-match razzmatazz and several new rules.

Nobody quite knew what to expect. Would Paris St Germain be competitive? Would they be embarrassed by a Sheffield Eagles side which had done so well in the last winter season? Would many locals even bother to turn up and watch?

In the end, the pessimists were proven wrong, as Maurice Lindsay's famous quote about reporters coming for a funeral would indicate. Paris won a magnificently entertaining game in front of a crowd of 17,873. Rugby League's first video referee, Martin Haigh, got his decisions right and everyone went home happy apart from those from Sheffield. He may have since won seven Grand Finals as the chief executive of Leeds Rhinos, but the Super League era got off to a less-than-satisfactory start for the Eagles owner and coach, Gary Hetherington.

The players came onto the field in twos, side by side, one from each team, position by position, when their names were announced to the crowd by Sky's Mike Stephenson. There had also been fireworks, pre-match entertainment and dancing girls. This was the brave new world that Rugby League had signed up to. With Queen's 'We Will Rock You' blaring over the public-address system, PSG's Freddie Banquet kicked off the new European Super League competition. The first hit-up came from the big Fijian winger Joe Dakuitoga and in the first set Ryan Sheridan made Super League's first clean break before being hauled down. On the last tackle, Dean Lawford kicked to Arnaud Cervello who was tackled by the kick chasers which gave Paris a zero tackle – teams got seven tackles when a player fielded a kick and was tackled without passing the ball. That rule change, like many in the summer era, didn't last long.

Jean-Marc Garcia, a Frenchman playing for Sheffield, made Super League's first handling error and Patrick Torreilles gave away the first penalty for using his hands in the ruck but the Eagles failed to find touch. Keith Senior was the first summer-era substitute to come on to the field, replacing the injured Dakuitoga.

The first video-referee decision came when Banquet dived for the corner and was tackled into touch by Senior and fullback Waisale Sovatabua. The try was disallowed with a scrum on the 10-metre line awarded to the visitors. A moment later, in the 11th minute, Banquet was successful, scoring Super League's first try by intercepting Johnny Lawless's juggle and beating Paul Carr to the line to score a try against his former club. Torreilles missed the first kick at goal. The try-scoring team restarted the game – another new rule which didn't last long.

The Eagles soon had their first try when the 18-year-old Dean Lawford beat Didier Cabestany after a run-around move with Sheridan. Matt Crowther kicked Super League's first-ever goal and Sheffield led 6-4 after 27 minutes. They were over again five minutes later when Andy Hay hit a Lawford short ball like a train to score on the short side, but just as it seemed that Sheffield were getting on top, Mikhail Piskunov touched down Patrick Entat's kick for a Paris try, which Torreilles converted. The teams were level at 10-10 as the half-time hooter sounded, although Stuart Cummings, amid all the noise, failed to hear it. The match restarted and went on for three tackles with the hooter in continuous operation, until one of the touch judges alerted the referee.

Darren Adams and Crowther exchanged tries ten minutes into the second half before Carr's try and Crowther's second goal put the Eagles 20-14 up. Paris came roaring back to give the neutrals the finish they wanted to see, with tries from Pierre Chamorin and Cervello, the latter with two, in a devastating 13-minute spell. Sheffield had the last word with

PARIS ST GERMAIN 30
SHEFFIELD EAGLES 24

PARIS
7 Laurent Lucchese
3 Mikhail Piskunov
15 Frederic Banquet
9 Pierre Chamorin (C)
19 Arnaud Cervello
16 Todd Brown
8 Patrick Entat
4 Gregory Kacala
14 Patrick Torreilles
21 Jason Sands
13 Darren Adams
23 Didier Cabestany
34 Jacques Pech
Subs:
25 Ian Turner
12 Vea Bloomfield
5 Regis Pastre-Courtine
10 Fabien Devecchi

Tries: Cervello 2, Adams, Banquet, Chamorin, Piscunov **Goals:** Torreilles 3

SHEFFIELD
14 Waisale Sovatabua
2 Joe Dakuitoga
3 Lynton Stott
4 Jean-Marc Garcia
16 Matt Crowther
6 Ryan Sheridan
18 Dean Lawford
8 Paul Broadbent (C)
9 Johnny Lawless
21 Danny McAllister
11 Andy Hay
23 Paul Carr
13 Mick Cook
Subs:
20 Keith Senior
7 Mark Aston
17 Anthony Farrell
25 Dale Laughton

Tries: Lawford, Hay, Crowther, Carr, Senior **Goals:** Crowther, Aston

Half-time: 10-10
Referee: Stuart Cummings
Crowd: 17,873

"*Some reporters came for a funeral, and had to write about a Super League party.*"

Sheffield's Johnny Lawless tries to escape from Paris St Germain's Patrick Torreilles

a try after the hooter by Senior, but the home side had won a famous 30-24 victory.

Critics pointed to the numerous free tickets given out which bolstered the impressive crowd figure and to the fact that many of the French players were having to double up with their club sides in the French Championship the following day. Long term, of course, the success of the

SUPER LEAGUE - FIRST WEEKEND'S RESULTS
Bradford Bulls 30 Castleford Tigers 18
Halifax Blue Sox 22 London Broncos 24
Leeds 18 Warrington 22
Oldham Bears 16 Wigan 56
Paris St Germain 30 Sheffield Eagles 24
Workington Town 0 St Helens 62

occasion proved to be a false dawn with the Parisian club run shambolically before it was closed down after just two seasons.

But on the night of 29th March 1996, most were just content that Super League and summer rugby had been launched in the most perfect way.

Saturday, 27th April 1996

GOULDING BOMBS THE BULLS

The thrill-a-minute Challenge Cup Final between St Helens and Bradford in 1996 shattered records galore and was the match which announced to the world that this new-fangled summer concept was well worth watching.

Coming just weeks after the sport had kicked off its revolutionary summer era, this wonderfully entertaining match, with more than its fair share of questionable defending, was a fitting representation of the new era's early days. Commentators debated whether it deserved to be ranked above the 1985 classic as Wembley's greatest final - and it provided a record aggregate score for a cup final, as well as the highest scores for both the winning and losing sides. The lead changed hands four times.

Robbie Paul, the youngest captain of a team at Wembley, won the Lance Todd Trophy as man of the match and a £10,000 bonus after becoming the first player to score a hat-trick in a Cup Final under the twin towers. He followed in the footsteps of Frank Whitcombe in 1948, Tommy Harris in 1960, Don Fox in 1968, George Nicholls in 1978 and Dave Topliss in 1979 by being named man of the match despite finishing on the losing side. But the match-winning contribution came from the inspirational St Helens skipper, Bobbie Goulding, who, in the best season of his career, engineered a stunning second-half comeback when all had seemed lost, although his goal kicking was uncharacteristically poor.

The fun and games started during the week when Bulls coach Brian Smith surprised everyone by naming prop Jon Hamer in the starting line-up for his first game of the season. Saints coach Shaun McRae mocked Smith, stating that Hamer wouldn't figure but the veteran forward did play, putting in a solid opening stint.

When Steve Prescott, the young Saints fullback, scored two early tries to have his side 8-0 up, it looked like being a long afternoon for the Bulls, but Jon Scales, their huge winger, got them back into the game by rounding Prescott to score after being sent clear by ex-Saint Paul Loughlin. Two goals by Paul

"We worked hard on the kicks in every single training session, and our call for the bombs was 'Graham!'"

Cook tied the match ten minutes before half-time, only for Danny Arnold to finish off a move instigated by Paul Newlove, who had moved from Odsal to Knowsley Road six months earlier. The last word of an exhilarating first half went to Paul, whose 38th-minute try allowed Cook to edge his side ahead at 14-12 with the conversion.

The Bulls went on to take charge of the game with the first two tries of the second half, scored by Bernard Dwyer – another player coming up against his former side – and Paul, who scored one of the great Wembley tries from acting–half, picking up the ball ten metres out, spinning out of two tackles and planting the ball down, despite the attention of four Saints players on the line. It was a remarkable try from a player who was one of the faces of the early Super League years. With little over 20 minutes remaining, Saints were faced with a 14-point deficit, more than any side had previously pulled around in a Challenge Cup Final - but those who believed that the game was over reckoned without Goulding's stunning leadership and positivity, as well as his masterful kicking game.

Seven incredible minutes later, Saints were 30-26 up after three steepling Goulding bombs led to tries for Keiron Cunningham, Simon Booth and Ian Pickavance. The skipper converted all three to crown an astounding passage of play. And when Karle Hammond, the Saints stand-off, set up Arnold's second it was Saints who had a 34-26 lead with just 13 minutes left. Surely Bradford were done for.

But this incredible see-saw game had yet another twist, because, at the other end, up popped Paul again to complete his hat-trick with another thrilling score. However, chances of the game's second miraculous comeback were snuffed out when Apollo Perelini restored Saints' two-try advantage by taking Goulding's drop-off pass. The captain's conversion took the score to 40-32, and Saints had finally seen off a superb Bulls challenge to win an amazing final. Goulding was accompanied up the Wembley steps by his two-and-a-half-year-old son Bobbie, a future Super League player with Wakefield. As Goulding senior lifted the famous trophy, some may have felt that he deserved the Lance Todd Trophy, too.

Brian Smith, the Bulls coach, was quick to defend Nathan Graham, his fullback who had been left bewildered by Goulding's bombardment. "All those who'd like to be at the back to catch those balls, with people coming through with baseball bats and hand grenades, should form a queue outside my office on Monday morning," he quipped.

A jubilant Goulding said: "We worked hard on the kicks in every single training session, and our call for the bombs was 'Graham!'. In the first half I thought he was outstanding but Shaun said to me to keep going at him and he would crack. He was just right."

Both clubs went on to enjoy an outstanding 1996, with Saints adding the inaugural Super League title to their Wembley success, while the Bulls established themselves as a force on and off the field, laying the groundwork for a magnificent decade of their own.

Bradford's Nathan Graham fails to deal with a Bobbie Goulding bomb for the third time, leading to Ian Pickavance's try

St Helens captain Bobbie Goulding lifts
the Challenge Cup, flanked by
Steve Prescott and Karle Hammond

Robbie Paul holds off Chris Joynt,
Ian Pickavance and Anthony Sullivan to
score his second try of the game

Vila Matautia takes on Paul Loughlin

ST HELENS 40
BRADFORD BULLS 32

ST HELENS
1 Steve Prescott
14 Danny Arnold
3 Scott Gibbs
4 Paul Newlove
5 Anthony Sullivan
6 Karle Hammond
7 Bobbie Goulding (C)
8 Apollo Perelini
9 Keiron Cunningham
17 Andy Leathem
11 Chris Joynt
12 Simon Booth
23 Chris Morley
Subs:
20 Tommy Martyn
10 Ian Pickavance
22 Vila Matautia
21 Alan Hunte

Tries: Prescott 2, Arnold 2,
Cunningham, Booth, Pickavance,
Perelini **Goals:** Goulding 4

BRADFORD
10 Nathan Graham
7 Paul Cook
20 Matt Calland
24 Paul Loughlin
5 Jon Scales
3 Graeme Bradley
1 Robbie Paul (C)
22 Brian McDermott
23 Bernard Dwyer
19 Jon Hamer
11 Jeremy Donougher
13 Sonny Nickle
18 Simon Knox
Subs:
21 Karl Fairbank
12 Paul Medley
9 Jason Donohue
17 Carlos Hassan

Tries: Scales, Paul 3, Dwyer
Goals: Cook 6

Half-time: 12-14
Referee: Stuart Cummings
Crowd: 75,994

TOUR DE FARCE!

The 1927 New Zealand tour of Great Britain was a shambles which had embarrassed Rugby League. Sixty-nine years later, the roles were reversed as a Lions tour descended into chaos and farce.

The tour had been going badly enough before Maurice Lindsay, architect-in-chief of the European Super League, shocked everybody by sending home a dozen players, with two Tests against New Zealand remaining, to save on hotel bills. It quickly proved to be a sizeable public-relations own goal and destroyed whatever morale was left in the squad.

The Australia leg of the tour had been cancelled due to the Super League War, before Great Britain's back-line was decimated by the unavailability of Jason Robinson, Gary Connolly, Paul Newlove and Shaun Edwards.

The Lions lost the first Test after a couple of late tries followed the sin-binning of the impressive young forward Adrian Morley. Halfbacks Bobbie Goulding and Iestyn Harris had failed to click, although Great Britain had led for most of the game and seemingly had something to build on.

Instead of that, Lindsay totally undermined his own position by dropping one of the biggest clangers in Rugby League's modern history, despite having regularly argued that the switch to summer would result in a new era of professionalism and good business practice. His foe Ken Arthurson, chief executive of the Australian Rugby League, Super League's big enemy down under, couldn't believe his ears – nor his luck. "It's a shocking indictment on Super League," he said. "This is amateur stuff. Incompetent is a strong word, but what else is it?"

In one stroke of a pen, Rugby League became a laughing stock as TV3, a national channel which had shown little interest in the tour, filmed the outcasts drowning their sorrows in Rowland Phillips' hotel room. The big Welshman had penned an amusing poem about the fiasco and read it to the cameras, while midweek skipper James Lowes was interviewed, clearly the worse for wear. Back in the UK, 'The Observer' queried: "What has happened

> **"It's a shocking indictment on Super League. This is amateur stuff. Incompetent is a strong word, but what else is it?"**

The Great Britain squad wait in Port Moresby airport

to Murdoch's millions?" They concluded, scathingly, that "Lindsay's vision was too grand by half." The front page of the next 'League Express' carried three headlines which summed up the feelings of many: "League in crisis", "Tour de farce" and "Should Maurice go?"

The wounds were entirely self-inflicted and the game was made to look badly run and amateurish. Rather ironically, at a time when the Rugby Football League needed a strong response to the horrendous publicity, Lindsay had just sacked the game's media manager, Paul Harrison.

The midweek team had just been beaten 40-28 by a Maori XIII in Whangarei. On the next morning, they were informed that they would be catching the 2.30pm plane home on the Thursday. Training was cancelled and was replaced by an impromptu pool party.

The players to be sent home were Lowes, Phillips, Steve Prescott, Keith Senior, Tulsen Tollett, Jon Roper, Brian McDermott, David Bradbury and Neil Harmon, while Jason Critchley, Joey Hayes and Mick Cassidy were injured anyway. The dozen weren't with the players who were in Palmerston North preparing for the second Test, and therefore didn't have the chance to say their farewells. Some had already arranged for their partners to fly out at the end of the tour.

Just 20 players remained with two Tests still to play and an injury to Daryl Powell meant that the Keith Senior decision was reversed. Tony Smith, with an arm infection, joined those leaving early. Days later Tollett was asked to return from Sydney and be on stand-by for the third Test. McDermott's fiancée was due to join him in Sydney for their wedding. He was another player asked to stay, but having already rearranged his partner's flights, he refused. The RFL then inadvertently wired his tour payments into the bank account of Barrie McDermott, who hadn't even toured.

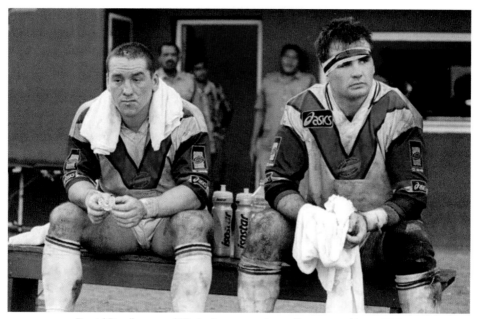

David Bradbury and Chris Joynt ponder a disastrous Lions tour

The usually upbeat skipper Andy Farrell said: "Everybody is really down. What is hurting us all, and especially me as captain, is not being able to say thanks and goodbye. The powers-that-be have taken this decision and it's left a nasty taste."

It had been anticipated that the tour of Papua New Guinea, Fiji and New Zealand would make a profit, although a fiscal headache was always likely with the Ashes series cancelled. The first two destinations were never likely to return a profit, but the Kiwi leg had been poorly supported and Lindsay was quick to blame the New Zealanders for over-estimating receipts at the gate. One tour match in Wellington – a 30-22 defeat to a New Zealand XIII – attracted a crowd of just 3,000. Before that, the full Test team had opened the New Zealand part of the tour against a Lion Red XIII and had only managed a draw in front of a mere 5,000 spectators. "The financial projections of gate receipts given to us by the NZRL have been widely optimistic to say the least," Lindsay protested.

The tour manager, Phil Lowe, a former Lion himself, fumed: "It is ridiculous. Things have happened on this tour that no other tour has had to put up with. It stinks. We don't have the money to pay the guys and we have been told we have to get it out of the New Zealand Rugby League from gate receipts." The players even had to pay their own taxi fares to Auckland airport and then a departure tax. According to Prescott, the returning players "were dumped in London, after flying economy class all the way home. In the end we paid for our own connecting flight back to Manchester."

Great Britain lost the Test series by three matches to nil and what had been a tremendously upbeat year for the sport in the UK as Super League was launched, ended in embarrassment.

Sunday, 28th September 1997

KNIGHTS WIN GREATEST GRAND FINAL

Having torn itself apart in the most exasperating way for two-and-a-half years, Rugby League in Australia desperately needed something to cheer and that moment came on the last Sunday of September in 1997 when Darren Albert's try for Newcastle against Manly, with seven seconds remaining in the ARL Grand Final, sparked wild scenes of celebration in the Hunter Valley and put smiles back on the faces of millions of fans.

For the city of Newcastle, which had been devastated by an earthquake three days after Christmas in 1989 that had killed 13 people and injured another 160, Albert's try precipitated pure jubilation. The Grand Final was played in the club's tenth year, and the city's 200th. Newcastle Workers Club, which had been destroyed in the earthquake, had never seen such intense scenes of celebrations. They later hosted the victorious players.

For the Knights' British coach, Malcolm Reilly, it was a well-deserved high in an excellent coaching career. Having won the Challenge Cup and the Australian Premiership as a player with Castleford and Manly, he had now completed the same double as a coach.

The build-up to the game was almost as dramatic with Sydney's 'Daily Telegraph' proclaiming that Andrew Johns, the superstar Knights halfback, "could die" if he took to the field with a punctured lung. Johns had cracked three ribs when scoring a try against Parramatta and when a painkilling injection went wrong during half-time of the next game against Norths, he was left with the damaged lung. But they were supremely confident, especially after a team meeting the night before, in which the club's long-serving loose forward, Marc Glanville, due to play his final match for the club, broke down in tears when explaining what a win would mean to him.

1996 premiers Manly, coached by Bob Fulton, were clear favourites and had beaten Newcastle in their last 11 meetings. They took a commanding 10-0 lead, albeit against the run of play, with tries from John Hopoate and Craig Innes before the Newcastle fullback, Robbie O'Davis, scored a fine individual

"We softened Manly's pack up so much that by the last ten minutes of the match, when we made our final surge, they had nothing left."

Lee Jackson leads the Newcastle celebrations following a thrilling Grand Final win

try. Shannon Nevin scored his side's third to give Manly a 16-8 lead at half-time. The scoreboard surprised few, although the sheer physicality of the game had been a revelation. Opposing Kangaroo props Mark Carroll and Paul Harragon had collided on several occasions with the latter hell bent on smashing anybody he could. Manly captain Geoff Toovey, in particular, was in the wars, at one point collapsing after attempting a tackle before stumbling again as he tried to stand up. "We softened Manly's pack up so much that by the last ten minutes of the match, when we made our final surge, they had nothing left," said Harragon.

The second half was tight and tense, setting the stage for the most incredible of endings. Johns's penalty reduced his side's deficit to six but, as the game went on, the Knights appeared to have little left. Johns, too, was suffering badly, but the message from Reilly was that he was to stay out there as he knew his side couldn't win without its talisman. Meanwhile, nobody was sure how Toovey remained on the field after Adam MacDougall trod on his head.

On 63 minutes, Nevin missed a penalty which would have put Manly ahead again by two scores. Albert returned the ball and made 40 metres but the set came to nothing. In the commentary box, Ray Warren noted that Newcastle's kicking game had had little purpose all afternoon while, at the other end, Albert needlessly conceded a goal-line drop-out. Warren's colleague Peter Sterling noted that Newcastle were "absolutely out on their feet" and that he couldn't see them "hanging on in this next set of six." Somehow, they did. A couple of minutes later the veteran Manly half, Cliff Lyons, missed a field-goal attempt from in front. It was reminiscent of Benny Elias in 1989.

The Knights managed to find the energy to get back up field and when, with six minutes to go, Johns found O'Davis, the eventual Clive Churchill medallist, under the shadow of the Manly posts, he seemed to be well marked. But he spun out of a tackle, beat Nevin and reached out to place the ball on the line to give Johns a simple conversion to level the scores.

Matthew Johns launched a drop-goal attempt with two minutes left but, after hanging in the air for an age, the ball thudded against the upright. Ninety seconds later, another attempt from the same player was charged down and the ball squirted to the right side of the field. The tension was unbearable. Six more tackles were awarded. Albert was tackled on the 20. Andrew Johns, at dummy-half, ignored his brother who wanted to attempt another one-point shot, and nipped down the blindside before slipping a pass to Albert. The defensive line opened up and the winger evaded Carroll's attempted ankle tap to score the most famous of Rugby League tries. There were just seven seconds left on the clock. It was the ultimate Roy of the Rovers ending, the like of which may never be repeated.

NEWCASTLE KNIGHTS 22
MANLY SEA EAGLES 16

NEWCASTLE
1 Robbie O'Davis
2 Darren Albert
3 Adam MacDougall
4 Owen Craigie
5 Mark Hughes
6 Matthew Johns
7 Andrew Johns
8 Tony Butterfield
9 Bill Peden
10 Paul Harragon (C)
11 Wayne Richards
12 Adam Muir
13 Marc Glanville
Subs:
15 Troy Fletcher
16 Scott Conley
18 Lee Jackson
19 Steve Crowe

Tries: O'Davis 2, Albert **Goals:** Johns 5

MANLY
1 Shannon Nevin
2 Danny Moore
3 Craig Innes
4 Terry Hill
5 John Hopoate
6 Geoff Toovey (C)
7 Craig Field
17 David Gillespie
15 Anthony Colella
10 Mark Carroll
11 Steve Menzies
12 Daniel Gartner
13 Nik Kosef
Subs:
8 Neil Tierney
9 Cliff Lyons
14 Scott Fulton
16 Andrew Hunter

Tries: Hopoate, Innes, Nevin
Goals: Nevin 2

Half-time: 8-16
Referee: David Manson
Crowd: 42,482

Saturday, 2nd May 1998

SHEFFIELD STUN WIGAN AT WEMBLEY

*"*The Crazy Gang have beaten the Culture Club," concluded John Motson as the 1988 FA Cup Final ended. The unthinkable had just happened.

Wimbledon, a minuscule club who only came into the bottom division of the Football League in 1977, had beaten the all-conquering Liverpool.

Ten years later, an almost identical story unfolded in Rugby League as Sheffield Eagles, a club which had only been conceived in 1984, beat Wigan, who had won even more trophies than Liverpool. Despite the generally accepted rhetoric, both Wimbledon and the Eagles were far better teams than they were given credit for. Sheffield had been in the top flight for six years, and had never been in danger of relegation, regularly proving to be a thorn in the sides of the top clubs. Their props and halfbacks, such vital positions, were at least on a par with those of their illustrious opponents.

As they proved, Sheffield were indeed capable of beating Wigan, as they had done before, but what made their achievement so remarkable was that they were a tiny organisation. Those calling the club with a general enquiry would sometimes find the phone answered by the team coach, John Kear. In many ways they weren't much bigger than an amateur club. Yet they were competitive and over the years had assembled a fine side, even though the driving force of the club for many years, Gary Hetherington, was now in charge at Leeds. A couple of Great Britain internationals, Daryl Powell and Lee Jackson, had also moved on.

Wigan's domination of the sport had ended in 1996 and a year later they struggled badly, limping home in fourth place in Super League. They were also beaten by a 12-man St Helens team in the Challenge Cup and, like most English teams, were subjected to regular batterings in the extended World Club Championship. They rebuilt for 1998 and boasted a star-studded backline along with a more-than-competent pack.

When Wigan were at Wembley in 1984 playing Widnes, Sheffield were

"They said that we were the underdogs. They didn't realise that we had a pack full of Rottweilers, backs who were Yorkshire Terriers, 13 bulldogs and every one could run like a bloody greyhound."

yet to play a match. The seeds of the club had been sewn in 1982 when Hetherington missed out on the coach's job at York. With the encouragement of his wife, Kath, he decided that the best way to secure such a position was to set up his own club. At the eleventh hour, the club's major sponsor, Telvista, went bust, putting into doubt the very existence of the club and after plans to play home games at Bramall Lane had fallen through, the Eagles moved into the much smaller Owlerton Stadium. They posted a crowd of 1,214 for their opening match against Rochdale Hornets in September 1984, in which a hat-trick from Paul McDermott, older brother of future Leeds coach Brian, helped them to a 29-12 win. Hetherington kicked a drop goal.

Fifteen years later, having beaten Leigh, Egremont, Castleford and Salford, the Eagles had reached Wembley. The Headingley semi-final against the Reds had been a classic, decided by a late Dale Laughton try. Then they had four Super League matches to play before the big day. They lost the first three, two of them at home, but bounced back to beat the bottom side Huddersfield. However many had written off their chances of winning the final - after all, Wigan were top of Super League having won all four of their matches, including a comprehensive win at St Helens at Easter.

The bookmakers may have given the Eagles a 22-point start, but they got off to a great start when Mark Aston's fourth-minute kick was plucked out of the air by Nick Pinkney, who touched down. Twenty-four minutes later they were over again through Matt Crowther in the corner. Aston

SHEFFIELD EAGLES 17
WIGAN WARRIORS 8

SHEFFIELD
1 Waisale Sovatabua
2 Nick Pinkney
3 Whetu Taewa
4 Keith Senior
6 Matt Crowther
22 Dave Watson
7 Mark Aston
8 Paul Broadbent (C)
9 John Lawless
10 Dale Laughton
11 Paul Carr
12 Darren Shaw
19 Rod Doyle
Subs:
15 Darren Turner
17 Michael Jackson
24 Martyn Wood
25 Lynton Stott (dnp)

Tries: Pinkney, Crowther, Turner
Goals: Aston 2 **Drop goal:** Aston

WIGAN
1 Kris Radlinski
2 Jason Robinson
3 Gary Connolly
4 Danny Moore
5 Mark Bell
6 Henry Paul
7 Tony Smith
17 Stephen Holgate
9 Robbie McCormack
10 Tony Mestrov
11 Denis Betts
12 Simon Haughton
13 Andy Farrell (C)
Subs:
8 Neil Cowie
14 Mick Cassidy
16 Terry O'Connor
20 Lee Gilmour

Try: Bell **Goals:** Farrell 2

Half-time: 11-2
Referee: Stuart Cummings
Crowd: 60,669

Mark Aston and Paul Broadbent lift the Challenge Cup

Sheffield celebrate Darren Turner's try as Wigan captain Andy Farrell looks on

goaled the second try for a 10-0 lead. Wigan captain Andy Farrell pulled back two points but Aston's drop goal gave the Eagles a nine-point half-time advantage.

Three or four Wigan tries in the second half would have surprised nobody, but they had to settle for just one, from winger Mark Bell, and even that came after Sheffield's third try which was scored by substitute hooker Darren Turner under the posts. Aston, who would win the Lance Todd Trophy, kicked the simple goal. Farrell thought he had scored soon after Bell's try but Stuart Cummings ruled that he had been held up, awarding a scrum to Wigan five metres out. The Warriors captain lost his temper with the referee and was penalised. The incident was a microcosm of Wigan's miserable day.

Sheffield's chairman Tim Adams, appointed MBE in 2017, had bet £1,000 at odds of 33-1 at the start of the season that his side would win the Cup. He summed up the day better than anybody. "They said that we were the underdogs. They didn't realise that we had a pack full of Rottweilers, backs who were Yorkshire Terriers, 13 bulldogs and every one could run like a bloody greyhound."

CARIGE MELTDOWN AS CANTERBURY REACH FINAL

B reathtaking comebacks happen, as do late tries, but what also made this 1998 NRL semi-final so memorable was the display of Paul Carige, who suffered the Rugby League version of the yips at the worst possible time. The bizarre nature of his mistakes went hand in hand with the incredible disintegration of his Parramatta team in nine agonising minutes, in which they blew an 18-2 lead.

The Eels hadn't won a Premiership since 1986 when such legends as Brett Kenny, Peter Sterling, Mick Cronin and Ray Price graced their team, but they enjoyed a promising season in 1998, finishing in fourth, just two points off the Minor Premiers Brisbane Broncos. They beat North Sydney Bears and even the mighty Broncos in the play-offs to move to within one match of the Grand Final.

Canterbury, on the other hand, had been less consistent, finishing ninth, and were only rescued by the NRL's one-off decision to have a ten-team play-off. But, free from public expectations, they beat eighth-placed St George and fifth-placed North Sydney. A week later, the Bulldogs looked dead and buried, finding themselves 16 points behind an Andrew Johns-inspired Newcastle, before storming back to win 28-16 in extra-time. That game marked the last in the Australian coaching career of the Knights' Malcolm Reilly. "People can keep writing us off," said the Dogs stand-off Glen Hughes. "But we'll keep proving them wrong." Someone at Parramatta should have listened.

Before a packed Sydney Football Stadium, the Eels were in complete control of the semi-final. Ball-handling loose forward Jim Dymock was on top form, whereas Canterbury looked like a side who were waiting for the end of the season. Two tries from winger Shane Whereat and another from Clinton Schifcofske had the Eels 18-2 up with just ten minutes left. In the Channel Nine commentary box, Sterling was purring. At last, it looked like Parramatta might have a team to compare to his champions.

When the Bulldogs' influential but inconsistent halfback Craig Polla-Mounter scored with ten minutes to go, it seemed pretty meaningless, especially

"He's made some of the dumbest plays I've ever seen in a game of Rugby League."

239

when super-boot Daryl Halligan, the Kiwi winger, surprisingly missed the goal. Rod Silva then took Robert Relf's offload three minutes later to scorch over the try line, and when Halligan kicked the goal from near the left touchline, suddenly the Dogs were back to within six points and Parramatta's worst nightmare was beginning to unfold. They were running out of steam at the worst possible time.

The Dogs smelt blood and when their left centre Willie Talau got on the outside of the defence to score out wide, everything hinged upon Halligan's attempted goal. With two minutes left on the clock, he nailed a magnificent kick from near the touchline. It remains one of the NRL's most famous moments, and it came in the first season of the newly named competition.

The Eels were shot, and that was no better illustrated than in the last minute when Carige, upon hearing the final hooter, inexplicably, on the first tackle, hoofed the ball forward for no apparent reason from under the shadow of his own posts. Polla-Mounter fielded the ball on halfway and responded with a snap drop-goal.

Time stood still as the ball hung in the air. Noise levels peaked. Polla-Mounter celebrated wildly with his teammates, but referee Bill Harrigan wisely consulted with the video referee. Fortunately for Carige, Polla-Mounter's kick had dropped centimetres short. The game was still alive.

Carige's nightmare continued in extra time even though he had been shifted from fullback to the left wing. Twice he caught the ball and stepped into touch. He had already conceded

---

CANTERBURY BULLDOGS 32
PARRAMATTA EELS 20
(after extra-time)

CANTERBURY
1 Rod Silva
2 Gavin Lester
3 Shane Marteene
4 Willie Talau
5 Daryl Halligan
6 Craig Polla-Mounter
7 Corey Hughes
8 Darren Britt (C)
9 Jason Hetherington
10 Steve Price
11 Tony Grimaldi
12 Robert Relf
13 Travis Norton
Subs:
15 Troy Stone
16 Glen Hughes
17 Matt Ryan
19 David Thompson

Tries: Polla-Mounter 2, Silva, Talau, Norton **Goals:** Halligan 5 **Drop goals:** Polla-Mounter 2

PARRAMATTA
1 Paul Carige
21 Clinton Schifcofske
3 Karl Lovell
4 Stuart Kelly
5 Shane Whereat
12 Jason Smith
7 John Simon
8 Dean Pay (C)
9 Aaron Raper
10 Mark Tookey
11 Jarrod McCracken (C)
15 Nathan Hindmarsh
13 Jim Dymock
Subs:
14 David Penna
6 Jason Bell
16 Nathan Cayless
17 Dallas Weston

Tries: Whereat 2, Schifcofske **Goals:** Schifcofske 3, Simon

Half-time: 2-12
Referee: Bill Harrigan
Crowd: 36,841

Jason Hetherington and Troy Stone jump for joy after the Bulldogs' extra-time win

a needless goal-line drop-out "He's made some of the dumbest plays I've ever seen in a game of Rugby League," moaned an exasperated Sterling.

Polla-Mounter lined up another drop goal 40 seconds into extra-time and this time was successful. He followed it up with a try a couple of minutes later and then another one-point kick to cap a wonderful individual performance. When Travis Norton scored the clinching try on 98 minutes, it sealed a comeback of stunning proportions. Sterling was too upset to speak, according to his colleague Ray Warren.

Canterbury's momentum was finally killed off by the Broncos in the second half of the Grand Final, but the Bulldogs had displayed a never-say-die attitude in the preceding fortnight which had captured the imagination of those who had been lucky enough to see them play.

Paul Carige didn't play again in the NRL, fleeing the Sydney media and angry Eels fans, moving to Salford in 1999. He failed to shine at The Willows, staying for just one year. The Eels bounced back in 2001, winning the Minor Premiership in style, but again fell agonisingly short when they were beaten in the Grand Final by Newcastle despite being overwhelming favourites to win the trophy.

Friday, 9th July 1999

ELLERY HANLEY ROUNDS ON ST HELENS DIRECTORS

Shaun McRae left St Helens after three seasons as head coach at the end of 1998, having won two Challenge Cups and a Super League title. The club decided not to renew his contract and instead, in what was a genuine coup, deciding to bring in Ellery Hanley for his first major club head-coaching role.

Hanley had worked on the coaching staff when he played for Leeds and had coached Great Britain in the 1994 Ashes series and England in the 1995 European Championship. He had since ended his playing career with Balmain Tigers in Australia. Despite being away from British Rugby League for three and a half years, he remained its biggest name. He would only stay at Knowsley Road for one full season - but what an incredible rollercoaster it turned out to be. Having endured a disappointing 1998, Saints won 13 of their first 14 Super League fixtures under Hanley, although that was followed by four defeats in five.

On the morning of Friday 9th July, a bombshell was dropped. Hanley had conducted one of the most stunning interviews that anyone in Rugby League could remember, telling 'Total Rugby League', the sister paper of 'League Express', that the club directors were endangering the health of their young players. "Everybody is saying that we have gone through a form dip, but we haven't," he said. "The problem is that our squad is not strong enough. If we are going to be successful we need an injection of players. I am having to blood kids of 17, some of whom have only had one game, and that's unfair on them."

Hanley went on to criticise the club's "disappointing and disgraceful" directors, pointing out they failed to telephone Halifax's Martin Moana who was willing to join the club and that they would not increase their offer to New Zealand's Jarrod McCracken, who wanted an extra £10,000. "We need fresh blood upstairs, in the club's hierarchy," he said. "If the St Helens directors really do have the club's best interests at heart, they have to broaden their horizons. The problem is the dinosaur-like thinking of the directors. We need to start afresh. I know for sure that there are so many people out there who would love to take over St Helens. They can't do a worse job that what's happening now."

The interview perhaps galvanised the squad as they won 21-16 at

PRACTICE IS USELESS
WITHOUT
QUALITY
AND
INTENSITY

Sheffield 24 hours later, with Hanley receiving a rousing reception from the travelling Saints fans before telling the media: "If [the directors] want to come and tell me that my services are no longer required, then that is completely up to them." Hanley also pointed to a strained relationship with the Saints' chief executive. "The fact that Eric Hughes doesn't talk to me is pretty poor really. All I am trying to do is run a football side to the best of my ability, and everyone has got to pull in the same direction." Twenty-five people called a Greater Manchester Radio phone-in, with 23 supporting the former Great Britain captain.

"It's true that socially we don't talk," Hughes responded. "Our worlds are miles apart but my office door is ten yards from his and it's always open. For nearly a decade he wouldn't talk to the press. Why has he suddenly become a big pal of the media now? I can only speculate, but I just wonder if it is because we've lost four games out of five." Hughes also claimed that Hanley had wanted to get rid of star players Keiron Cunningham and Tommy Martyn in favour of little-known Hunslet hooker Richard Pachniuk and Leeds stand-off Graham Holroyd. Hanley emphatically denied having any knowledge of such deals. He was also keen to point out that the signing of the little-used Australian prop Phil Adamson was nothing to do with him. The player hit

"Ellery Hanley does not eat humble pie!"

back at Hanley's treatment of him.

The board met three days after Hanley's initial interview and decided to suspend him. "I think he expected it," said the club chairman, Howard Morris, a solicitor. With a legal dispute inevitable, Hanley's own lawyer, Richard Cramer, said: "My initial instructions from Ellery are that he would like the suspension lifted." Hanley missed one match – a 74-16 win over bottom-place Hull during which such banners as "Sack the board and Hughes" and "Bring back Ellery" were spotted on the terraces. Some of the crowd even booed the club physio Jeanette Smith, the girlfriend of Hughes.

With the suspension lifted, Hanley returned to work for a vital trip to Challenge Cup winners Leeds and issued the following statement: "I regret my involvement in the events of the last couple of weeks and my comments suggesting that the board is in any way old-fashioned and unprofessional," but he rounded on journalists after a fine win at Headingley who suggested he had been forced into an embarrassing climbdown. "Ellery Hanley does not eat humble pie!" he pointed out rather forcefully to the perpetrator of the suggestion.

With Hanley back in charge, St Helens finished second in Super League behind Bradford, but in a play-off match at Odsal they were thumped 40-4. A fortnight later, they produced a defensive masterclass to turn the tables on the Bulls, beating them 8-6 in a wonderfully entertaining Grand Final at Old Trafford three months to the day after Hanley's interview.

1999 remains one of the most action-packed years in the glorious history of St Helens and it did much to fuel the mysterious legend of Ellery Hanley, but six months later he was out of a job, sacked for apparently making inappropriate comments at a sponsors' lunch, for failing to conduct an interview with the BBC before a match and for his alleged non-attendance the launch of the new Super League season. Hanley has never coached in the top flight since, but he did lead Doncaster to promotion in 2007 – his only subsequent year as a head coach. His absence from top-flight coaching since 2000 has been Rugby League's loss.

Friday, 22nd September 2000

WIDE TO WEST!

For 78 minutes Dwayne West, the son of the former Wigan and New Zealand forward Graeme, sat on the bench at Knowsley Road watching his St Helens side struggle at home to Bradford Bulls in the first match of the 2000 Super League play-off series.

He was a bit-part player, who had started just three matches all season. In fact, in three seasons he'd been selected in the starting 13 in just eight games, and would leave the club at the end of the season and play Super League no longer. A blood-bin injury to the former Great Britain centre Paul Newlove meant that West would play some part in this game but, with his side losing and only two minutes remaining, nobody was expecting miracles.

However, West was to play a huge role in the most sensational 60 seconds in Super League's short history and was memorably featured in one of the most famous pieces of Rugby League commentary as he took Sean Long's pass, set off downfield and released his captain, Chris Joynt, who took the ball and finished off a quite unbelievable try.

Eddie: "That's going to be the match for Bradford."

Stevo: "He's given a penalty."

Eddie: "Oh he has!"

Stevo: "He'd called held there. They're still not out of it. They've taken a short one. They know they've only got ten seconds. Will they get this play-the-ball in? They're holding him down."

Eddie: "Sculthorpe wants to get on with it. Bradford counting down."

Stevo: "Kick and chase!"

Eddie: "This is the last play. Long kicks it wide to Iro. Iro to Hall. Hall is trapped. Back it goes to Hoppe. Over the shoulder to Hall. There is Jonkers. Here is Long. And Long fancies it. Long fancies it! It's wide to West. It's wide to West! Dwayne West. Inside to Joynt. Joynt. Joynt! Jooooynt! Oh! Ohhh! Fantastic!"

Stevo: "I don't believe it!"

Eddie: "They've won it! They've won it! Chris Joynt, Chris Joynt has won it. It is unbelievable here. It is frankly unbelievable! Chris Joynt has won the match for St Helens."

"It is unbelievable here. It is frankly unbelievable!"

245

Super League had never seen anything like it. This immortal try has since been christened 'Wide to West' after the wonderful commentary of Sky Sports' Eddie Hemmings which, itself, has gone down in Rugby League folklore. It even made the Bradford coach, Matthew Elliott, fall off his chair. The celebrations went on for minutes, with the St Helens mascot St Bernard in the middle of them. Long wanted to take the conversion with St Bernard's head on, but referee Russell Smith wouldn't allow it.

A week earlier, Saints had been hammered 42-4 at home by Wigan in a match to decide which of the north-west giants would finish top of the table. Saints' turnaround was stunning, especially as it came against Bradford, the Challenge Cup winners and a side who had topped the table for much of the season. "Forget what a great try it was," said Joynt, modestly. "Just marvel at a great game. If you look over the 80 minutes it was a quality game from two great sides vying for a place in the next round and it was a great performance from St Helens to come back like that."

St Helens had fallen behind to a 24th-minute try from Jamie Peacock, who had gone through a weak Newlove tackle to go over at the scoreboard end of the ground. It was the only score of an absorbing half as Henry Paul missed the goal, but two tries in four minutes midway through the second half saw the hosts exert their authority. First, Kiwi Sean Hoppe scored in the corner. Then Tommy Martyn, who had been named in the Dream Team earlier in the week along with Peacock and Long, dummied his way over in the 59th minute to make it 10-4 to Saints. Leon Pryce then took

---

ST HELENS 16
BRADFORD BULLS 11

ST HELENS
17 Paul Wellens
15 Sean Hoppe
3 Kevin Iro
4 Paul Newlove
5 Anthony Sullivan
20 Tommy Martyn
7 Sean Long
8 Apollo Perelini
9 Keiron Cunningham
10 Julian O'Neill
11 Chris Joynt (C)
22 Tim Jonkers
13 Paul Sculthorpe
Subs:
14 Fereti Tuilagi
26 John Stankevitch
24 Steve Hall
21 Dwayne West

Tries: Hoppe, Martyn, Joynt
Goals: Long 2

Sin bin: Joynt

BRADFORD
28 Stuart Spruce
3 Leon Pryce
5 Michael Withers
20 Scott Naylor
2 Tevita Vaikona
6 Henry Paul
7 Paul Deacon
22 Brian McDermott
9 James Lowes (C)
10 Paul Anderson
12 Mike Forshaw
19 Jamie Peacock
13 Brad Mackay
Subs:
29 Stuart Fielden
1 Robbie Paul
15 Hudson Smith
4 Nathan McAvoy

Tries: Peacock, Pryce **Goal:** H Paul
Drop goal: H Paul

Half-time: 0-4
Referee: Russell Smith
Crowd: 8,864

Wild celebrations begin as Chris Joynt scores St Helens' last-gasp winning try

Sean Long and Chris Joynt join the jubilant St Helens fans after a stunning win

Long's kick close to his own line and went the length of the field to score the Bulls' second try. Paul's touchline goal locked up the game with 15 minutes left.

Joynt had a try disallowed before Paul kicked the Bulls into an 11-10 lead with a little under nine minutes to go. Technically speaking, they actually did hold out for those nine minutes as Joynt's crushing blow came after the hooter. As for Joynt, there was a degree of irony in the fact that such a mild-mannered and modest man should score Super League's most famous try, yet see it named after somebody else.

The Bulls recovered to hammer Leeds the following week before their season ended at Wigan a week before the Grand Final. Joynt's try, on the other hand, ignited an unstoppable Saints charge. They were crowned Super League champions at Old Trafford a few weeks later after beating Wigan 29-16.

STERLING ACCUSES LEEDS OF RACIAL DISCRIMINATION

As Leeds Rhinos began their week's training ahead of a trip to Odsal for their side's elimination play-off match with Bradford in 2000, a bombshell was dropped. News emerged that Paul Sterling was taking the club to an employment tribunal on the grounds of racial discrimination. The three-day hearing ended just three days before the game. It was a sad episode for a sport which had done more than most to eradicate racism and for a club which has always led the way in so many areas during the summer era.

It had been a difficult year for the Rhinos, the first after Graham Murray's fondly remembered two-year reign. New coach Dean Lance had initially struggled in the position, having to contend with fans singing the name of his predecessor. Leeds were joint bottom of Super League when they faced table-topping Bradford in the Challenge Cup Final at Murrayfield at the end of April. They may have only lost 24-18, but the score flattered Leeds.

By this stage of the season, Sterling was yet to appear in the side. He had been told by Lance on 9th February, four days before the first game of the season, that he was sixth in the pecking order for the wing spots and that he would not be selected, irrespective of performance.

"I sought advice from the Commission for Racial Equality and the Leeds Racial Equality Council, as the only explanation I could think of was that I was being discriminated due to race," Sterling, then 36, told the tribunal. He also claimed that "all the other black players felt alienated. He [Lance] didn't start speaking to them until I submitted this claim."

The club's chief executive, Gary Hetherington, supported Lance and claimed that he "investigated [Sterling's] claim very thoroughly. I questioned other players, and they all said there was no evidence at all of racial discrimination. We have more black players than any other club, and we have been more active than any, as far as I am aware, in implementing the anti-racism policies developed by the RFL."

Lance was asked if black players played Rugby League in Australia and replied, rather ill-advisedly, that "those boys" play basketball and other sports. He denied Sterling's claim, maintaining that he had been excluded from the side because his training and fitness levels had been below the required standards and that other players were ahead of him in the pecking order.

Sterling made his first appearance of the season on 26th May in a 26-19 win over Wigan - the first of 13 consecutive wins, which took the club from eighth to fourth, where they finished the season. Before the Wigan game, Lance had told the media: "We need a winger who is in form and has confidence. I told Paul he would get a chance when his fitness and form warrant it, and he has forced his way back into the team - deservedly so. He said he'd be back, and he has put his money where his mouth is. I am not going to hold back on him." Earlier in the season, Francis Cummins and Keith Senior had started on the wing, with the latter moving into the centres when Paul Bell sustained a season-ending injury. Before Sterling's first appearance, Karl Pratt also featured on the wing, as did Leroy Rivett, Chev Walker and Marcus St Hilaire.

In September, Lance and Sterling returned to training without knowing the outcome of the tribunal. The winger was named on the bench for the match at Odsal, despite an injury concern. Sterling played more than half the match, scoring a late try as the hapless Rhinos were thrashed 46-12. The coach denied that the week's extraordinary events had affected morale. "It has been a difficult week but the boys were jumping out of their skin on Thursday and Friday. The effort was there. We just didn't play great." Barrie McDermott, on the other hand, believed the opposite, according to his autobiography. "It would have been nice for Moz [Adrian Morley] to bow out of Leeds with a Super League Grand Final appearance in 2000, but that was never really on the cards considering what was going on behind the scenes at Headingley at the end of that season."

The tribunal reached its decision at the end of October, broadly coming down in favour of Sterling. The club was criticised for demonstrating "a lack of understanding of insidious and unconscious race discrimination". It was also ruled that they had failed to investigate Sterling's complaints properly. Sterling's allegation, however, that there was evidence of "ethnic cleansing and racial discrimination within the club" were dismissed. The tribunal stressed its belief that Lance was a "professional and honourable man," but that his pre-season comment to Sterling that he would not play for the side "irrespective of performance" had been ill-considered. As for Lance's "those boys" comment, the judge concluded: "that remark rang alarm bells in the mind of each member of this tribunal." The club was advised not to take "a disproportionate view of [Lance's] culpability." Hetherington said: "We are naturally pleased that many serious allegations have been completely rejected but we are mindful that lessons must be learned and we will be conducting a thorough review of our internal procedures."

On 15th December the Tribunal ruled that the club should pay the player £16,000. This comprised a £10,000 payment for injury to feeling, £5,250 for loss of opportunity to win match bonuses and an interest payment just over £750. They were also ordered to hand Sterling, whose annual salary was

"Those boys play basketball."

Paul Sterling and Dean Lance (*below*) both encountered a turbulent season in 2000

£19,500, a playing contract for 2001. The club appealed the decision which put the winger's new deal on the back-burner, meaning he had to train on his own. "The appeal means I can't go back to the club and you could be into June or July for when the appeal will be conducted," said the player. "Obviously I'm in limbo in that time."

Sterling eventually announced his retirement from the game on 12th April 2001, citing a loss of appetite for Rugby League whilst launching a sports-management company on the same day. "As a direct result of the problems with Leeds Rhinos, I have decided to retire," he said. "Last year was extremely difficult for me bearing in mind that I was racially discriminated against in February and was exonerated in October. I had to play the whole season knowing that I had been unfairly treated. I could have moved down a division but the desire had gone and there was no point staying."

It was a sad ending to a sorry episode.

KANGAROOS RATTLED
BY A WELSH WHIRLWIND

The Rugby League World Cup has thrown up an abundance of drama down the years, but the night Wales scored 20 unanswered points in the first half of a crazy semi-final against runaway favourites Australians has to rank with anything it has ever produced.

Those glorious moments took place in Huddersfield on a Sunday night in November 2000 when British Rugby League morale was at its lowest point since 1982, due to England's shellacking at the hands of the awesome Kiwis the day before. The tournament had fallen way below everybody's expectations, and Australia were expected to run up a huge score in the second semi-final.

It all seemed so simple for the Kangaroos when Brett Kimmorley and Wendell Sailor scored early tries. A team that also boasted world-class talent like Darren Lockyer, Brad Fittler, Shane Webcke, Gorden Tallis and Trent Barrett looked to be on course to rack up a point a minute.

Suddenly, from nowhere, Australia were hit by the most incredible Welsh whirlwind, and what made it even more miraculous was that they had several players from lower-division clubs, as well as Paul Moriarty and John Devereux, who hadn't played Rugby League for five years before the tournament. They and Jason Critchley, who had all been playing rugby union, had 'unattached' written next to their names on the team sheets. Wales were the ultimate rag-tag team, but they played with a spirit and determination that England could only dream of.

Firstly, Ian Watson, who played his club football in the Northern Ford Premiership with ninth-placed Swinton in 2000, crossed next to the posts after an offload from the Leeds forward Anthony Farrell. Then Salford's Kris Tassell scored after a bad bounce had wrong-footed the green-and-gold defence. Sky Sports' Eddie Hemmings was enraptured, summing up the feelings of complete disbelief as well as he could.

Then came a truly iconic World Cup moment. Iestyn Harris, nursing an injured shoulder at fullback, launched a huge up and under. The on-rushing Lee Briers timed his jump perfectly to beat the great fullback Lockyer to the ball, and

"We knew we could give them a fright and it was one of the proudest days of my career."

Ian Watson scores Wales' first try, despite the challenge of Darren Lockyer

somersault over the line in delight. Few could believe what they were seeing. Harris's goal had the Welsh in dreamland at 18-8, but they still weren't finished. At the end of the next set, Briers booted a long-range drop goal, and then, in the most surreal fashion, he did exactly the same at the end of the next set.

Wales had now scored 20 consecutive points against the best Australian tour party in many a year. The Rugby League World Cup had never seen anything like it, although Fittler halted the Welsh momentum by pulling a try back. The Welsh lead was cut to just 20-14 at half-time after the most extraordinary 40 minutes in World Cup history.

Wales still had the audacity to open the scoring in the second half with a Harris penalty, although that was as good as it got for them. Even so, it wasn't until the hour mark that the Australians actually hauled them back. Bryan Fletcher scored a try, Lockyer got two, with another Fittler try in between. Late on, Craig Gower and Ben Kennedy gave the score line an unrealistic edge and it finished 46-22.

The Huddersfield crowd was only 8,114 - a far cry from the Welsh 1995 semi-final crowd of 30,042 against England at Old Trafford - but those present will never forget what they witnessed in that unbelievable first half.

Briers recollected: "Did we believe we could win? Probably not, but we knew we could give them a fright and it was one of the proudest days of my career," he said. "The togetherness and spirit in the team was fantastic. It was a special day despite the eventual defeat. In Iestyn Harris's book he likened the Welsh to a club side. I certainly thought that when I came into the set-up. We didn't have many players to choose from so there's continuity there. England have so many to choose from that they sometimes struggle for the continuity and camaraderie which is massive in sport. It's there straightaway with Wales."

Australia went on to win the competition, comprehensively beating the Kiwis in the final, but it was that Welsh performance on that incredible Sunday evening in West Yorkshire, which captured the imagination of the Rugby League public.

Keiron Cunningham collared by Australia captain Brad Fittler

Kris Tassell dives past Darren Lockyer to score Wales' second try

Nathan Hindmarsh takes on Justin Morgan

AUSTRALIA 46 WALES 22

AUSTRALIA
1 Darren Lockyer
2 Adam MacDougall
3 Ryan Girdler
4 Matthew Gidley
5 Wendell Sailor
6 Brad Fittler (C)
7 Brett Kimmorley
8 Shane Webcke
9 Craig Gower
10 Michael Vella
11 Gorden Tallis
12 Bryan Fletcher
13 Scott Hill
Subs:
14 Trent Barrett
15 Robbie Kearns
16 Ben Kennedy
17 Nathan Hindmarsh

Tries: Kimmorley, Sailor, Fittler 2, Fletcher, Lockyer 2, Gower, Kennedy
Goals: Lockyer 4, Girdler

WALES
1 Iestyn Harris (C)
2 Chris Smith
3 Kris Tassell
4 Jason Critchley
5 Anthony Sullivan
6 Lee Briers
7 Ian Watson
8 Anthony Farrell
9 Keiron Cunningham
10 Paul Moriarty
11 Justin Morgan
12 Paul Highton
13 Chris Morley
Subs:
14 Wes Davies
15 Paul Atcheson
16 John Devereux
17 David Luckwell

Tries: Watson, Tassell, Briers
Goals: Harris 4
Drop goals: Briers 2

Half-time: 14-20
Referee: Russell Smith
Crowd: 8,124

LANGER'S AMAZING RETURN

Seven days after one of the most unexpected selection announcements in Australian Rugby League history, Allan Langer produced a virtuoso display in his State of Origin comeback to help the Maroons clinch an unlikely series win on 1st July in 2001. Australians who signed for Super League clubs in England did so knowing that their representative careers were over. The only people who had flown to Australia from England to play a part in Origin were referees Billy Thompson and Robin Whitfield, but in 2001 that all changed.

From the moment it had been announced by Gene Miles, chairman of the Queensland selectors and himself a former Maroon great, Langer's shock call-up from mid-table Warrington had dominated the Australian media all week. It was even reported that he had been booked onto a flight under a false name, as the Queensland Rugby League kept the move under wraps for as long as they could.

The Sydney media scoffed at the move, labelling it desperate. Peter Sterling, the New South Wales legend who had been retired for nearly ten years, joked that he might get a call-up too. The Blues' confidence was sky high. After all, the Maroons had been hammered 26-8 in game two, losing the series lead they had established with a fine 34-16 win in the first game. They were also without their fearsome captain Gorden Tallis, who had been ruled out for the season with a neck injury.

The Langer factor ensured that the build-up was huge. He strode onto the field behind skipper Darren Lockyer looking as fit and as ready as anyone, but Queensland's bubble was burst almost immediately when Blues centre Ryan Girdler scored the try quickest in Origin history after just 39 seconds following John Buttigieg's knock-on on the first tackle of the match. His finish was superb, dummying Wendell Sailor and handing off Darren Smith to score. The Blues centre converted his own try from out wide.

Eight minutes later Chris Walker got the Maroons on the board, finishing off a move that included impressive offloads from Lockyer and Brad Meyers.

"Bloody Alf! You flew 16,981km to break our hearts. Now, please go back to England!"

The centre took Lote Tuqiri's pass to score in the corner and although Lockyer missed the goal, Queensland, having gained a foothold in the match, dominated from here on in, with Langer and Lockyer in typically great form. Paul Bowman reached out to score in the 15th minute but Lockyer missed another conversion - this one very kickable, and his profligacy was punished as Girdler levelled the scores with a penalty. Lockyer eventually broke his duck with a simple penalty and when Langer set up a Dane Carlaw try with a great step and delayed offload, the skipper kicked another goal to set up a 16-8 lead. The multi-talented Test fullback then broke through from the back and kicked ahead for Walker to score his second. Lockyer had now found his kicking range and landed one from near the sideline.

There was still time in the first half for the two magicians to combine and when Lockyer ran on to Langer's inside ball to score, the game was up as Lockyer's fourth goal took the interval score to 28-8. Not in their wildest dreams did the Queenslanders expect this. Alfie's presence had lifted his teammates to such an extent that New South Wales just couldn't live with them. The only thing the crowd still wanted to see was a try for Langer himself, and he didn't disappoint. Early in the second half he took John Doyle's dummy-half pass close to the line, dummied, stepped and reached over to score a try that brought the house down. The joyous fans had everything they had come for now.

The centre Paul Bowman added his second, beating Brad Fittler with ease before Girdler also completed a brace. The last word, however, went to the official man of the match Darren Lockyer who scored his second try from Carl Webb's break to take the final score to 40-14.

"This is probably the best day of my life," said Langer after the match. "The last two weeks have been a fairytale and now it's come to a great end." However the quote of the night came from Peter Beattie, the 36th Premier of Queensland, who simply said: "We'll call him Sir Alfred!" The next day, the

Allan Langer celebrates scoring for Warrington in a 2001 Challenge Cup win against Leigh

Allan Langer leaves the field with teammates Brad Meyers and Wendell Sailor

'Daily Telegraph' in Sydney devoted their front page to the game, with the memorable headline: "Bloody Alf! You flew 16,981km to break our hearts. Now, please go back to England!"

A year earlier Sydneysiders had predicted that the State of Origin concept was finished as a viable concept when they secured a series whitewash with an embarrassingly easy 56-16 win at Stadium Australia. But the return of Wayne Bennett as coach, the form of Lockyer, who was fast becoming a modern-day legend, and the incredible selection of Langer for the decider when all had seemed lost, proved them all wrong. Origin was alive and well.

For Langer, though, it was a case of after the Lord Mayor's show. He returned to England and lost his next Warrington match by 70-16 at St Helens.

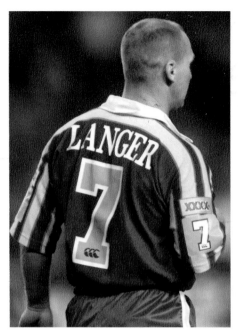

(*Above*) and (*below*):
A selection of photos from Allan Langer's
memorable Origin return in July 2001

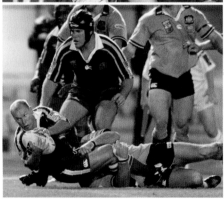

NEW SOUTH WALES 14
QUEENSLAND 40

NEW SOUTH WALES
1 Mark Hughes
2 Jamie Ainscough
3 Ryan Girdler
4 Matthew Gidley
5 Adam MacDougall
6 Brad Fittler (C)
7 Brett Kimmorley
8 Jason Stevens
9 Luke Priddis
10 Mark O'Meley
11 Bryan Fletcher
12 Adam Muir
13 Andrew Ryan
Subs:
14 Craig Gower
15 Michael Vella
16 Matt Adamson
17 Steve Menzies

Tries: Girdler 2 **Goals:** Girdler 3

QUEENSLAND
1 Darren Lockyer (C)
2 Lote Tuqiri
14 Chris Walker
4 Paul Bowman
5 Wendell Sailor
3 Daniel Wagon
7 Allan Langer
8 Shane Webcke
6 Paul Green
10 John Buttigieg
11 Petero Civoniceva
12 Brad Meyers
13 Darren Smith
Subs:
9 John Doyle
15 Kevin Campion
16 Carl Webb
17 Dane Carlaw

Tries: Lockyer 2, Walker 2, Bowman 2, Langer, Carlaw **Goals:** Lockyer 4

Half-time: 8-28
Referee: Bill Harrigan
Crowd: 49,441

CANTERBURY BULLDOGS GUILTY OF SALARY CAP CHEATING

Australian Rugby League was rocked to its foundations towards the end of the 2002 season, when the sensational news broke that its table-topping club Canterbury Bulldogs had been systematically cheating the salary cap for two years. Under the headline "Bulldogs bust the bank to stay on top", the 'Sydney Morning Herald' revealed that the club had breached the cap by $1.5 million in the 2001 and 2002 seasons.

Rumours that a big story was in the offing began to circulate one Friday midway through August as the Bulldogs were beating Parramatta 28-10 at the Sydney Showground. Intriguingly, David Gallop, the chief executive of the NRL, was attending the match as a guest of the club but this was the first he had heard of the story. Bulldogs Coach Steve Folkes and captain Steve Price were told the news after the game.

Clubs were allowed to spend $3.25 million on their top 25 players every year, but Canterbury were found to be at $4.05 million in 2001 and $3.95 million in 2002, which went a long way to explaining how they were top of the NRL table with 18 wins and a draw from 21 matches, which included a run of 17 straight victories.

It had long been rumoured that various clubs were cheating the cap with suggestions that they might give a player cash from one of the poker machines at their Leagues Club, or that they might employ a player's wife in some capacity, arrange for payments to be made from a sponsor directly to a player or that they might pay for a player's house renovations. The 'Herald' investigation even discovered payments being paid to a player's mother and an agent. It was also alleged that an unnamed NRL club had given one of its players an $8,000 fish tank. The Melbourne Storm coach, Mark Murray, said of the Bulldogs: "I'm not surprised, it's been going on for years."

The Bulldogs stand-off Braith Anasta, who had toured with the Kangaroos in 2001, had allegedly received an extra quarter of a million dollars on top of his $205,000 basic pay. Darrell Trindall took home an undisclosed $60,000 as well as his basic $115,000 with Kiwi Nigel Vagana reportedly being paid an under-the-table $50,000 as well as his contracted $200,000. It was inferred

"I'm not surprised, it's been going on for years."

that at least a dozen players were receiving undisclosed payments and that the illicit payments were made by the Canterbury Leagues Club, whose revenue came largely from lucrative poker machines, as was generally the case with the New South Wales clubs in the NRL.

At first the club was in denial, with the 20-year-old Anasta describing it as "a load of crap" and that he had done nothing wrong. His manager threatened legal action and Anasta broke down on a radio show on the Tuesday after the scandal broke. Bob Hagan, the Bulldogs chief executive, and Gary McIntyre, the Leagues Club

Bulldogs stand-off Braith Anasta

president also denied the allegations, but two days later, they admitted their guilt, apologised to the NRL and to the Bulldogs fans, whilst Hagan, a former Canterbury player, stood down from the NRL board and then from the club. "The Bulldogs have revealed today a quite deliberate, elaborate system of payments to players, devised to avoid detection by our salary-cap team," the NRL chief executive, David Gallop confirmed.

For the first few days, much of the conversation centred on what the club's punishment might be. For a side that had dominated all season, it was unthinkable that they would miss out on the play-offs which were just around the corner. Star forward Willie Mason was adamant that they deserved to be able to contest the title, but in reality, the NRL had no real option but to exclude them. The Bulldogs were subsequently stripped of all of their 37 competition points leaving them certain to win the wooden spoon instead of the J.J. Giltinan Shield. They were also fined half-a-million dollars. Steve Mortimer, the club's great halfback from the 1980s, took over as acting chief executive, vowing to restore the club's battered image.

New Zealand Warriors ended up topping the table and winning the accompanying $100,000 prize money before they were beaten in a memorable Grand Final by an Adrian Morley-inspired Sydney Roosters.

Eighteen months later the Bulldogs were on the front pages again when, on a pre-season trip to Coffs Harbour, a woman accused a number of their players of raping her. The case was dropped but the toxic headlines were harmful to both the club and the sport.

As for the salary cap, in April 2010 an almost identical situation occurred with the Melbourne Storm docked all eight of their points and told that they could collect no more for the rest of the year after being found to have cheated the cap in an even bigger way to Canterbury. Their 2007 and 2009 NRL titles were rescinded along with their 2010 World Club Challenge win and three Minor Premierships in 2006, 2007 and 2008.

Sunday, 9th February 2003

TWO YOUNG WARRIORS KILLED

Wigan Warriors were left stunned when two of their young players were killed in a road-traffic accident in the early hours of Sunday 9th February 2003. Neither had played for the first team, but it was believed that both had promising futures in Rugby League.

Billie-Joe Edwards, 20, was in the final year of his contract at the club and also worked as a development officer. He was the younger brother of club legend and former captain, Shaun. Craig Johnson, sibling of first-teamer Paul was a trialist at the club and was often paired with Edwards in the halves in the club's second team. He was just 18. The incident took place in Bury shortly after midnight when the car they were driving went out of control going around a bend on Turton Road in Tottingham.

The club were due to play amateur side Halton Simms Cross in the Challenge Cup fourth round later that day and, amid much sadness, the game went ahead with Paul, understandably, withdrawing from the side. He told 'League Express' in 2010: "I was lying in bed and the phone rang. It was my dad. He said I needed to get round to the house and I could tell something was wrong, so I got him to just tell me there and then what had happened and he said Craig had been killed in a car crash. I just slammed the phone down in shock. I got in the car and raced round to the house. I was worried that I'd drive past the accident but I didn't, although that made me think my dad had made a mistake and there'd been no accident. They were both drunk – drink driving. They hit a kerb and ended up hitting a wall. There were fibres from both of them to suggest they'd both been driving that night, but we'll never know who was driving at the time."

Edwards, by now working in rugby union, later recalled: "When he died I was down in London and drove straight up to Wigan. We had a game at Wasps that day and I asked Warren [Gatland] not to tell the players beforehand. We won the game and we always sing a song when we win. But they didn't sing it that day."

Wigan's community development manager Mick Hannan said: "Their

"They are a close-knit bunch of guys and this tragedy has affected the club deeply."

deaths leave me distraught. They were a couple of wonderful lads who will be greatly missed. They loved the game and were so determined to make the grade. Rugby League meant everything to them. They were dedicated training partners and were relishing playing together for the Under-21s. The Wigan set up is very closely knit. Everyone is gutted. Billy-Joe was also a first-class development officer for us. He was fantastic with kids. He did a wonderful job going out to schools on our Outreach scheme, promoting the game and helping youngsters. The children thought the world of him. I now have to go to these youngsters and tell them what has happened. Craig was another very quiet lad. He too was very dedicated and he was made up when he returned to Wigan from Warrington."

Billie-Joe Edwards

The Peugeot 106, which belonged to Johnson's father, clipped a kerb and hit two garden walls before overturning and sliding down the road on its roof. Johnson, just under three-and-a-half times over the drink-drive limit, was found 40 feet away from the car while Edwards, two-and-a-half times over the limit, was in the car with his legs out of the passenger-door window. Various personal effects were found in nearby gardens. The inquest heard that neither man was wearing a seatbelt and the investigation failed to determine who had been driving at the time of the accident. The coroner, Simon Nelson, recorded an open verdict and concluded that both were equally accountable for their actions.

"From the evidence I have heard, each of these young men were accompanying each other for the best part of the evening preceding this incident," he said. "They would have been present, each of them, when they were consuming alcohol. Therefore in my view the passenger would have been aware of the limitations of the driver and driver would have been aware of his limitations as well having known how much alcohol he had drunk."

After a minute's silence, the Warriors beat the Widnes-based amateur side 82-3 despite a Brian Capewell drop goal giving Halton a 1-0 lead. Among 15 tries, Kris Radlinski scored a hat-trick with Terry Newton, Andy Farrell and Sean O'Loughlin each scoring two. Wigan's coach Stuart Raper said after the game: "It was difficult day for the players. They are a close-knit bunch of guys and this tragedy has affected the club deeply."

The Warriors later inaugurated the Edwards-Johnson Memorial Trophy for their Under-20s player of the season. Halfback James Coyle was the first winner.

MORLEY'S 12TH-SECOND DISMISSAL COSTS GREAT BRITAIN

The opening kick-off in the 2003 Ashes series hung in the cold Wigan night air. In the blink of an eye, the Great Britain prop forward Adrian Morley clattered into his Australian counterpart Robbie Kearns. The crowd rose to cheer a thundering tackle which would set the tone for the entire series. Play was stopped on 12 seconds. Kearns was hurt. The incident happened so quickly that no one seemed to question its legality at first. It appeared that Morley had executed his trademark big hit which had made him such a star in the NRL with Sydney Roosters.

What got the former Leeds player into trouble was that Kearns needed treatment and during the break in play, the fourth official had time to study the incident and advise the referee Steve Ganson that Morley should be removed from the field. The official acted accordingly. This was the most extraordinary beginning to a Test match and even the stoniest of hearts must have sympathised with Morley as the Sky Sports cameras showed him disconsolate in the changing room. "I thought that it was my duty to get out there and show the rest of the team that they were beatable," Morley reflected a couple of years later, "but I was too aggressive and, looking at the video, I was seven or eight metres ahead of the other players. If I'd hit him cleanly, he'd have ended up in the stands but he stepped me and we all know what happened."

With a man down, how on earth could Great Britain compete with Australia, who had beaten them 64-10 in their last meeting, in July 2002 in Sydney? At least the Kangaroos were without numerous top players including Andrew Johns and Gorden Tallis. Under the circumstances, Britain's subsequent performance was of the highest order; perhaps even better than some of their previous wins over the old enemy. The record book does show a defeat, but it took a late Australian try to seal the match, something that would become a recurring theme through the series.

Phil Bailey scored Australia's opening try in the right-hand corner in the 11th minute when he ran onto a superb long pass from Darren Lockyer after

"If I'd hit him cleanly, he'd have ended up in the stands."

Brett Kimmorley's break. Craig Gower missed the goal, while at the other end Sean Long missed a sitter of a penalty. But despite being a man down, Great Britain still posed a threat with their ball movement. Richard Horne was sent clear down the left wing and, on the next play, Long put Connolly away and his beautifully timed pass sent Brian Carney to the corner. The Saints halfback again missed with the boot.

Lockyer engineered Australia's second try when his grubber kick on the last tackle was collected by Trent Waterhouse, who scored on his debut. Not for the first time in recent Anglo-Australian clashes, the Kangaroos posed a significant threat on the last tackle with Great Britain all too often predictable in the same situation. Craig Gower again missed the conversion as Australia went into half time leading 8-4.

There was mayhem in the stands when Great Britain struck ten minutes into the second half as Keith Senior got on Bailey's outside from a scrum base to score. The impossible was becoming a reality, especially with Michael Crocker in the sin bin for punching Carney. The scrum had come from a rare Lockyer error. Long finally succeeded with a conversion to put Great Britain 10-8 up. Britain were on top and Senior hared clear. As he was swallowed up by the cover near halfway, he offloaded to Kris Radlinski but the fullback couldn't take the pass and so the try went begging. Long did add a penalty to push the lead out to 12-8.

Great Britain tried to hold out but were punished on 69 minutes when Kimmorley ran the ball on the last tackle from dummy-half close

GREAT BRITAIN 18 AUSTRALIA 22

GREAT BRITAIN
1 Kris Radlinski
2 Brian Carney
3 Gary Connolly
4 Keith Senior
5 Richard Horne
6 Paul Sculthorpe
7 Sean Long
8 Stuart Fielden
9 Terry Newton
10 Adrian Morley
11 Jamie Peacock
12 Andy Farrell (C)
13 Mike Forshaw
Subs:
14 Paul Anderson
15 Barrie McDermott
16 Paul Deacon
17 Lee Gilmour

Tries: Carney 2, Senior
Goals: Long 2, Deacon

Dismissed: Morley

AUSTRALIA
1 Darren Lockyer (C)
2 Anthony Minichiello
3 Craig Wing
4 Phil Bailey
5 Shannon Hegarty
6 Craig Gower
7 Brett Kimmorley
8 Shane Webcke
9 Danny Buderus
10 Robbie Kearns
11 Steve Simpson
12 Craig Fitzgibbon
13 Luke Ricketson
Subs:
14 Petero Civoniceva
15 Willie Mason
16 Trent Waterhouse
17 Mick Crocker

Tries: Bailey, Waterhouse, Gower, Lockyer **Goals:** Fitzgibbon 3

Sin bin: Crocker

Half-time: 4-8
Referee: Steve Ganson
Crowd: 24,614

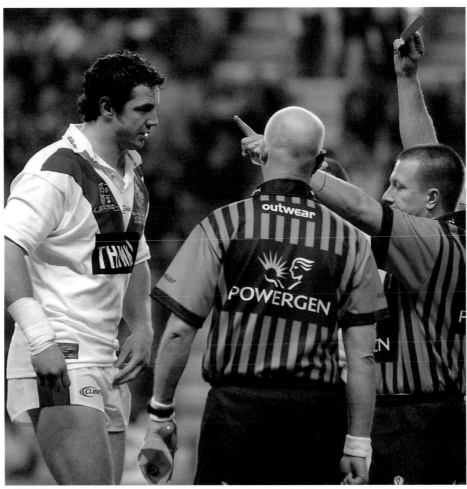

Adrian Morley is sent off by referee Steve Ganson as Robbie Kearns receives treatment

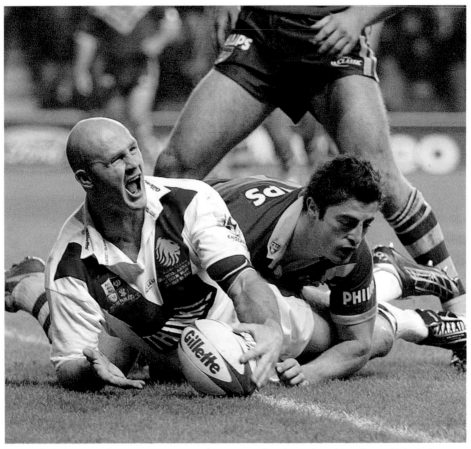

Keith Senior crashes over to score during another heartbreaking Great Britain loss

to the line and sent Gower to the line with a brilliant flat pass. Fitzgibbon was on the mark with the conversion to push the Kangaroos in front by two. But the try scorer spilled the kick off and, from the resulting scrum, Carney brought the house down by scoring his second try in the corner on the first tackle. Substitute Paul Deacon converted from the sideline to take the score to 18-14 with nine minutes to play. The JJB Stadium was alive with a raucous atmosphere. One of Test football's most gargantuan achievements was on the cards.

Australia know how to ruin parties though. Four minutes later, they ran the ball on the last tackle again, with Lockyer putting Craig Wing into the clear, and the inspirational Australian captain backed up on his inside to score the game's decisive try. Fitzgibbon converted and added a late penalty for the 22-18 victory. Once again Great Britain's inability to read a last-tackle play caused the maximum damage.

Australia had finally won this classic international, albeit by the skin of their teeth. They went on to win the second and third Tests with more late scores. Not for the first time, Great Britain were forced to focus on the positives after defeat in a series which had promised so much.

'DAILY MAIL' ACCUSES SAINTS DUO OF BETTING AGAINST OWN SIDE

When the St Helens coach, Ian Millward, fielded a weakened team for their fixture at Bradford Bulls on Easter Monday 2004, that was a big enough story in its own right. Saints, with five debutants and other inexperienced players in their line-up, were hammered 54-8 by the champions.

Millward was accused of bringing the game into disrepute by resting 11 regular players, although he had done the same thing at the same venue in 2002. On that occasion, amid much criticism, he rested key players to keep them fresh for the Challenge Cup Final, a game which they lost anyway.

This time Millward's antics opened up a can of worms in the most unwelcome way for both the club and the sport. In hindsight, it is likely that is was the beginning of the end of his time at the club. He was sacked in 2005 for other disciplinary issues, after a breakdown in his relationship with the board.

Armed with team information unbeknownst to bookmakers a day before Millward revealed his squad, Saints halfback Sean Long and centre Martin Gleeson decided to cash in. They opened telephone accounts in their own names with the Gibraltar-based bookie Stan James, with each seeking a £909 profit after staking £1000 on the Bulls to overcome a handicap of eight points at odds of 10-11. Had the bookies known the make-up of the Saints team, it is likely that the Bulls handicap would have been at least 40 points. They lost an estimated £1 million on the match.

Gleeson played in the match at Odsal, and even scored the first try while Long was one of many stars omitted by Millward. Three days later, Long was at home in Orrell watching an episode of 'Columbo' when he heard a knock on his front door. When he opened it, a photographer in a car on the street quickly took his picture and a journalist informed him that the 'Daily Mail' knew about the bets and that they intended to run with the story the following day. Long panicked.

When the story appeared splashed across the back page of Friday's paper, it was a sensation. Controversies like this rarely occurred in the sport and

*"It was not my bet.
I opened the account for my mate."*

267

Martin Gleeson in action against Bradford in the game at the centre of the betting storm

Rugby League barely ever made the back pages. Long was quoted in the piece saying that he had placed the bet for a friend. It didn't sound too convincing.

Under the headline "Star backed his team to lose", the article began: "Great Britain Rugby League star Sean Long last night admitted putting money on his own team to lose." Long had said: "It was not my bet. I opened the account for my mate. He didn't have the money in his account so I just said I'd put the money on for him and, obviously, he would give me the money if he lost and I would give him the money if he won." He agreed that the wager looked "dodgy".

Long and Gleeson's behaviour was "extremely naïve" according to James Eastham, the sports editor of 'Inside Edge', a gambling magazine. "It is unthinkable that they could have got away with it. Sportsmen would usually get friends to put a bet on for them - they seem to have done the extreme opposite. I just can't think of a similar case in recent memory."

Saints responded by banning the newspaper and its long-serving Rugby League correspondent, Richard Bott – a move which was rightly slammed by the paper and soon reversed. By the time the story hit the newsstands, the two players had scarpered. Long borrowed his wife's Fiat Punto, picked up Gleeson from his mother's house and hightailed it to Paul Sculthorpe's

Sean Long and Martin Gleeson after St Helens' 2004 Challenge Cup semi-final victory

caravan in Blackpool for a few nights.

Long claimed in his 2009 autobiography that numerous Saints players took advantage of the generous odds but were sensible enough to pay cash over the counter in the high-street bookies or to get friends to place the bet.

There were suggestions that the Great Britain pair could be banned for life, but in the end they were excluded from the game for a total of seven months. Long was banned for three months, and Gleeson four – an extra month because he had played in the game. Both returned to play for Great Britain in that autumn's Tri-Nations series with Australia and New Zealand. The players were also hit financially with estimates that the episode cost Long around £50,000 and Gleeson £40,000 in lost wages, fines and costs. Gleeson didn't play again for St Helens as they sold him to Warrington for £200,000.

The scandal also derailed the team's fortunes. Second at the time the pair's ban kicked in, they finished the season in fifth and exited the play-offs at the first stage at Wigan.

Long did go on to enjoy further success in the Red Vee, but the talented yet controversial scrum-half was back in the headlines two years later when he walked out on the Great Britain Lions touring party, who were competing in the Southern Hemisphere, in order to return home.

WIGAN ANNOUNCE MIKE GREGORY'S ILLNESS

It was an unremarkable Monday a couple of months into the 2004 Super League season when Wigan Warriors issued a statement to say that their coach, Mike Gregory, was suffering from a chronic bacterial infection which would require treatment in America. Gregory was due to leave his post after the Challenge Cup Final against St Helens in Cardiff on 15th May.

The news was greeted with incredulity among Rugby League fans, particularly those of Wigan. As the captain of Great Britain, Gregory had been as fit as a fiddle and, at the age of 39, he still possessed an indestructible aura. It was unthinkable that this could happen to such a fit man.

Shortly before Wigan's press release was sent, Gregory broke the news to his stunned squad. "He was clearly upset, and we were upset too," said the club's hooker Terry Newton. "It came as a surprise and a shock to us all and it took a while to sink in. But once we had been told, we all agreed that we were with him all the way. Greg's more than just a coach to us, he's one of the lads and we're all very close to him. We're going to dig deep for him."

Gregory didn't play for Wigan, his home-town club. Instead he excelled for Warrington, winning the Lancashire Cup Final as an 18-year-old in just his tenth senior game in 1982. He later won the Premiership trophy and another county cup before scoring in the 1990 Challenge Cup Final defeat to Wigan, capping a tremendous personal performance. He scored twice against France on his Great Britain debut in 1987. A year later, he ran 60 metres to score that wonderful try as the Lions finally beat Australia. He went on to captain Great Britain to series victories against New Zealand in 1989 and 1990.

Having also played for Salford, Gregory moved into coaching, working with Wales at the 1995 World Cup and then at St Helens under head coach Shaun McRae. He helped Saints to two Challenge Cups and a Super League title, before taking the top job at Swinton Lions. He enjoyed further success with the England Academy team when he coached them to their first-ever win over the Combined Australian High Schools in 2002. England won both Tests and most of the side went on to enjoy excellent professional careers.

"Mike's kids must know what an incredible man their father was."

Mike Gregory looks on during Wigan's 2004 Challenge Cup Final defeat to St Helens

By this time, Gregory had moved to Wigan, coaching them to Senior Academy success, after which he was promoted to Stuart Raper's assistant. When the Australian was sacked in July 2003, Gregory took over – initially on a caretaker basis - and a long unbeaten run saw them reach the Grand Final where they lost to Bradford. Gregory's impact had been substantial and he was an enormously popular coach.

The 2004 season delivered mixed fortunes in the first couple of months, but the Warriors did enough to reach the Cup Final - beating Widnes, Limoux, Wakefield and Warrington, before news of Gregory's illness broke. It later transpired that he had sustained a bite from an infected tick while coaching the England Sevens team in Australia in early 2003. He collapsed on the team bus in the days before the 2003 Grand Final. His speech became slightly slurred. He struggled to grasp a tumbler of water and noticed other symptoms, too. Gregory was eventually diagnosed with Borrelia and Progressive Muscular Atrophy in 2004. Although he would remain Wigan coach in name, the Cardiff final against St Helens, which Wigan lost 32-16, was to be the last match he coached. Before the game, Ellery Hanley had given him his winner's medal from the 1990 final.

Unfortunately Gregory's relationship with the Warriors broke down. The club believed that he had Motor Neurone Disease and saw no way that he could return as coach. They honoured his contract by continuing to pay him during his time away but Gregory and his wife, Erica, maintained that he was able to return to work. The club disagreed, blocking his return so Gregory took legal action which was eventually settled out of court, with the club paying out £17,500 in 2006.

Gregory said: "This was my dream job. I was proud to lead my team out into two finals. The supporters had belief in me and the team. I would never have betrayed this loyalty by returning to the job, if I felt incapable of doing it. My health was no different when I wanted to return to work than it had been at the Challenge Cup Final at the Millennium Stadium. However, I was 'frozen out' from that then on. I feel the management of the club failed to do their duty as a good employer. Never once did I feel they were trying to aid my return to work."

Typically, the Rugby League community rallied around Gregory. In September 2006, a crowd in excess of 5,000 attended a testimonial match at Wigan St Pat's. He died on 19th November 2007 and his death remains one of the most tragic of Rugby League stories.

Kris Radlinski, who played in the Wigan side that Gregory coached, paid him the following tribute: "Mike's kids must know what an incredible man their father was, and that his wife fought long and hard for him. He was honest and his family should be extremely proud of him. His legacy will live on forever."

COOKE'S LATE TRY STUNS LEEDS

After Katherine Jenkins delivered the first verse of the traditional Challenge Cup Final hymn, 'Abide With Me', at the Millennium Stadium in 2005, the BBC cameras showed a Hull FC fan unashamedly weeping and wiping away his tears with his black-and-white scarf - a poignant image of a Rugby League supporter wrapped up in the tension and emotion. It demonstrated to the watching nation just how much the grand old Challenge Cup still meant.

A couple of hours later Paul Cooke's late try, after he dummied his way through the Leeds defence, allowed Danny Brough to add the winning points. Those six points earned Hull a sensational and unexpected 25-24 success to give them their first Challenge Cup success since the 1982 Elland Road replay against Widnes. According to their coach John Kear, the success ranked even higher than his extraordinary 1998 triumph with Sheffield Eagles against Wigan. This was because to get to lift the Cup, they had beaten the three best sides in the country - Bradford, St Helens and Leeds.

The drama began the night before when their popular fullback Shaun Briscoe was struck down with a bout of appendicitis. He was replaced at the back by the former Australia Test winger Nathan Blacklock, who, conveniently for Kear, had successfully filled in at fullback for St George-Illawarra in the 1999 NRL Grand Final, scoring a brilliant try in the process.

Leeds also had fitness concerns, notably with Keith Senior injuring his ankle a week earlier in a 42-10 home defeat to Bradford Bulls. The will-he-play-won't-he-play saga went on all week with Kear playing a central role. "One of the first things I did ... on Monday morning was sit down with our physio Simon Pope and watch the Senior incident again," he wrote in his autobiography. "He said to me: 'There isn't a hope in hell of Keith playing in the final, or if he does play, he'll be a passenger.' From the moment Simon said that, I wanted Keith to play. Obviously I couldn't pick the Leeds team, but I did try to manipulate the opposition camp. I made a point of saying: 'If Keith Senior plays in the final, I'll put my boots on and play against him.'

"Obviously I couldn't pick the Leeds team, but I did try to manipulate the opposition."

[Tony Smith] is a superb coach but he is very bloody minded. If you tell him something isn't going to happen, he will do everything he possibly can to make sure it does."

Senior did play, but was withdrawn at half-time after a laboured performance, which was heavily criticised by the BBC pundits. Most of his teammates had also been well below their best.

The scoring was opened in the 12th minute with a rare penalty try. Mark Calderwood chased Kevin Sinfield's bomb and when the ball roamed free in the in-goal area, and with Calderwood favourite to touch down the ball, Gareth Raynor grabbed his shorts and held him back. Richard Horne went close for Hull, before the scores were levelled in the 20th minute when Motu Tony chipped over Marcus Bai and beat Ali Lauitiiti and Richie Mathers to score the try. Brough goaled from out wide to tie the scores. Kirk Yeaman had a try disallowed and so the score remained the same until half-time, but there were three early tries in the second half.

Firstly, Raynor collected Blacklock's overhead pass to put Hull ahead but Danny Ward hit back for Leeds after taking Sinfield's offload. Richard Whiting then restored Hull's advantage after a horrendous in-goal error from Marcus Bai. The Papua New Guinean was being held behind the try line when he attempted to offload to Mathers, only for Whiting to intercept. When Brough kicked a 58th-minute drop goal, the Airlie Birds were seven to the good.

The Rhinos came roaring back, turning the game on its head with a devastating four-minute blitz.

HULL FC 25 LEEDS RHINOS 24

HULL
2 Nathan Blacklock
14 Motu Tony
30 Richard Whiting
3 Kirk Yeaman
5 Gareth Raynor
6 Richard Horne
21 Danny Brough
8 Ewan Dowes
9 Richard Swain (C)
20 Garreth Carvell
11 Shayne McMenemy
12 Stephen Kearney
13 Paul Cooke
Subs:
10 Paul King
15 Jamie Thackray
16 Tommy Saxton
17 Chris Chester

Tries: Tony, Raynor, Whiting, Cooke
Goals: Brough 4 **Drop goal:** Brough

LEEDS
1 Richard Mathers
2 Mark Calderwood
3 Chev Walker
4 Keith Senior
5 Marcus Bai
13 Kevin Sinfield (C)
7 Rob Burrow
8 Ryan Bailey
9 Matt Diskin
15 Danny Ward
11 Ali Lauitiiti
12 Chris McKenna
20 Gareth Ellis
Subs:
6 Danny McGuire
14 Andrew Dunemann
16 Willie Poching
18 Jamie Jones-Buchanan

Tries: Calderwood 2 (1 penalty try), Ward, Bai **Goals:** Sinfield 4

Half-time: 6-6
Referee: Steve Ganson
Crowd: 74,213

Paul Cooke is mobbed by teammates Garreth Carvell and Shayne McMenemy after scoring Hull FC's dramatic winning try *(inset)* in the 2005 Challenge Cup Final

John Kear, Chris Chester, Garreth Carvell, Jamie Thackray and Ewan Dowes celebrate

Calderwood scored his second, punishing Horne's knock-on by scoring from a scrum base 50 metres out, before Bai's try, with 12 minutes left, from Mathers' kick, converted by Sinfield, saw Leeds lead 24-19. It was at this stage of the game that the man-of-the-match voted were collected and, with the Rhinos seemingly on course to win the Cup, the media voted for Sinfield to win the Lance Todd Trophy.

Ten minutes later, Leeds' dreams lay shattered when Cooke received the ball from Horne on the left, dummied and scampered between Sinfield and Ward to cross the line, sparking bedlam among the Hull supporters. This was Boys' Own stuff for a club starved of success for so long. Brough still had to convert the try, but even with Don Fox's infamous 1968 miss going through his mind, he made no mistake. There was still time for Sinfield to line up a drop-goal attempt, but the incomparable Richard Swain - who may well have won the Lance Todd had it been voted for at the end of the match - managed to charge it down.

The final was the first to be played in August after the Rugby Football League moved it from its traditional springtime slot. They were rewarded with a crowd of 74,213, all of whom witnessed one of the most dramatic Cup Finals ever played.

Saturday, 26th November 2005

AUSSIES FINALLY BEATEN

There were times when it looked like this day would never come. Australia hadn't lost a Test series since 1978 when the French had beaten them.

They were too good, the experts thought, to lose a series in the modern era. Great Britain didn't have the requisite quality in the key positions. New Zealand possessed neither the consistency nor the requisite strength in depth to be lifting silverware on the biggest stage - or so we thought. But they did have a man called Stacey Jones, and the genius halfback's presence in the Kiwi side of 2005 went a long way to ensuring that the Australians finally came up short.

The Kiwis had threatened their winning run on a few occasions, most notably in the 1999 Tri-Nations final when the Australians won 22-20 - a match which Jones missed with a broken arm. They had also won a one-off Test in 1987. But ahead of the 2005 final, they didn't look a realistic threat. A fortnight earlier, Brian McClennan's boys had been hammered 38-12 by Great Britain. A week before the final, the Kiwis had been deeply unimpressive in squeezing past France in a friendly, having trailed after 71 minutes.

Australia, meanwhile, had been typically efficient on the British leg of the competition, without quite being at their imperious best. They beat the hosts 20-6 at Wigan and 26-14 at Hull and were never really in danger of losing either game. Yet not only did they lose to the Kiwis in the Elland Road decider, they were nilled for the first time since September 1985, when New Zealand had beaten them 18-0.

What made the Kiwis' achievement even more impressive was that Jones had flown to New Zealand and back for the birth of his son. Their preparation was in constant disarray throughout the competition, unaware as they were from game to game of his availability. He returned to the UK just the day before the final.

"I'd told Bluey [McClennan] that I could only play in the first two games before the UK leg of the competition," said Jones, "but then Lance Hohaia got injured and Brian was left short so he persuaded me to play in

"No-one expected us to win the final but what a great performance we put in."

London. The following week, Lance got injured so Bluey was back on the phone persuading me to play again in Huddersfield. So I played in that and then against France. After that, I flew to New Zealand for the birth and then came back for the final against Australia. No-one expected us to win the final but what a great performance we put in."

A key tactical move for the Kiwis proved to be playing Bradford centre Shontayne Hape at loose forward. Not only did he have a great game in an unfamiliar position, but he was key to New Zealand's regular deployment of the 'mousetrap' dummy-half move which saw him regularly go into acting-half, dummy a pick-up, only to allow another player to come in for the ball. The tactic disorientated the Kangaroos' defensive structures and it took less than four minutes for McClennan's side to take the lead when the winger Jake Webster got to Jones's cross-field kick ahead of Matt King and centre Paul Whatuira touched down. A fight broke out in the 19th minute, after which the Kiwis extended their lead when Jones, Louis Anderson and Clinton Toopi combined to send powerhouse winger Manu Vatuvei to the corner.

Six minutes later, Vatuvei beat Brent Tate to another Jones high kick to score his second. Jones failed to convert any of the three tries, but he did land two penalty goals in the last five minutes of the half. At 16-0, the Kiwis were in dream land.

The usual script was that Australia, led by Brisbane Broncos super coach Wayne Bennett, would mount a comeback. Just three converted tries would do the trick, but no green-and-gold stirring was to

NEW ZEALAND 24 AUSTRALIA 0

NEW ZEALAND
1 Brent Webb
2 Jake Webster
3 Paul Whatuira
4 Clinton Toopi
5 Manu Vatuvei
6 Nigel Vagana
7 Stacey Jones
8 Paul Rauhihi
9 Motu Tony
10 Ruben Wiki (C)
11 David Kidwell
12 Louis Anderson
13 Shontayne Hape
Subs:
14 David Faiumu
15 Roy Asotasi
16 David Solomona
17 Ali Lauitiiti

Tries: Whatuira, Vatuvei 2, Webb
Goals: Jones 4

AUSTRALIA
1 Anthony Minichiello
2 Matt King
3 Mark Gasnier
4 Matt Cooper
5 Brent Tate
6 Trent Barrett
7 Craig Gower
8 Petero Civoniceva
9 Danny Buderus (C)
10 Jason Ryles
11 Luke O'Donnell
12 Craig Fitzgibbon
13 Ben Kennedy
Subs:
14 Craig Wing
15 Willie Mason
16 Mark O'Meley
17 Steve Price

Half-time: 16-0
Referee: Steve Ganson
Crowd: 26,534

New Zealand's Stacey Jones leaves the Elland Road pitch with the Tri-Nations trophy

materialise, thanks largely to magnificent Kiwi defence. "I was confident [at half-time] we could play better than the first half, but we didn't," Bennett said after the game. "We didn't give ourselves a chance. They played tremendously well and coming into half-time their ball control was almost 100 per cent. We were 50." The subsequent backlash in Australia was so fierce that Bennett left the airport via a back entrance to avoid the media.

Eleven minutes into the second half, the game was up, courtesy of a try by an Australian in the Kiwi ranks. Brent Webb, who played for New Zealand through the residency rule, burst onto Jones's pass and put the game beyond doubt. The man-of-the-match halfback converted and added a penalty six minutes later to bring an end to the night's scoring.

Webster had a try disallowed for a Whatuira forward pass and Jones missed with a drop goal, but nothing could deny the Kiwis their glory. To put it simply, it was the most momentous of games. Australia finally had to watch someone else lift a trophy.

Thursday, 21st September 2006

NEWS BREAKS OF
STEVE PRESCOTT'S ILLNESS

Rumours had circulated for over a week that all was not well with the former St Helens and Hull FC fullback Steve Prescott, whose playing career had ended three years earlier. And sure enough, the Rugby League community was plunged into shock on 21st September 2006 when Hull confirmed that Prescott had indeed been diagnosed with cancer at the age of 32.

Entitled 'Hull FC support Steve Prescott in difficult times', the press release read: "Hull FC would like to send their support to former player Steve Prescott who is suffering from cancer. The 32-year-old former Hull FC, St Helens and Great Britain fullback is currently awaiting further medical news and all at Hull FC would like to wish Steve and his family all the best in this difficult time. Hull FC, St Helens RLFC and the wider world of Rugby League are currently initiating fundraising efforts and will keep supporters informed as the coming days and weeks progress. Steve Prescott would like to thank all Rugby League supporters for their overwhelming messages of support."

His mother, Pat, told the St Helens Reporter: "It is dreadful, really dreadful. We are trying to take it in and just want to support him without breaking down. It's getting your head around it really. It's a shock to the system, we are totally devastated."

Details were sketchy at first with no mention of the terminal diagnosis of pseudomyxoma peritonei. This rare cancer literally means false (pseudo) benign tumour with mucinous features (myxoma) of the abdomen (peritonei). It is sometimes known as "jelly belly" and is the disease which had killed the actress Audrey Hepburn.

It was a shock to many that somebody so fit and so young, who had so recently been at the top of his game, could now have such a serious illness. Stunned fans of his former clubs staged a bucket collection for him at their Super League fixture on 29th September.

The 32-year-old had been diagnosed 13 days before the news became

**"It is dreadful, really dreadful.
We are trying to take it in and just want to
support him without breaking down."**

public and given just months to live. The news was delivered hours after the birth of his second child, Koby. When he asked a nurse how long he had to live, they replied: "months … a year maximum. Don't worry, you'll see Christmas."

Prescott, in fact, would see in seven more Christmases after embarking upon the bravest of fights against the condition. He went to Basingstoke for an operation in the hope it would rid him of the disease, but, although most of it was taken away, some remained. The operation stabilized him. Eleven months after the initial diagnosis, he set up his eponymous Foundation which broke through the £1 million barrier in 2016 for the Christie Hospital in Manchester and 'Try Assist', the Rugby League's Benevolent Fund, which aids injured or sick ex-players.

Despite his debilitating illness, Prescott ran, cycled, climbed and rowed his way through many grueling physical challenges. He was appointed MBE in 2009 for his Herculean efforts and came closer than many imagined to winning his battle. After a transplant in the autumn of 2013, he was finally cancer-free, but his body rejected the donor's anti-bodies and Prescott ultimately died of graft-versus-host disease.

News of his death began to circulate on the morning of England's last World Cup group game against Fiji at Prescott's former home ground, the KC Stadium in Hull. A minute's silence was observed immaculately by the 25,114 spectators.

Six months after his death, the Rugby Football League confirmed that the Man of Steel would be named after Prescott. St Helens and Hull, meanwhile, now compete annually for the Steve Prescott Cup. The Steve Prescott Foundation continues to raise funds and awareness and in the autumn of 2015 staged a game of Rugby League at the top of Mount Kilimanjaro with Barrie McDermott, Terry O'Connor, Lee Briers and Adrian Morley joining a host of other Rugby League personalities and supporters in taking part.

Prescott's career saw him win Challenge Cup Finals at Wembley in 1996 and 1997 before he moved to Hull FC. He was transferred to Wakefield in 2000 before returning to Hull a year later after financial problems at Trinity. He played for England in 1996, setting a points-per-game record against France with 22 in a European Championship match, before he went on to become a British Lion at the end of the year on their tour of New

Steve Prescott lifts the Challenge Cup in 1996 with Karle Hammond and *(below)* in action for Great Britain and Hull FC

Zealand, Papua New Guinea and Fiji. In 2000, after switching nations, he reached the World Cup quarter-finals with Ireland.

He won his sole county cap with Lancashire in 2003, but that War of the Roses match at Odsal was to be the final match of an impressive career. Three weeks after signing a two-year contract extension with Hull, having scored 18 tries in 19 matches that season, he came off the bench and sustained a career-ending broken knee-cap.

Steve Prescott's admirable playing career won him many admirers, but his remarkable battle against the most appalling adversity between 2006 and 2013 ensures that he will be forever regarded as a giant of Rugby League.

RHINOS BEAT BULLS IN MAGIC WEEKEND FARCE

As long as there is Rugby League, referees will be criticised. Sometimes it is wholly unjustified. At other times, such as in Cardiff in May 2007, they get everything they deserve. The most infamous refereeing decision in Super League history took place in its 12th season as Steve Ganson and video referee Ashley Klein unwittingly handed Leeds a thoroughly undeserved win over Bradford at the end of the inaugural Magic Weekend in the Welsh capital. In fact, in the sport's history it is hard to think of many bigger officiating mishaps. The fact that it happened in the final minute of the sport's brand-new showpiece event made it a much bigger story.

Even without this incredible ending, the weekend had generated considerable interest and plenty of column inches. It was a brave decision by the Rugby Football League to take an entire round of matches to one stadium with players, fans and journalists split over how successful it would be. In particular, St Helens were dead-set against the idea but, on the whole, it was deemed that the concept of six Super League fixtures over two days in one stadium had been a success, although it was clear that there were many ways in which it could be improved.

In the opening match, played in front of a sparse crowd, Harlequins beat Catalans 32-28. That was followed by a sweet moment for Paul Cooke, whose new side Hull Kingston Rovers beat the club he had recently and controversially left, Hull FC, by 14-10. In the last game of the first day, Saints beat Wigan 34-18, a game which saw a few mystifying decisions from the officials. Day two began with an out-of-form Warrington hammering Salford 50-18 before a dull match between Huddersfield and Wakefield saw the former claim a 36-12 win. With neither any real quality nor excitement on offer thus far, it was then up to the Rhinos and the Bulls to produce a spectacle befitting of the occasion.

With 19-year-old winger Ryan Hall making his senior debut, Leeds trailed the three-time world champions 38-36 in the dying seconds. Brent

"Steve Ganson has ended this weekend with a nonsense. A total, complete and utter mess from the officials at the end."

Webb had scored three for the Rhinos, with Michael Platt crossing twice for the Bulls in what had been an entertaining game, even if there had been an alarming lack of intensity.

As the game wound down, Bradford's Matt Cook was penalised for picking the ball up in an offside position, giving Kevin Sinfield the chance to grab a point for Leeds with a long-range penalty, although replays clearly demonstrated that the call was incorrect because the ball had come to Cook via Gareth Ellis's boot and not from Iestyn Harris. It later transpired that Klein had wrongly advised Ganson to award the penalty and not only had that call been wrong, the referees' boss Stuart Cummings later admitted that Klein had no business to interfere even if he had been correct.

That was only a small part of the controversy!

Sinfield's penalty hit the crossbar and bounced down. The ball popped back up and hung in the air for what seemed like an age, before it was eventually grabbed by a joyous Jordan Tansey, who powered over to score. Jamie Jones-Buchanan and Sinfield, celebrated like they had won a Grand Final.

In what was a rarity for this match, Ganson awarded the try without checking with the video referee, but, to the horror of the Bulls, replays showed Tansey had been several metres offside when Sinfield struck the shot at goal. Ironically, the referee had already used Klein's services on no fewer than eight occasions during the match.

The abiding image of the game was Sinfield somersaulting through the air in celebration as an incandescent Harris berated Ganson

---

LEEDS RHINOS 42
BRADFORD BULLS 38

LEEDS
1 Brent Webb
2 Scott Donald
3 Clinton Toopi
4 Keith Senior
5 Lee Smith
6 Danny McGuire
7 Rob Burrow
15 Jamie Thackray
13 Kevin Sinfield (C)
8 Kylie Leuluai
11 Jamie Jones-Buchanan
18 Ian Kirke
12 Gareth Ellis
Subs:
25 Ryan Hall
14 Ali Lauitiiti
22 Carl Ablett
23 Jordan Tansey

Tries: Jones–Buchanan, Webb 3, Senior, Burrow, Tansey **Goals:** Sinfield 7

BRADFORD
19 Michael Platt
2 Nathan McAvoy
3 Ben Harris
17 James Evans
5 Lesley Vainikolo
6 Iestyn Harris
7 Paul Deacon (C)
8 Joe Vagana
9 Terry Newton
10 Andy Lynch
15 Matt Cook
26 David Solomona
13 Jamie Langley
Subs:
24 Dave Halley
16 Ian Henderson
22 Craig Kopczak
18 Sam Burgess

Tries: Platt 2, Vainikolo, Henderson, B Harris, Lynch **Goals:** Deacon 7

Half-time: 26-18
Referee: Steve Ganson
Crowd: 26,447

Iestyn Harris confronts referee Steve Ganson as Leeds celebrate a controversial win

for his incompetence. The Leeds skipper's conversion was the final act of the game, which his team won 42-38.

"Steve Ganson has ended this weekend with a nonsense," concluded a stunned *Sky Sports* commentator, Eddie Hemmings. "A total, complete and utter mess from the officials at the end."

A few days later, Bradford publicly appealed for the Rhinos to give them the two points. Their desperate plea fell on deaf ears.

For Bulls supporters, the game evoked painful memories of Chris Joynt's 'Wide to West' try seven years earlier. On both occasions, Hemmings had prematurely declared the Bulls the victors in his commentary, only to realise a penalty had been awarded. On both occasions the winning try had come after the final hooter. At least at Knowsley Road, the Bulls had been undone by a thrilling try.

For the Bulls halfback Paul Deacon, who played in both matches, it was the most agonising case of déjà vu, only with the most astonishing incompetence thrown in by the officials this time around.

ANDREW JOHNS GIVES SENSATIONAL LIVE-TV INTERVIEW

When Andrew Johns, the former Australia, New South Wales and Newcastle Knights genius, was arrested at a London tube station in August 2007 for fare-dodging and being in possession of an ecstasy tablet, that would have been an interesting enough story in its own right. Four days later, back in Australia, an emotional Johns bared his soul to the viewers of Channel Nine's 'The Footy Show' and spoke candidly about his regular use of recreational drugs. It made for the most compulsive viewing.

Player misbehaviour has been a considerable problem throughout the NRL era, even among the most high-profile of names, but given Johns' stature and the length of time it had been going on, this was a huge story. It also emerged that he was suffering from bipolar disorder, a condition which had affected him for years. In front of a stunned audience, Johns, regarded by many as the greatest Rugby League player ever, divulged the incredible secret which had originally been intended for his forthcoming autobiography. And that was that for the vast majority of his career, he had wilfully taken recreational drugs and had successfully cheated the NRL testing system.

Quizzed by Phil Gould, his old State of Origin coach, on the popular free-to-air programme, Johns said of his arrest: "It was probably the scariest moment of my life. I was in a cell of my own but in the other cells there were a couple of crazy men just running and charging into the walls, screaming out constantly. It shook me up. I haven't slept in days and I haven't eaten. I just can't describe how bad I felt sitting there this morning trying to explain to my seven-year-old son what I'd done in London. My past 10 or 12 years have been like a fairy tale. I think about some of the great times I had and they've been destroyed by drugs. I look back now and I'm so ashamed of it. I know I'll never touch drugs again. The way I felt being handcuffed and being in that London lock-up in jail. It's just a feeling I can't describe. I'll never go near it again."

Asked how long he had taken the drug, he replied: "Probably ten years. I've taken it on and off, generally during the off-season. But there's times during the season I've run the gauntlet and played Russian roulette and taken it. It wasn't drug dependency. I had an alcohol problem but it was more in the off-season I'd do it. I was about 19, 20, 21 when I started. I used it to escape the pressure. To me, the problem was alcohol. I would never intentionally go to take drugs but I'd have six or eight beers and not care."

Hinting towards his bipolar which he would go on to talk about extensively in his book, 'The Two of Me', Johns continued: "There's medical reasons that contribute to my reckless behaviour but I don't want to make excuses. I'm so ashamed of it. People ask 'how do you avoid the drug testers?' If you play Friday night, and you don't train Saturday and Sunday times generally it's out by Monday. I've lived with it for ten years. It adds to the paranoia. You go out Friday night and hammer yourself and then you don't know where you've been for two days. You can get really down."

Gould asked Johns how long he had suffered from depression. "I have for the last five years or so – constantly," he said, and that he "was diagnosed by a club doctor and a professor in Sydney. It stabilised me and took away the incredible highs, but invariably after the highs I crashed to lows where I wouldn't leave the house for four days. One minute I could be literally willing to take the world on and that's when I was at my creative best when I was playing. Then one day I'd turn up to the field and not want to talk to anybody."

Johns had finished playing at the start 2007. He was hurt by a collision with Sonny-Bill Williams in round one of the new NRL season, missing the next match but returning in round three against Canberra. It would be his final match. Again, he was injured in a tackle and scans showed a bulging disc in his neck. Johns decided to retire from the sport.

He and his successor as Australian captain, Darren Lockyer, who was injured at the time, were invited to the Challenge Cup Final at Wembley Stadium between St Helens and Catalans Dragons. Due to British Airways losing his luggage, Johns had gone a week without taking his bipolar medication. It was the day after the match that he was arrested. He had been drinking in the popular all-day club, 'The Church', in Kentish Town.

His book was published a few weeks later and, buoyed by the numerous column inches following his arrest, it was a huge success. In it, he admitted that the London episode had left him the closest he had ever been to taking his life.

After a lengthy public debate, Johns was named in Australia's Team of the Century in 2008 and as the eighth Rugby League 'Immortal' in 2012. But there were those, like his former international teammate Shane Webcke, who believed that his drug use should have discounted him from both honours. In the end, the former Bronco didn't get his own way and Andrew Johns is rightly recognised as one of the greatest players to have played Rugby League.

"I think about some of the great times I had and they've been destroyed by drugs."

Tuesday, 22nd July 2008

THE FIRST LICENSING ANNOUNCEMENT

After months of speculation, D-Day finally arrived in July 2008 when the Rugby Football League announced the recipients of the first Super League licences, following the momentous decision to rescind promotion and relegation. The RFL made the disastrous decision of including Celtic Crusaders at the expense of Widnes, on the flawed basis that the Vikings' previous owners had taken the club into insolvency.

Those in favour of licensing claimed it would end the game's boom-and-bust culture, with clubs no longer needing to sack coaches nor panic buy to avoid relegation or secure promotion. On the other hand, there were those who claimed that such a move effectively made Super League a closed shop, that too many sides would have little to play for and that interest in the lower divisions would plummet.

The 12 Super League clubs in 2008 - Bradford, Castleford, Catalans, Harlequins, Huddersfield, Hull, Hull KR, Leeds, St Helens, Wakefield, Warrington and Wigan - were eventually given the go-ahead to compete in the competition for a further three years, despite suggestions that one or two of them might be under threat. Six of them only received a 'C' grade - Castleford, Catalans, Harlequins, Huddersfield, Hull KR and Wakefield. Hull, Leeds and Warrington were given 'A' grades, with Bradford, St Helens and Wigan having to settle for a 'B'.

The big debate throughout the preceding weeks surrounded which clubs might join them, with applications from Celtic Crusaders, Featherstone Rovers, Halifax, Leigh Centurions, Salford City Reds, Toulouse Olympic and Widnes Vikings. Many seemed to believe that the two successful clubs would come from the Crusaders, Salford and Widnes. Of those, Widnes had the advantage of a stadium which satisfied the criteria, compared to the Crusaders' run-down Brewery Field and Salford's ancient Willows. They were also led by Steve O'Connor, a successful businessman who many Super League clubs would have loved to have, but the previous Widnes regime had taken the club into insolvency in October 2007 and it seemed likely that that would be taken into consideration by the decision makers. In the end this proved to be the issue that cost them dear. The RFL concluded: "The club has been in a difficult position of seeking to take into account the club's historical attendance and playing record but naturally distancing itself from the previous regime's financial record." To a hero's reception at their next game, O'Connor vowed to remain at the club and win them a licence three years later.

Featherstone, Halifax, Leigh and Toulouse also missed out, with the Centurions particularly angered by the decision. Their chief executive Allan Rowley claimed to be "disgusted with the Celtic inclusion" and that the powers that be at Red Hall should "hang their heads in shame". He was right to criticise their inclusion, but his club palpably wasn't ready either.

Salford and Celtic were instead awarded 'C'-grade licences, allowing them to join Super League in 2009. "Despite previous relegations from Super League [Salford] has a long history of financial stability," reported the RFL. "The club's commercial and marketing plans appear well developed and will allow them to make use of a new stadium and access to the Salford and Manchester conurbations. The club's player-performance strategy is very diligent in every area and there is a strong infrastructure."

As for the Crusaders, the RFL's summary concluded: "In the medium term the club recognises the need to develop a new facility and appears to be working with the local public agencies to deliver this. As with any new venture, financial projections are more subjective but the club has demonstrated financial stability during its progress through the National Leagues. The club has built good relationships with commercial partners and TV channel S4C offers exciting opportunities. There is supportive independent market research for Super League in South Wales, although inevitably this can only be fully tested by participation in the competition. The playing infrastructure is very good in places but the club is understandably at the early stages with its scholarship and academy teams."

The Crusaders' inclusion provided a huge talking point, with 'Rugby League World' magazine pundits Jon Wells and Garry Schofield seeing things from differing perspectives. "I think this decision, albeit a controversial one for Rugby League traditionalists, represents the clearest signal of the sport's intentions to expand since the introduction of Les Catalans in 2006, and I don't think you'll find many people who will want to argue that the sojourn into the South of France has been anything other than a resounding success," wrote Wells. Schofield, meanwhile, said: "It's the wrong decision to put Celtic Crusaders into Super League. If it's a purely geographical decision then Richard Lewis needs to have a long hard look at himself. The game has been badly burned before doing this. All I can ask is how on earth did Celtic Crusaders get a 'C' grade when clubs like St Helens and Wigan only got a 'B'?"

The Crusaders proved to be a deeply unsuccessful Super League club, with numerous things going wrong. Even though the RFL seemed set to repeat their mistake three years later by awarding them another licence, the club was honest enough to admit they were out of their depth and withdrew their application at the 11th hour.

The licensing concept was soon scrapped and replaced by the Super Eights system, which was used for the first time in 2015.

"How on earth did Celtic Crusaders get a 'C' grade when clubs like St Helens and Wigan only got a 'B'?"

BILLY SLATER THROWS AWAY THE WORLD CUP

With one game left in the 2008 calendar, the Australian fullback Billy Slater was a racing certainty to be crowned the world's best player by winning the coveted Golden Boot award, presented by 'Rugby League World' magazine. His performances with Melbourne Storm had been of the highest order and he had helped Queensland to win the State of Origin series for the third year in a row. Australia had thrashed everybody in sight en route to the World Cup Final and Slater's hat-trick against England led to a 52-4 thrashing. Channel Nine pundits were suggesting that he might just be the greatest attacking player in the history of the game.

With 20 minutes to play in the World Cup Final, his country needed him more than ever. New Zealand had overturned a 10-0 deficit at Suncorp Stadium to take a two-point lead midway through the second half. But Australia were the masters of the late comeback. They hadn't lost in nine World Cup Finals. No-one was worried just yet.

On the hour mark, Benji Marshall kicked into the corner where Slater fielded the ball. He stepped inside and flirted with the idea of taking on Manu Vatuvei on the outside. Suddenly, he was heading for touch. Recklessly, he flung the ball infield and it bounced perfectly for Marshall to pick up and score.

Few could believe what they had just witnessed. Slater's error evoked memories of the infamous Australian cricketing sledge "You've just dropped the World Cup mate," allegedly aimed at a South African fielder nine years earlier. It was one of the most incredible passages of play seen in 13 World Cups, although Ricky Stuart, the Australia coach, refused to blame Slater after the game, saying, "If I asked Billy Slater to take that out of his game, he wouldn't be the Billy Slater that we all love."

The goal was missed so the Kiwis led by six at 22-16. They remained in front for the rest of the game, despite a Greg Inglis try five minutes later. After another extraordinary passage of play, they were home and dry. With ten minutes to play, Nathan Fien kicked into Australia's in-goal from the

"If I asked Billy Slater to take that out of his game, he wouldn't be the Billy Slater that we all love."

New Zealand celebrate with the World Cup after defeating Australia

20-metre line. The ball bounced awkwardly for the defence and, as Lance Hohaia challenged for the ball, he was impeded by Joel Monaghan. Australia claimed that Slater would have beaten Hohaia to the ball anyway, but the English video referee Steve Ganson awarded a penalty try, which as good as confirmed the Kiwis' win. The simple goal opened up an eight-point lead. Australian spectators were stunned.

For once the Australians fell away in the closing stages and further salt was poured into their gaping wound when Adam Blair grabbed a loose ball on the Aussie line and touched it down. New Zealand, with a 34-20 win, were the world champions of Rugby League for the first time. Rookie coach Stephen Kearney, a former Test captain, had done a magnificent job, aided by his assistant Wayne Bennett, a former Kangaroo coach.

The final was preceded by one of the best hakas ever seen. In a moment of pure theatre, the Australian players advanced towards the New Zealanders as they began to perform their usual pre-match war cry until the players were nose to nose. It set the tone for an extraordinary evening.

After Darren Lockyer and David Williams had scored early tries, it appeared Australia would canter to victory, but Jeremy Smith halted their momentum with a try under the posts after Lockyer had had another chalked off by the video referee. Jerome Ropati was next over, although Lockyer's second and Thurston's second goal ensured Australia took a four-point lead into the interval. Hohaia got the Kiwis over the line again early in the second half and by this stage it was obvious to all that a modern-day classic was unfolding.

Australia coach Ricky Stuart crassly blamed the officials and players told journalists in the changing rooms where to go. Stuart was fined $20,000. Australian fans, on the other hand, were magnanimous in defeat, knowing they had witnessed an incredible game and a performance from New Zealand to rank alongside anything in their history. The competition itself had also lived up to the most optimistic expectations. It went a long way to making up for the damp squib of a World Cup in 2000.

Despite the events of the World Cup Final, Slater was crowned the winner of the Golden Boot a week later. He was the almost unanimous choice of a judging panel made up of several members of the worldwide media and former winners.

AUSTRALIA 20 NEW ZEALAND 34

AUSTRALIA
1 Billy Slater
2 Joel Monaghan
3 Greg Inglis
4 Israel Folau
5 David Williams
6 Darren Lockyer (C)
7 Johnathan Thurston
10 Petero Civoniceva
9 Cameron Smith
15 Brent Kite
11 Glenn Stewart
12 Anthony Laffranchi
13 Paul Gallen
Subs:
14 Karmichael Hunt
16 Craig Fitzgibbon
17 Anthony Tupou
22 Anthony Watmough

Tries: Lockyer 2, Williams, Inglis
Goals: Thurston 2

NEW ZEALAND
1 Lance Hohaia
2 Sam Perrett
3 Simon Mannering
4 Jerome Ropati
5 Manu Vatuvei
6 Benji Marshall
7 Nathan Fien
8 Nathan Cayless (C)
9 Thomas Leuluai
10 Adam Blair
11 David Fa'alogo
12 Bronson Harrison
13 Jeremy Smith
Subs:
14 Issac Luke
15 Greg Eastwood
16 Sam Rapira
17 Sika Manu

Tries: Smith, Ropati, Hohaia 2 (1 penalty try), Marshall, Blair
Goals: Luke 3, Marshall 2

Half-time: 16-12
Referee: Ashley Klein
Crowd: 50,599

Sunday, 22nd March 2009

WAKEFIELD STUNNED BY
SECOND TRAGEDY IN SIX MONTHS

Rugby League fans hoping to catch Celtic Crusaders' match against Wakefield Trinity Wildcats in March 2009 would have been confused to find Sky Sports instead showing the previous season's Grand Final between Leeds and St Helens. Occasional messages popped up to explain that match from the Brewery Field had been postponed, but no reason was given.

Speculation began to rage on the Rugby League message boards and social media, but few knew the truth. Gradually the rumours became more accurate and when online messages hinted at the reality, they were quickly deleted by frantic moderators. That was because the real story was so appalling. Wakefield player Leon Walker had lost his life earlier that afternoon after collapsing in the 63rd minute of a reserve match against the Crusaders at nearby Maesteg. An air ambulance had taken him to Swansea's Morriston Hospital, but he was pronounced dead upon arrival. When Walker's family had been informed of the desperate news, the reason for the postponement was finally revealed to horrified supporters on Sky Sports by the club's chief executive, Diane Rogerson. Walker was just 20. It had been a long time since a player had died in such circumstances.

The consultant surgeon, Richard Johnson, said at the inquest: "Two opposing players were involved in the tackle - one person goes in high, one goes in low. To start with his breathing was laboured and he had a pulse but then it dropped. We gave CPR, oxygen and used a defibrillator to try to shock his heart into beating. But it did not work."

For John Kear, the Wildcats coach, and his players, the pain was unbearable. Just months earlier, the club's popular prop forward Adam Watene had died after collapsing in the gymnasium. Watene and Walker were never teammates, with the latter joining the club from Salford, a month after the Cook Islander's passing. The club had coped admirably, but Walker's death pushed the popular coach over the edge. Comforted by his friends at Sky Sports, Eddie Hemmings and Mike Stephenson, Kear broke down in tears.

Walker's father, Steve, had been a professional player himself with Bramley in the 1983-84 and 1984-85 seasons. He and his family made the grim journey to south Wales to identify their son. Mr Walker was later keen to point out that the Crusaders player involved in the tackle was categorically not

Wakefield fans observe a minutes' silence in memory of Leon Walker

to blame. Rugby League personalities rallied around both club and family, and five days later, with the Walkers' blessing, the club's home match with St Helens went ahead, preceded by a beautiful tribute to Leon.

Salford's Jordan Turner, who went on to play for St Helens, was traumatised by the news. "I was at a mate's house and we were flicking through the channels looking for the Celtic-Wakefield game," he said. "But the 2008 Grand Final was on instead. At that point, a mate rang and told us the news. I just had to go home because I couldn't hold back the tears. He was not just a teammate, but a mate I went into town with. It was good to be at Wakefield for their game at St Helens. His family and friends had a private box and as we watched the build-up on the screen, everyone was in tears. Wakefield should be proud of themselves for the way they've handled this."

Walker attended Morley High School and played at amateur level for Churwell Chiefs before he joined Leeds, the club his grandfather, Dave, had played for. He played for the Rhinos' Under-16 Foundation team in 2005, before moving onto Salford where he was named Junior Academy player of the year at the conclusion of his first season.

He was coached at The Willows by the former Great Britain player Alan Hunte, who said of him: "Leon was just a bubbly personality and just eager to play the game. He was very honest and tried to do everything at 100mph.

"How far could he have gone? Who knows? But I can say that there were no obstacles he wouldn't have charged right through."

Adam Watene tragically passed away just a few months before Leon Walker

During his three years with us, he won two player-of-the-year awards and was vastly appreciated by his teammates for the effort and honesty he gave the team on the field. It was disappointing for me to see him leaving us at Salford without playing for our first team. How far could he have gone? Who knows? But I can say that there were no obstacles he wouldn't have charged right through."

When the Wildcats signed him, their player performance manager, Richard Tunningley, said: "Leon is an excellent young prospect, and we're delighted to have him here. He's earned honours with Yorkshire and England already and we're sure he'll develop further during his time here." He figured in the first-team Boxing Day friendly against Leeds at Headingley, and remained in the team for another pre-season match against Doncaster.

The inquest into Leon Walker's death revealed that he had died from natural causes. He had a rare undiagnosed heart defect and could have died at any time. "He had a flap of tissue which blocked the opening of his heart during rigorous exercise," said the pathologist, Richard Jones. "The right coronary artery followed a strange and precarious course through big blood vessels. When it expanded and contracted during exercise the artery would become squashed reducing the amount of oxygenated blood to the heart. In Leon's case this would have caused an abnormal rhythm and this led to his heart attack. Death could have occurred at any time but the risk was increased during exertion or exercise."

The Wakefield team responded magnificently to the twin tragedies, finishing in fifth position, one place above Wigan, to secure their second play-off spot in the summer era.

Sunday, 26th September 2010

TERRY NEWTON FOUND HANGED

A s Sky Sports broadcast the Championship One Grand Final between Oldham and York at the Halliwell Jones Stadium in Warrington in September 2010, rumours began to circulate online that Terry Newton, the former Great Britain hooker, had been found dead at his home in Orrell, near Wigan. Before the kick-off to the next game – the Championship Grand Final between Featherstone and Halifax - presenter Eddie Hemmings confirmed the news to disbelieving viewers. The 31-year-old was survived by his wife and two daughters.

Police had been called to his house just after 2pm on Sunday, 26th September following a report of concern for his welfare. He was found hanged in his garage. He had posted on Facebook shortly before his death with the last message reading, "Luv U all but it's end time." His death followed that of his sister, Leanne, in 2008 from pneumonia.

Popular with his own fans, disliked by the opposition's due to his aggressive style of play, Newton enjoyed a lengthy career with Leeds, Wigan and Bradford. He had also played 15 times for Great Britain before signing with Wakefield for the 2010 season. The hooker was as controversial as he was talented. In his final game for Wigan, he badly injured two Great Britain teammates, Lee Gilmour and Sean Long, and after just two games for the Wildcats, news broke that he had tested positive for a human growth hormone, making him the first sportsperson in the world to be caught with the substance in his system. He was banned from Rugby League for two years, with Trinity terminating his two-year contract.

In the months after his ban, Newton released a contrite autobiography, which looked to the future with a note of positivity. He hoped to work with the game's governing body to educate young players about the perils of banned substances. He took over a pub and appeared to have moved on. In the epilogue to his book he wrote: "When I started taking hGH I ought to have known I'd be the first person in the whole damn world to get busted for it. But one of the many texts I received in the days after I got banned, the one that struck a chord, was from my former Wigan teammate Matty Johns. 'We all make mistakes … the bigger men get over them.' And I have done."

"Luv U all but it's end time."

Three of Newton's closest friends, Terry O'Connor, Barrie McDermott and Brian Carney, were working for Sky Sports on the day of his death. The latter two were with Hemmings when the stunning news was delivered with O'Connor reportedly too upset to remain on the set. "He was ready to go to the next stage of his life," said an emotional Carney. "His Rugby League career was going to be behind him, but we don't know sometimes. There were obviously some deeper things troubling Terry and he obviously

Terry Newton is consoled by Craig Smith following Wigan's 2003 Super League Grand Final defeat to Bradford

couldn't find a way out of what was troubling him." McDermott added: "I remember speaking to him saying 'don't let this [the ban] be the thing that defines you, Tez. Get on with the rest of your life.' We cared for him. We care for him the way you would a very good friend. His heart and soul was in the game." O'Connor said later that he had seen Newton on the day of his death and did not believe that he had seen anything that was troubling him.

It transpired that the 31-year-old had taken cocaine, amphetamines, steroids and alcohol on the Saturday night, which could have impaired his judgment according to the coroner. He left a number of notes stating his wish to die and was found with several cuts to both wrists, measuring up to four centimetres, although they were deemed superficial. "I cannot be sure beyond all reasonable doubt that at the time Mr Newton did that act that he had the capacity at the relevant time to form an appropriate intention to end his own life," Jennifer Leeming told the inquest at Bolton Coroner's Court, as she recorded an open verdict.

Forensic toxicologist Julie Evans reported that prolonged use of particular steroids could affect the way that the brain deals with moods, resulting in such side-effects as paranoid jealousy, irritability, delusions and impaired judgment. The inquest was also told that the family of the former international had detected changes in his behaviour when using other drugs.

Six days later, after a minute's silence, his former club Wigan beat St Helens in the Super League Grand Final with Martin Gleeson, who was close to Newton, scoring the opening try of the match in the fourth minute. Fittingly, when he rose to his feet, he gestured to his wristband, whereupon there was a tribute to his late friend.

Three-quarters of suicides, it was soon reported, are males, with the most likely to do so being those between the ages of 15 and 35. For all men in that bracket, suicide is the most common cause of death. Therefore, in the wake of Newton's death, a campaign called State of Mind was set up. With the aid of NHS experts, volunteers, players, the RFL and the Rugby League Cares charity, they seek to promote positive mental health among sports men and women in order to prevent suicides. Their website can be found at stateofmindrugby.com.

ENGLAND'S SEMI-FINAL HEARTACHE

The clock had gone past 79 minutes and England, ahead by four points, were on the verge of beating the reigning world champions in the 2013 World Cup semi-final.

New Zealand were 40 metres short of the England line with four tackles used up when they were handed a lifeline. A penalty. The big prop Frank-Paul Nuuausala drove forward. Issac Luke played the ball under the English sticks. Thirty seconds remained.

From acting-half, Nuuausala looked left and found his gifted halfback Shaun Johnson 15 metres out. A desperate Kevin Sinfield surged forward but Johnson stepped around the England captain and beat George Burgess to break the heart of every England supporter by planting the football down and kicking the goal that put his side into the World Cup Final.

It was déjà vu for many of those in Wembley who had witnessed numerous gut-wrenching late defeats for Great Britain and England since 1990, but at least the 14th Rugby League World Cup itself had exceeded all expectations. It was the first such competition to be held in the UK since the disappointing 2000 tournament and England had clearly improved on the horror showings in 2000 and 2008.

Yet their build-up had been horrendous. England had lost a pre-tournament match with Italy, with Gareth Hock subsequently booted out of the squad for disciplinary reasons. James Graham was also stood down from the opening match against Australia which was lost 28-20.

England came through the group stages and a quarter-final with France to set up a third-consecutive World Cup semi-final with New Zealand, but they had failed to spark. Coach Steve McNamara, therefore, chose stand-off Gareth Widdop instead of Rangi Chase for the semi-final – a popular decision with fans. With Sinfield, the captain, next to him at scrum-half, England looked balanced in the halves for the first time in years.

The decision to use Wembley for a double-header of semi-finals was rewarded with a bumper crowd of 67,545, and with the game live on the BBC, it was just like the good old days. All that was needed was for England

"So near, yet so far."

to deliver and although they fell agonisingly short, they played their part in a classic international.

England failed to start well and had to prevent Luke and Jason Nightingale from scoring. A seventh-minute penalty did finally take England into the opposition half and when they exerted sustained pressure, they produced a gem of a try. The ball was shifted left where James Graham found Sam Burgess with his trademark before-the-line pass and the South Sydney forward offloaded for Sean O'Loughlin to score near the left corner. It was a beautiful move crafted by three wonderfully talented forwards and Sinfield converted magnificently. England continued to threaten and Sam Burgess's sidestep opened up New Zealand. O'Loughlin put the pass down but a penalty was awarded, for a Kiwi interference on Widdop, which Sinfield sent between the posts for an 8-0 lead.

On a rare New Zealand attack, a misdirected pass from Luke sailed towards the touchline. Dean Whare didn't it give up and grabbed the ball, which had crossed the line, in mid-air, without putting a foot out of play. In an astonishing piece of skill, without looking, he spun the ball into play behind his back to Roger Tuivasa-Sheck, who crossed for a sumptuous try, which Johnson goaled. For all their dominance England had only mustered one first-half try and they even lost their lead when Johnson kicked a penalty just before half-time to lock the scores at 8-8.

The second period proved to be of the great halves in World Cup history, with the outcome of the match only decided by its final piece of play.

England were undone after just

ENGLAND 18 NEW ZEALAND 20

ENGLAND
1 Sam Tomkins
2 Josh Charnley
3 Kallum Watkins
4 Leroy Cudjoe
5 Ryan Hall
6 Gareth Widdop
7 Kevin Sinfield (C)
8 James Graham
9 James Roby
10 Sam Burgess
11 Brett Ferres
12 Ben Westwood
13 Sean O'Loughlin
Subs:
14 Rob Burrow
15 George Burgess
16 Chris Hill
17 Carl Ablett (dnp)

Tries: O'Loughlin, Watkins, S Burgess
Goals: Sinfield 3

NEW ZEALAND
1 Kevin Locke
2 Roger Tuivasa-Sheck
3 Dean Whare
4 Bryson Goodwin
5 Jason Nightingale
6 Kieran Foran
7 Shaun Johnson
8 Jared Waerea-Hargreaves
9 Issac Luke
10 Jesse Bromwich
13 Simon Mannering (C)
12 Sonny-Bill Williams
17 Elijah Taylor
Subs:
14 Frank-Paul Nuuausala
15 Sam Kasiano
16 Ben Matalino
19 Alex Glenn

Tries: Tuivasa-Sheck 2, Johnson
Goals: Johnson 4

Half-time: 8-8
Referee: Ben Cummins
Crowd: 67,545

A jubilant Shaun Johnson dives over to score his last-gasp winning try and break English hearts

Sam Burgess crashes over and *(inset)* a devastated James Graham reflects on defeat

three and a half minutes, Johnson sparking a right-side attack which Tuivasa-Sheck finished in the corner. After another Johnson penalty, England were now six down. Typical of the see-saw nature of this magnificent game, they weren't behind for long. England swarmed up-field and in the 58th minute received another set of six tackles on the Kiwi line. It took just a couple of plays to crack the defence when Sinfield's majestic cut-out pass found the centre Kallum Watkins running a beautiful line, although the captain missed the relatively simple conversion.

England continued to attack and a sensational short ball from Sinfield allowed Sam Burgess to charge through, side step Kevin Locke and put his side in the lead, sparking delirious scenes in the stands. This time the skipper converted and England were 18-14 up. Burgess was having the game of his life.

New Zealand put the kick off out on the full, allowing England to attack again, but their subsequent attack came up short and they didn't register another point. All they had to do, instead, was protect their line. But they failed to do so, and so the greatest of the code's 14 World Cups ended without the host nation in the final.

So near, yet so far!

Saturday, 11th October 2014

GRAND FINAL RED-CARD SENSATION

Grand Finals aren't supposed to start like this.

Showpiece matches are usually tight in the opening stages, with both sides prepared to build pressure, but the incredible 2014 Grand Final was blown wide open in the second minute when Wigan's Welsh prop, Ben Flower, was sent from the field for two punches aimed at the head of Saints' Lance Hohaia. The second was thrown as the Kiwi playmaker lay unconscious.

It was a disgraceful attack which shocked everybody who saw it, especially Shaun Wane, the Wigan coach, who was caught on camera looking absolutely stunned, barely able to comprehend what his player had done. The Welshman was subsequently banned for six months, the longest initial suspension of the Super League era.

On the last tackle of a promising early set for Wigan, Blake Green hoisted a kick to the corner and as Flower ran past Hohaia, he deliberately knocked him over. The ball came free and bounced invitingly to the prop with the unguarded try line just ten metres away. Had he collected it, a try was a near certainty. That in itself would have been the most dramatic of openings to a Grand Final.

Perhaps enraged at having been felled or possibly with an element of schadenfreude, Hohaia flew at the Wigan prop, banging into him. The New Zealander wasn't without blame for the incident but that was no excuse for Flower flooring him with an inch-perfect right hook which landed on the button, knocking Hohaia out. Then, in an action which stunned viewers all over the world, Flower, kneeling over his victim, punched him again on the left cheekbone, just below the eye, as he lay vulnerable. A brawl resulted and when it ended, Phil Bentham sent Flower from the field.

"[He's] completely lost the plot!" shouted Mike Stephenson, the Sky Sports co-commentator. Wane looked on bewildered, as his team's status as odds-on favourites now lay in tatters. Hohaia was taken from the field, not to return. He played eight more games for Saints in 2015, before announcing his retirement with immediate effect at the end of April that year.

The incident has taken its place among the most notorious events in

"He's completely lost the plot!"

Paul Wellens lifts the Super League trophy, flanked by his victorious St Helens teammates

the game's history and Flower's place in Rugby League's Hall of Shame is forever guaranteed. His second punch usurped Mick Cassidy's flying elbow on Adrian Morley in a 1998 Super League match between Wigan and Leeds as Super League's most outrageous piece of violence. Within minutes, Flower's actions had gone viral on various social-media platforms.

Wigan had to play for 78 minutes a man down. Winning a big match in such circumstances is possible – Great Britain did so in 1989 and 1994, and Wigan lost Challenge Cup matches to St Helens in 1997 and Leeds in 1999 despite the opposition having had a Great Britain international sent off in the first half. But in the new millennium, with a quicker ruck, such examples are harder to find.

Matty Smith did kick Wigan ahead with a penalty only for Mark Percival to reply in kind for St Helens. Saints attacked again with Josh Jones bundled into touch as he attempted to score in the corner, but it was a rare attack as they struggled to find any rhythm, with all their halfbacks out with injury. The sending-off appeared to have affected them more than Wigan and they had been below-par for some weeks leading into the game. It was Wigan who scored the first try, with seconds left in the first half, when Joe Burgess touched down Green's cut-out pass in the corner. The goal was missed but Wigan held

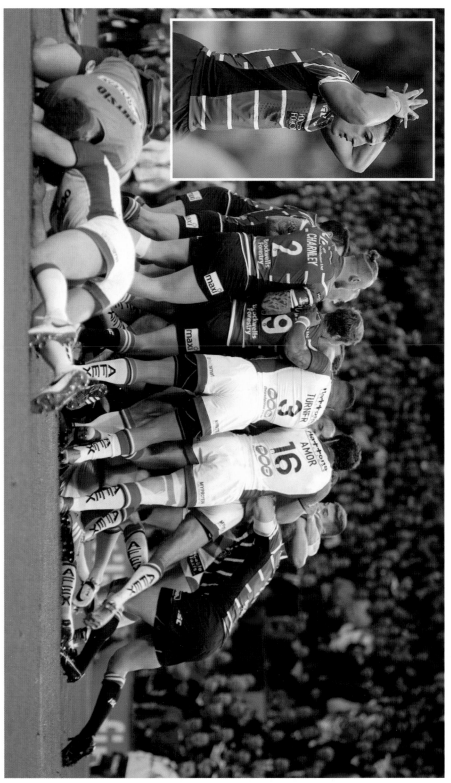

Lance Hohaia receives treatment as tempers flare, and (inset), Ben Flower makes his way to the Old Trafford dressing rooms

a valuable 6-2 advantage at the break.

Unfortunately for them Sia Soliola forced his way over from close range 14 minutes into the second half and Percival kicked the goal. Saints were in front by two, but they still didn't look too convincing. Despite the numerical disadvantage, Wigan were far from out of this and Tommy Makinson had to be at his best to bring down Liam Farrell. On the next play, Matty Bowen blew an overlap and Saints survived. Bowen then sent Charnley free but he was felled by Josh Jones, who held on for too long. Smith missed the very kickable penalty.

Wigan had had their chances, but wasted them. With 11 minutes remaining, Paul Wellens, the veteran fullback, hoisted a clever kick from out wide towards the posts where Makinson beat Bowen and Smith to score the clinching try. Few victories had tasted so sweet for the jubilant St Helens supporters. They had been written off by everybody as no-hopers. Admittedly without the red card it is unlikely they would have won, but when Wellens hoisted aloft the Super League trophy, no-one connected to the club cared about that. Flower's faux pas had been as stupid as it was costly, and everyone at Wigan suffered for it.

Months later Hohaia walked away from the game with everybody's best wishes. He and Flower had long since buried the hatchet but sadly, in 2016, the episode reared its ugly head again with the New Zealander critical of Saints' treatment of him during his recovery. The club were quick to refute his allegations in the strongest possible tone.

ST HELENS 14
WIGAN WARRIORS 6

ST HELENS
17 Paul Wellens (C)
2 Tommy Makinson
22 Mark Percival
4 Josh Jones
5 Adam Swift
15 Mark Flanagan
6 Lance Hohaia
16 Kyle Amor
9 James Roby
8 Mose Masoe
10 Louie McCarthy-Scarsbrook
11 Iosia Soliola
3 Jordan Turner
Subs:
28 Luke Thompson
13 Willie Manu
18 Alex Walmsley
27 Greg Richards

Tries: Soliola, Makinson **Goals:** Percival 3

WIGAN
1 Matt Bowen
2 Josh Charnley
5 Anthony Gelling
23 Dan Sarginson
32 Joe Burgess
6 Blake Green
7 Matty Smith
10 Ben Flower
19 Sam Powell
17 Dominic Crosby
11 Joel Tomkins
12 Liam Farrell
13 Sean O'Loughlin (C)
Subs:
22 Eddy Pettybourne
24 Tony Clubb
25 John Bateman
27 George Williams

Try: Burgess **Goal:** Smith

Dismissed: Flower

Half-time: 2-6
Referee: Phil Bentham
Crowd: 70,102

THE DEATH OF DANNY JONES

When the Keighley players set off to the New River Stadium for their fixture with London Skolars in May 2015, spirits were high. The Cougars were enjoying an excellent League One campaign in response to relegation at the end of 2014. As usual, their stand-off, the Welsh international Danny Jones, was at the centre of the camaraderie. The bus stopped in Coventry, which is usual for Keighley's forays south, and Jones took it upon himself to ensure that his teammates resisted the temptation of having any Yorkshire pudding with their food.

The bus stopped again, four miles from the stadium, for the players to stretch their legs. Jones remained his usual exuberant self, joking around with Ash Lindsay, the team's loose forward. The players were driven to the stadium and prepared for the match. All appeared well with Jones. He was in a confident mood, having kicked the winning drop goal a week earlier in a 23-22 win over North Wales Crusaders. He had played and scored in all seven of the Cougars' matches in the new campaign.

Four minutes into the game he had to be substituted, having complained of feeling unwell. He walked from the field, aided by the club physio. He hadn't been involved in any collision which could have led to an injury. Five minutes later, as the Cougars scored their second try, Jones collapsed by the side of the field. He was given emergency cardiopulmonary resuscitation (CPR) in front of the visitors' dug-out which lasted for the best part of an hour. The match was abandoned when it became clear that the stricken Jones was in trouble.

The physios, the on-site doctor, the paramedics and then the air-ambulance doctor all tried to treat him. Jones received four cardio shocks. Adrenaline was administered. He had four canisters of oxygen. Finally, he was taken to hospital in a state of cardiac arrest with the CPR machine attached to his chest and oxygen still being administered. One of the doctors was in tears.

Danny Jones was pronounced dead shortly after arriving at the hospital. It was later revealed that he had undiagnosed hypertrophic cardiomyopathy. He was 29. He was survived by his wife, Lizzie, and their five-month-old twins, Bobby and Phoebe. His parents, and his brother and sister, drove to London to see him one last time.

Teammates and club officials, naturally, were devastated. "We all miss Danny Jones," said the club's chairman, Gary Fawcett. "His professionalism, his leadership, his life and soul and his cheeky grin. We'll miss the grin and we'll miss Danny Jones very much at Keighley Cougars. Rest in peace, our friend."

A day after the tragedy, the club announced that it would retire the number-six jersey that Jones had graced with so much class. By the end of the turbulent week which followed, the club's main grandstand had been renamed The Danny Jones Stand. A fund for the twins was set up, and went on to pass the targeted £250,000 mark with so many in Rugby League eager to contribute. A crowd of over 4,000 turned up to Cougar Park seven days after Jones's death to watch the team beat Coventry 52-10. Player-coach Paul March played in Jones' position and scored one of the nine tries. Hooker James Feather scored three more of them. Over £10,000 was raised in a bucket collection for the fund.

"I'm proud of the players; not just for today but ever since the event," said March, a veteran of lower-division football. "There are 17 lads who took the field today, but we've got a squad of 30 who are all feeling it in different ways, which has been hard to manage. We're going to do more and more fundraising because he's never going to leave us."

Jones scored 33 tries, 444 goals and seven drop goals in 153 games in two spells for the Cougars. He also played for his home-town club, Halifax, for whom he featured in one Super League match as a 17-year-old at the end of the 2003 season. In two spells for Keighley, he played in 53 matches, scoring 17 tries, 132 goals and two drop goals. Jones made his Wales debut in 2010 against Italy and played in the 2011 Four Nations and the 2013 World Cup. He played a dozen times for the Welsh.

Nearly four months after his death, Lizzie Jones, Danny's widow, enthralled everybody inside Wembley Stadium, and the millions watching on television, by leading the traditional cup-final hymn, 'Abide With Me'. It became one of the enduring images of the Rugby League year and it was released as a single. She sang 'Danny Boy' in Belfast towards the end of the BBC's Sports' Personality of the Year show, in which Kevin Sinfield, the outgoing Leeds captain, came second in the main award. As she sang, images of those sportsmen and sportswomen who had lost their lives during 2015 were shown, culminating with the face of her husband as her performance came to an end. The song provided a fitting end to the sporting year and it provided a poignant reminder that Rugby League will never forget Danny Jones.

Lizzie has since campaigned successfully for free Echocardiograms to be available for all professional players – not just those who play in Super League - and for defibrillators to be present at all amateur clubs.

In May 2015, Danny Jones joined the saddest of professional Rugby League rollcalls. As a result of his wife's campaigning, hopefully Jones will remain the final name on the list.

"We all miss Danny Jones. His professionalism, his leadership, his life and soul and his cheeky grin. We'll miss the grin and we'll miss Danny Jones very much at Keighley Cougars. Rest in peace, our friend."

Danny Jones in action for Keighley in 2015 and *(inset, above)*
Lizzie Jones with twins Bobby and Phoebe at Wembley

SOL MOKDAD IMPRISONED

As Rugby League approached its 120th birthday, it was almost inconceivable that it was still having to contend with rugby union trying to kill it off in various parts of the world. The jailing of Sol Mokdad, who ran Rugby League in the United Arab Emirates, was a shocking story, underlining the lengths that at least one rugby union governing body was prepared to go to in order to stamp out its rival.

The 30-year-old had been trying to get the 13-man code off the ground since 2007, and with sponsors like Nissan and Fitness First on board, had done a commendable job. However, things aren't as simple in the UAE for someone like Mokdad as they might be in other countries. Sports must be recognised by the government and all forms of rugby have to come under one umbrella - the UAE Rugby Federation. Rugby League, therefore, would have to be controlled by the rugby union authorities if it was to be formally recognised by the government. Mokdad carried on regardless, without an official stamp of approval.

In 2015 he conducted a newspaper interview in which he spoke of his ambition of the UAE hosting the 2021 Rugby League World Cup. When the article was translated into Arabic, Mokdad was, through no fault of his own, incorrectly identified as the rugby union president. A complaint was made, resulting in his arrest and imprisonment upon charges of fraud, pretending to represent rugby union and accepting a sponsorship from Nissan under false pretences.

A letter to the players of the Dubai Sharks team from their management, explaining why their match against the Wasps could not go ahead, was leaked to the Australian journalist Steve Mascord. It confirmed the reasons for Mokdad's imprisonment and that Rugby League was effectively illegal in the UAE. In order to be released from prison, it was put to Mokdad that he should issue a public apology to the UAERF and that he should play no further part in promoting or organising Rugby League in the UAE. He agreed to those conditions and walked free, having served 13 days in jail.

"We apologise to the UAE country and the UAERF for our illegal behaviour, and the announcement of forming a rugby federation," read Mokdad's rather contrived statement. He also apologised for "forming a group of players and calling this team an Emirates Rugby League team and organising a local tournament called Emirates Rugby League without obtaining permission from UAERF. We committed a mistake by doing that. It was a mistake in newspapers and all different kinds of media about [the] Emirates hosting the Rugby League World Cup [in] 2021. We broke all protocols and traditions of using the name [of the] country without any rights to do so. We had no official or unofficial status, and everything we did was wrong and a mistake and we will never do it again."

Mokdad immediately left the UAE, and headed for England, where he was interviewed by Mascord, who set the scene in his 'Rugby League Week' article by pointing out that "rugby union has done some dastardly things to Rugby League over the past 120 years – the French injustice of the Second World War will hopefully never be outdone – but having a League official thrown in jail holds a unique place in the troubled history of the two codes."

Mokdad explained: "UAE Rugby League was formed in 2007, even though we weren't registered with the government. UAE rugby union was registered in 2009 or 2010 by Emirati people. Rugby union had been there for about 40 years. When I approached the General Authority of Youth and Sports [GAYS], they said 'play the game, get Emiratis involved, grow the game and then we'll give you recognition'. When we started getting big enough, through to the first weekend of our competition in 2015, which was a huge success thanks to everyone involved, there was a press release from UAE Rugby in conjunction with the GAYS that we weren't allowed to use the UAE name and if we did use the UAE name, there would be criminal charges against us.

"The first thing we did was we rebranded … we changed all our social media and I sent an email to the rugby union because they said they wanted to meet with me. I said I'd love to meet with them. No reply. That's when I made a statement about hosting the 2021 World Cup and it hit the fan. They translated it and said I was the president of the rugby union. I sent an apology to the general secretary of the rugby union … I copied in the European Federation. No reply. I sent another one, just to him. No reply. I managed to get a meeting with the general secretary of the rugby union – which was cancelled.

"I was invited to go to the Sports Industry Forum at the Sofitel Hotel in Dubai – by the organiser. Then a friend of mine texted me saying 'get out of there, they're coming to arrest you.' "As soon as I got outside, there were two guys who took my phone, put me in a van and took me to the general headquarters of the police station.

"When I got there, I waited for an hour. They [had arrested] me for fraud and embezzlement. They claimed that I said I was president of the rugby union and they said that I took a substantial amount of money from the sponsors. One of the questions was 'what did you do with the 800,000 dirhams from Nissan?' and that's ridiculous. We didn't even take any money off them. Before they paid, this whole thing went down."

The actions of the UAERF appear to have had the desired effect. With Mokdad gone, Rugby League in the United Arab Emirates withered and died.

> ***"Having a League official thrown in jail holds a unique place in the troubled history of the two codes."***

Sunday, 4th October 2015

COWBOYS IN DREAMLAND

The North Queensland Cowboys winger Kyle Feldt kicked off. The ball hung for an age in the night air. As it spiralled down, it was dropped by poor Ben Hunt, the Brisbane halfback. A scrum formed under the posts and the world's greatest player, Johnathan Thurston, prepared to drop a goal which would win the 2015 Grand Final for the Cowboys. The defence rushed up and prevented the one-point attempt, but three tackles later, the indigenous superstar was in the same position and, from Jake Granville's dummy-half pass, he sent over the kick which secured the club's maiden Premiership.

In his glorious first spell at the Broncos, Wayne Bennett had coached six Grand Final wins in 21 years, before leaving for pastures new in 2008. Now in 2015, in his first year back at the club, he was in another final. He is Rugby League's greatest-ever coach.

North Queensland played their first match in 1995. In those 20 years, they had only been to one final, which they lost in 2005. They were hoping that their 20th anniversary would be kinder to them than the tenth, but they started badly against the Broncos.

After five minutes, the Brisbane loose forward, Corey Parker, kicked his side into a two-point lead from 40 metres. From the kick off, the Broncos then produced one of the great Grand Final tries. On the second tackle, on their own 10-metre line, prop Adam Blair offloaded superbly to the stand-off Anthony Milford who took play forward ten metres before releasing Jack Reed. The English centre, in turn, found his winger, Corey Oates, with 65 metres to run. He had too much speed for the cover defence. For the 21st time of the season, Bennett's men had scored the first try in a match. Parker kicked another goal, and it was 8-0.

The Cowboys came straight back with a clever try. Matt Gillett lost the ball in a heavy tackle on the second tackle after the restart and hooker Granville, positioned at the back of the scrum, dummied and made a half break before offloading to centre Justin O'Neill on his inside. Thurston's goal ensured his side was back to within two points. The Cowboys were soon in the lead when James Tamou touched down next to the posts in the 25th minute, with Granville earning another assist. Thurston's second conversion took the score to 12-8.

North Queensland players and fans celebrate Johnathan Thurston's winner

At the other end, Andrew McCullough failed to find Parker on his inside when a try seemed certain. Minutes later, Gillett atoned for his earlier error when his offload on the Cowboys 20-metre line sent Jack Reed in for a try which was converted, this time by winger Jordan Kahu. Brisbane were back in front at 14-12 and a breathless half of football was soon at an end.

The lead was extended to four in the 43rd minute when Kahu kicked another goal and the score remained 16-12 throughout much of the second half. On the hour mark, when Thurston seemed to have put Kane Linnett over the line, the Scottish international centre dropped the ball. Minutes later, Lachlan Coote was denied by a double-movement ruling.

With two minutes to go, Sam Thaiday hammered Thurston on the fourth tackle before Granville's grubber was cleaned up by Reed. It looked like the Premiership was heading back to Brisbane, especially when Milford broke

"He's gone from a captain to a legend and probably Rugby League immortality."

into the Cowboys half, but the ball was stolen and there was still time for one more Cowboys set.

On the last tackle, with 20 seconds remaining, Matt Scott played the ball inside the Broncos 20-metre line. Granville passed to Thurston on his left but the defence shut him down. The Test halfback retreated out of the 20 and lobbed the ball to his stand-off, Michael Morgan, who produced the play which blew the final wide open. He cleverly got on the outside of a defender and, as Reed and Oates moved to shut him down, he got away a brilliant one-handed offload as the hooter was sounding. Feldt caught the ball and placed it over the line before running in joyous celebration to the mass of fans behind the posts.

Thurston was left with a touchline conversion to win the Grand Final. "He's thinking about the biggest moment of his career," said Phil Gould in the commentary box, as the tension built. He lined it up meticulously and his right boot struck the ball sweetly. As usual, when kicking from the right, he set it to the outside of the near post, hoping it would curl in. It did bend, but his projection was an inch out. The ball struck the post. Thurston's face was etched in agony. Golden-point extra time loomed.

Unperturbed by his miss, he soon made up for it by landing the winning point, which led Gould's colleague Ray Warren to observe: "He's gone from a captain to a legend and probably Rugby League immortality." Four months later, Thurston was crowned the world's best player for a record third time when he received the Golden Boot from 'Rugby League World' magazine.

NORTH QUEENSLAND COWBOYS 17
BRISBANE BRONCOS 16

NORTH QUEENSLAND
1 Lachlan Coote
2 Kyle Feldt
3 Justin O'Neill
4 Kane Linnett
5 Antonio Winterstein
6 Michael Morgan
7 Johnathan Thurston (C)
8 Matt Scott (C)
9 Jake Granville
10 James Tamou
11 Gavin Cooper
12 Ethan Lowe
13 Jason Taumalolo
Subs:
14 Rory Kostjasyn
15 John Asiata
16 Scott Bolton
17 Ben Hannant

Tries: O'Neill, Tamou, Feldt
Goals: Thurston 2 **Drop goal:** Thurston

BRISBANE
1 Darius Boyd
2 Corey Oates
3 Jack Reed
4 Justin Hodges (C)
5 Jordan Kahu
6 Anthony Milford
7 Ben Hunt
8 Sam Thaiday
9 Andrew McCullough
10 Adam Blair
11 Alex Glenn
12 Matt Gillett
13 Corey Parker
Subs:
14 Jarrod Wallace
15 Mitchell Dodds
16 Joe Ofahengaue
17 Kofi Nikorima

Tries: Oates, Reed
Goals: Parker 2, Kahu 2

Half-time: 12-14
Referees:
Ben Cummins & Gerard Sutton
Crowd: 82,758

ROBINS RELEGATED IN THE MOST EXTRAORDINARY FASHION

Just past the hour mark in the Million Pound Game of 2016, Terry Campese kicked a 40-20. His Hull Kingston Rovers team were already 18-10 up against an exhausted Salford side. He punched the air, screamed with delight and hugged his teammates. A try in the ensuing set would surely preserve his team's Super League status and see the Red Devils relegated. But after winning the scrum, their attack fizzled out. By the skin of their teeth, Salford were still alive.

The Million Pound concept was introduced to Rugby League in 2015, after the abject failure of the licensing system. Promotion and relegation were back on the table, but not in the traditional one-up one-down format. At the end of 23 rounds, the clubs in the top two divisions split into three groups of eight to determine the destination of the game's major prizes. The middle group comprised Super League's bottom four and the leading quartet from the Championship. After the teams had played each other once, the top three were awarded places in the following year's Super League, and would be joined by the winner of fourth against fifth, in the crassly termed Million Pound Game. Super League's Wakefield beat Championship side Bradford Bulls in the 2015 match, to the surprise of few.

A year later, the Championship's top club, Leigh Centurions, finished second in the middle-eight grouping, meaning that two Super League clubs, Hull KR and Salford, would contest the Million Pound Game. Rovers had come fourth and were awarded home advantage. For the first time since Salford themselves in 2007, a top-flight club would be relegated. Everything was on the line. What made the fixture even more interesting was that Salford's director of rugby, Tim Sheens, had signed a contract with Rovers to coach them in 2017, regardless of the outcome. With an obvious conflict of interest looming, he wisely stepped away from his Salford employment.

All seemed to be going well for Rovers when early tries from Adam Walker and Josh Mantellato had them 10-0 up, but Ben Murdoch-Masila and Niall Evalds hit back for the visitors. Rovers led 12-10 at half-time and increased

"I've been at Sky for 18 years and I've never seen anything like it."

the lead by six points 17 minutes into the second half when Thomas Minns crossed and Mantellato goaled. The score remained 18-10 until the closing stages.

"We sent a call out with five minutes to go," the Salford coach Ian Watson later revealed. "We were under the pump defending our line but we told them to believe." But no-one else believed in them. They looked exhausted and beaten. Some players were off injured, others were playing through the pain barrier. When O'Brien threw the ball into touch in his own 20-metre area with four minutes left, the Sky Sports commentators, Bill Arthur and Terry O'Connor, understandably consigned them to the inevitable.

There were less than three minutes to go when Rovers centre Iain Thornley kicked the ball dead. Needing two tries, Salford tapped on the 20, drove upfield and kept the ball alive. By the last tackle, they were deep in Rovers territory and when they moved the ball to the left, Josh Griffin released Evalds, who touched down. No more than a consolation, surely. O'Brien missed the conversion, leaving the gap at four points. But there was still time for one last set of six. They had less than one minute to go the length of the field and save their future.

After three tackles, they were still in their own half. Suddenly, an offload. A quick ball to the left. Man-of-the-moment Griffin made a break. The unthinkable was on. He found Evalds, who was grassed 15 metres short with seven seconds left. Mantellato and Ken Sio had the chance to execute a textbook professional foul to stop the quick play the ball, but,

HULL KINGSTON ROVERS 18
SALFORD RED DEVILS 19

HULL KR
18 Ben Cockayne
1 Ken Sio
21 Thomas Minns
4 Iain Thornley
2 Josh Mantellato
32 Terry Campese (C)
22 Matty Marsh
17 Dane Tilse
9 Shaun Lunt
8 Adam Walker
11 Maurice Blair
13 Chris Clarkson
15 James Donaldson
Subs:
10 Mitch Allgood
12 Graeme Horne
31 Will Jubb
34 Jamie Peacock

Tries: Walker, Mantellato, Minns
Goals: Mantellato 3

SALFORD
14 Gareth O'Brien
18 Greg Johnson
33 Josh Jones
4 Junior Sa'u
3 Josh Griffin
6 Robert Lui
7 Michael Dobson (C)
35 Luke Burgess
19 Logan Tomkins
10 George Griffin
11 Ben Murdoch-Masila
12 Weller Hauraki
13 Mark Flanagan
Subs:
1 Niall Evalds
8 Craig Kopczak
16 Olsi Krasniqi
34 Sean Kenny

Tries: Murdoch-Masila, Evalds 2, Johnson
Goals: O'Brien **Drop goal:** O'Brien

Half-time: 12-10
Referee: Phil Bentham
Crowd: 6,562

Gareth O'Brien wheels away and celebrates after kicking Salford to safety

crucially, neither did. Had they done so, the Robins would have remained in Super League. Play was shifted to the right and five passes later, with Hull KR outnumbered, Greg Johnson touched down near the corner. The hooter had gone. Marwan Koukash, the club's flamboyant owner banged a table in celebration. Fans spilled onto the pitch. But the conversion, which would have won them the game, was missed by O'Brien. Golden point extra

Salford owner Marwan Koukash enjoys the moment with delirious Red Devils fans

time loomed with so much riding on it. Pitch side, the Rovers chairman Neil Hudgell and Koukash shook hands. A touching moment.

Rovers kicked off the extra period and the Red Devils got to the last tackle of what looked to be a routine set. There didn't seem to be much on for O'Brien who caught the ball on halfway, but the Rovers markers were slow. He moved forward unchallenged and, on the run, let fly with an audacious, long-range drop goal attempt 50 seconds into extra time. It sailed between the sticks. Salford were reprieved, but after ten seasons of top-flight football, Hull Kingston Rovers were relegated. The Sky Sports cameras focused on a devastated Rovers coach, James Webster. His expression spoke volumes.

Spectators flooded onto the pitch again. Koukash joined them and was mobbed. Chaos reigned. Among the pandemonium was Sky Sports' Angela Powers, trying to do her job amid almost impossible circumstances. "I remember standing there with my mouth wide open when Salford came back," she said. "I've been at Sky for 18 years and I've never seen anything like it. It's hard to know what to ask when doing interviews like that, because every question seems a bit stupid. But the story made itself – it didn't matter what I asked. When O'Brien kicked the drop goal, everything started to go crazy. Among the Rovers players I was near, everyone just stopped still. Everyone was incredulous. They just stopped and stared. Had it really happened? In the tunnel afterwards, there were so many people in tears. It's a small area at Hull KR and so on one side there were people high fiving and hugging their wives and on the other people looked like death. One of my most vivid memories is of James Webster's wife and two kids on the bench with me. She was crying her eyes out. It was very emotional, and I disappeared off after the interviews and found myself filling up. It was really overwhelming."

Rovers were stunned. Jamie Peacock's playing comeback, having retired a year earlier, hadn't worked out. He and fullback Ben Cockayne had been scathing of the Million Pound Game during the week. It sounded like they wanted to be anywhere else – music to the ears of Salford players, surely. Most crucially of all, the decision to drop the talented playmaker Albert Kelly for the rest of the season for discipline reasons, had proved absolutely disastrous.

It had taken 16 years for Chris Joynt's 'Wide to West' try to be usurped as Super League's most incredible moment. When it finally happened, the repercussions couldn't have been greater.

With thanks to: *The British Heart Foundation, Tim Butcher, Phil Caplan, John Coffey, David Coon, Mike Critchley, Anita de la Rivière, Katy de la Rivière, Jason Emery, Bryce Eulenstein, Sean Fagan, Dave Gilbank, Allan Green, Mick Gledhill, Tony Harrison, Gareth Hodgson, Newtown Jets, Mike Latham, Grace Lee, Lewis Mills, Alex Murphy OBE, Brian Noble, Angela Powers, David Richards, Martyn Sadler, Garry Schofield OBE, Tim Sheens, Mandy Skayman, Daniel Spencer, Keith Tomlinson, Chris Westwood, Gav Willacy & Chris 'Jocky' Wilson.*